Webcasting

and

Push Technology Strategies

Effective Communications for Intranets and Extranets

Bohdan O. Szuprowicz

Computer Technology Research Corp.
6 North Atlantic Wharf, Charleston, South Carolina 29401 U.S.A.
Telephone: (803) 853-6460 • Fax: (803) 853-7210
E-mail: reports@ctrcorp.com • World Wide Web: http://www.ctrcorp.com

About the Author...

Bohdan Szuprowicz is an authority on leading-edge, interactive multimedia technologies. He is the president of 21st Century Research, a consulting firm specializing in strategic technology research and investment. He also directs Interactive Multimedia Communications, a continuous research program dedicated to investigating new markets, ventures, and strategic implementation of new technologies.

He developed numerous concepts, applications, and product reports for McGraw-Hill/DATA PRO and is a member of the Workgroup Computing Multimedia Solutions services advisory board and completed "Multimedia Databases" and "Portable Multimedia Applications" reports. He is also the author of the "Multimedia Networking" book published by McGraw-Hill Professional Book Division.

Mr. Szuprowicz holds a bachelor of science degree in Aeronautical Engineering from the Imperial College of Science and Technology of the University of London and studied Industrial Management and Photojournalism at Columbia University in New York and UCLA. He was born in Poland, educated in France and England, and has traveled throughout the world in more than 60 different countries.

Webcasting and Push Technology Strategies: Effective Communications for Intranets and Extranets

First Edition - 1998

ISBN: 1-56607-999-3

Published by Computer Technology Research Corp., Charleston, South Carolina, U.S.A.

Library of Congress Cataloging–in–Publication Data

Szuprowicz, Bohdan O., 1931–
Webcasting and push technology strategies : effective communications for Intranets and Extranets / Bohdan Szuprowicz.
p. cm.
ISBN 1-56607-999-3
1. Webcasting 2. Push technology (Computer networks)
3. Electronic commerce--Technological innovations. I. Title
TK5105.887.S99 1998
070.5' 797--dc21 97-46546
CIP

WEBCASTING AND PUSH TECHNOLOGY STRATEGIES:

EFFECTIVE COMMUNICATIONS FOR INTRANETS AND EXTRANETS

TABLE OF CONTENTS

Introduction 1

1. Executive Summary 7
How Webcasting and Push Technology Differ 7
The Simplicity of Push Technology 8
Why Push Technology? 9
A Whole New Marketplace 10
The Inevitable Trend 10
The Problems with Push Technology 11
A Narrowcasting Solution 11
Converting Web Pages to Channels 13
The Promise of Multicasting 14
Are Enterprise Web Channels Really Necessary? 14
Where Webcasting Will Be Most Effective 15
Resulting Changes in E-commerce 16
Creating a Smart Push Organization 19
Immature Webcasting Products and Services 20
Who Are the Early Adopters? 22

2. Anatomy of Webcasting 23
Webcasting Alternatives 24
The Pure Push 25
The Selective Pull 26
The Distributed Push/Pull 27
Webcasting Content Delivery 28
Push Client Features 29
Subscriber Connectivity 30
User Flexibility 30
Customization Profile 31
Information Transfer Persistence 31
Bandwidth Efficiency 32
New Content Integration 32
Client Notification 32
Push Security 33
Client Protocol Issues 33
Content Webcasters 34

Web Extenders 35
The Automated Pull Technology 35
Push/Pull Webcasting 36
Software Implementation Webcasting 37
Webcasting Concepts in Videoconferencing 37
One-to-One Operation 39
One-to-Many Distribution 40
Many-to-Many Enterprise 40
Powerful User Interaction Potential 41
Digital Broadcasting: The Technology of the Future 42
Consumers of Web-based Information 43
Providers of Web-based Content 44
Targeting Special Interests 44
Efficiently Distributing Data Packets 45
Replicating Data Traffic from a Single Source 45
Audio and Video on the Internet 45
Digital Video Production 46
Digital Audio Production 47
Radio and TV Broadcasting Sources 47
Multiple Encoding Requirements 48
Webcasting: The New Form of Multimedia 49
Instant Updating Capabilities 49
Conclusion 49

3. Multicasting Solutions 53
Multicasting Advantages 53
How Multicasting Works 54
TCP's Inefficiency for Multicasting 56
The User Datagram Protocol 57
IP Multicast Protocol 57
Internet Group Management Protocol 58
Multicast Routing Protocols 59
Distance Vector Multicast Routing Protocol 60
Multicast Open Shortest Path First Routing Protocol 61
Protocol Independent Multicast 61
Multicasting on LANs and WANs 62
Multicast File Distribution 62
The MBone Initiative 63
How MBone Works 64
Internet Multicasting Channels 64

IP Multicast Initiative 65
The ISP Role in Multicasting 65
Concerns About Multicasting 65
Toward More Reliable IP Multicasting 66
Developing Reliable Multicast Protocols 67
Reliable Multicast Protocol 68
Scalable Reliable Multicast 68
Reliable Multicast Transport Protocol 69
Multicasting Tools and Services 69
Multicast Services Using Satellites 70
Conclusion 70

4. The Search for E-commerce Solutions 73
Intranets, Extranets, and the Internet 74
E-commerce Defined 75
The Quest for Web Site Revenues 76
Surfing and Browsing Inefficiencies 78
Information Overload 78
Conserve Bandwidth 79
Disadvantages of Search and Metasearch Sites 79
Customized Content Delivery Dilemma 80
Controlled Information Delivery 80
Targeted Advertising 81
Growth in Interactive Advertising 81
Linking Brands to Consumers 82
User Targeting Factors 82
Targeted Keyword Advertising 82
Pinpointing Target Audiences 83
Controlling Information Distribution Reach 83
Determining Distribution Frequency 84
Measuring User Response 85
Reporting on User Interaction in Cyberspace 85
The Quest for a Total Solution 86
The Interactive Broadcasting Medium Is Born 86
Conclusion 87

5. The Web Information Push Alternative 89
The Push Alternative 89
The User Subscription Model 89
User Interests and Needs to the Forefront 90
Mass Distribution of Real-time Information 91

Eliminating Keyword Searching Inefficiencies 91
Unicasting 92
Webcasting as Broadcasting 92
Multicasting 93
A Narrowcasting Solution 94
Developing Reliable Multicasting Technology 95
Collaborative Computing 95
Multiuser Videoconferencing 96
The Impact of Push Technology on Revenues 96
The Disadvantages of Push Technology 97
Conclusion 97

6. From Web Pages to Channels 99
Internet Cyberspace 100
Broadcast Channels 100
The Biased Traditional Media 100
The Convergence of Two Technologies 101
Creating the Broadcast Paradigm on the Web 101
Psychographics of Webcasting and Push Technology 102
The Emergence of the Web Page 102
Transmitting Text and Graphics 103
Including Animation 103
Adding Audio and Video Elements 104
The Full Multimedia Web 104
The Internet as a Delivery Channel 105
What Is a Web Channel? 106
The Company Channel Idea 106
Quality of Service Issues 107
Digital TV Standards 108
The Push/Pull Broadcasting Solution 108
Conclusion 109

7. Creating Enterprise Channels on the Web 111
Ideal Push and Webcasting Characteristics 112
Real-time Chatting 113
Creating Web Content for Push Applications 114
Specialized Intelligent Agents 115
Multimedia on Demand 115
Preparing Multimedia Content for Webcasting 116
Webcasting: Another Form of Multimedia 116
Multimedia Webcasting Software Requirements 116

Multimedia Content Encoding and Decoding 117
Streaming Multimedia Characteristics 118
Use of Animation in Web Channels 119
Audio Streaming on the Web 119
Creating a Web Radio Channel 120
Streaming Video Channels 120
Audio and Video Newscasting on the Web 123
The Enterprise Training Channel 123
Emerging Streaming Multimedia Services 124
The @Home Network 125
Streaming Multimedia Standards 125
The NetChannel Concept 125
Multiuser Multimedia Conferencing 126
Consider Channel Replication 126
Creating Remote Push Channels 127
Virtual Private Networks on the Web 128
Webcasting Development Studio Idea 129
Streaming Multimedia Industry Trends 130
Conclusion 130

8. Major Push Applications 133
Enterprise Push Applications 134
Audience Targeting 136
Delivery Applications 137
Distributing Time-sensitive Information 137
News Services 137
Electronic Software Distribution 138
Software Implementation and Maintenance 138
Financial Services 139
Consulting Communications 139
Trading Support Systems 140
Sales Force Automation 140
Competitive Intelligence 142
Strategic Marketing 142
Interactive Advertising 142
Netfomercials 143
Product Distribution Support 143
Legal Information 144
Collaborative Computing 144
Multicasting Applications 145

Web Conferencing 146
Streaming Live Events 146
Promoting and Distributing Online Music 146
Online Travel Applications 147
Internet Webcasting Growth 147
Audio and Video Broadcasting 148
Conclusion 148

9. Webcasting and Push Business Strategies 151
How to Become a Webcasting Organization 151
Determining Webcasting User Categories 152
Push Objectives for Small Businesses 153
Midrange Market Push Program Developers 154
Major Webcasting Publishers 154
Content Branding 155
Selecting the Minimal Complement of Push Components 155
Building Push Communities 156
Resolving Bandwidth Shortages 157
Establishing Connections 158
Push Technology on the LAN 159
Facilitating Multimedia Traffic 160
Considering Multicasting Tools and Services 161
Anticipating User Operating Problems 161
How Much Push? 162
Selecting Notification and Delivery Features 162
Effective Web Site Development 163
Selecting Authoring and Development Tools 164
Evaluating Push Technologies 166
Selecting the Necessary Skills 166
The Cost of Webcasting 167
Push: An Advertiser's Nightmare 168
Digital TV 169
Monitoring Digital Broadcasting Services 170
Evaluating Digital Broadcasting Alternatives 171
End-user Orientation 173
Immature Push Industry Instability 173
Maintain Awareness of Future Developments 174
International Webcasting Association 174
Conclusion 175

10. Webcasting and Push Browser Capabilities 177

Netscape Communications 177
Microsoft 178
Comprehensive Webcasting Tools 180
Affinicast 182
BackWeb Technologies 183
Cognisoft, Inc. 184
DataChannel 185
Diffusion 186
Intercast 186
Lanacom 187
Marimba, Inc. 189
My Way Online, Inc. 191
Wayfarer 192
Other Webcasting Tools 193
Conclusion 194

11. Webcasting and Push Services 195
Growth of Third-party Webcasting Services 195
Intelligent Search Engines 198
AirMedia, Inc. 199
Amulet 199
AudioNet 200
Berkeley Systems 200
BroadVision 201
Caravelle 201
Desktop Data, Inc. 202
Desktop News 204
The DoubleClick Network 204
Empirical Media 205
Farcast 205
inCommon 206
Individual, Inc. 207
InfoBeat 207
Intermind 208
News-Alert 209
NETdelivery 209
Open Sesame 210
PointCast 211
Tibco Software 213
WavePhore 214

Conclusion 215

12. **Webcasting and Push Case Studies..217**
ABN-AMRO Bank NV...219
AT&T Wireless Services..220
Barnes & Noble 220
Bechtel 221
Ben & Jerry's 221
Bloomberg..222
Capital Market Risk Advisors..223
Chicago Board of Trade 224
Compaq Computer 224
Conference Plus, Inc. 225
Dell Online..225
Dow Jones Interactive 226
Ernst & Young 226
Ford Motor..227
Fruit of the Loom 227
Heineken 228
IBM AS/400 Division 228
IntelliHealth 229
KPMG 229
Lufthansa 230
MagicMaker..230
Merrill Lynch...230
NationsBank..231
TCI, Ingenius...232
Conclusion 232

13. **Conclusions..235**
If You Build It, They May Not Bother to Come... 235
The Virtual Mall Lessons 236
Business-to-Business Success 236
Streaming Multimedia Will Make It Happen.......................................237
The Importance of Multicasting 237
Web Content Provides the Real Challenges 238
Creating Web Channels Is Not a Trivial Task.....................................238
Webcasting Money-making Potential 239
The Risk of Webcasting 240
Unstable and Emerging New Industry..240
Watch the Early Adopters 240

The Webcasting Idea Is Widespread 240

Glossary 243

LIST OF FIGURES

1.1 Push Process Concept 9
1.2 Web-based Training Market 16
1.3 Most Probable Web Marketing Sites 17
1.4 Prospects for Insurance Markets on the Web 18
1.5 Projections of Online Travel Markets 18
1.6 Online Advertising Revenue Projections 19
1.7 Example of an Enterprise Smart Push Installation 20
2.1 The Push Food Chain 23
2.2 Pull and Push Technologies Compared 24
2.3 Pure Push Service 26
2.4 Selective Pull Service 27
2.5 Distributed Push/Pull Alternative 28
2.6 Forms of Conferencing 39
3.1 Multicast Island Concept 55
3.2 Multicasting Network Concept 56
3.3 1997 Multicast Use Study Results 67
4.1 Projected Explosion in Internet Revenues 73
4.2 Growth in Number of Clients on the Web 76
4.3 Projected Web Sales by the Year 2000 77
5.1 General Concept of Multicasting 94
7.1 Streaming Video Frame Size Relative to Full Screen 119
7.2 An Example of a Virtual Private Network on the Web 128
8.1 Example of an Integrated Architecture 141
9.1 A Gigabit Intranet Network Example 158
9.2 The Multimedia Datacasting Concept of WavePhore 172
10.1 AIM Implementation Concept 183
10.2 IntelliServ Implementation Example 185
10.3 HeadLiner Use in Enterprise Applications 188
10.4 Marimba's Castanet Elements 190
10.5 The MindShare Concept 192
10.6 INCISA System Architecture 193
11.1 Desktop Data Service Overview 203
11.2 Downtown Channel Selector Screen 206

11.3 InfoBeat Home Page 208
11.4 The PointCast Home Page 212
11.5 Illustration of TIBnet 213

LIST OF TABLES

1.1 Webcasting Versus Push 8
1.2 Narrowcasting Solutions Defined 12
1.3 Webcasting Companies 21
2.1 Summary of Push Client Features 29
2.2 Forms of Videoconferencing 38
3.1 Summary of Multicasting Protocols 59
7.1 Push Technology Selection Factors 112
7.2 Summary of Streaming Multimedia Products for the Web 122
8.1 Potential Enterprise Push Application Categories 134
9.1 Major Webcaster User Categories 153
9.2 Push Community Characteristics 156
9.3 Summary of Web Authoring and Development Tools 165
9.4 Pricing Policies of Push Vendors 168
10.1 Summary of Browser-based Delivery Technologies 180
10.2 Representative Webcasting Tools 181
11.1 Representative Webcasting and Push Services 196
12.1 Early Adopters of Push Technology 217

Introduction

The Internet has sparked a revolution in computing. It is truly becoming a global information medium. From the Web to E-mail, the Internet has become a delivery channel for audio, video, graphics, and text. Because of the current information overload created by the Internet's phenomenal growth, manually searching the Web is no longer a productive option.

The difficulties associated with gathering information on the Internet has been squarely addressed by a new suite of programs designed to cut through Web clutter using principles borrowed from broadcasting. With these products, users can select specific topics, such as news, weather, or business information. The software program works as an intelligent agent, searching the Internet and delivering relevant information into the user's broadcasting system. This process, known as webcasting, represents a new means of exploiting Web technology by significantly reducing the time required to locate specific information.

The webcasting concept is simple: It is the process of transmitting audio and video over the Internet. To receive information, users visit the Web page where the content is located and specify which channels and topics they would like to receive. Users also have the option of specifying how often they would like to receive updates. Webcasting software diligently monitors the Web on the user's behalf. Once information is located, the program notifies the user via a pop-up message or a scrolling ticker. When the user clicks for more information – actively seeking the information – the program links to the site with that information.

In light of the controversy surrounding the value of webcasting and push technologies, this report is designed to provide executives and information technology (IT) personnel with an overview of push technologies and strategies required to launch a webcasting operation. In addition, it provides information regarding the development of intranet and extranet applications, and for designing webcasting promotions and Internet marketing program implementations for both small and large businesses.

The report presents an analysis of the emerging webcasting solutions using push technologies in intranets, extranets, and the Internet. It outlines the intense search for effective E-commerce solutions, the development of webcasting, the creation of specialized Web channels, and the use of specific software tools to implement those concepts.

The report is divided into three segments:

1) The initial chapters examine the overall E-commerce environment, webcasting as an information distribution alternative, and the conversion of existing Web sites and pages into webcasting channels
2) Several chapters discuss the existing webcasting infrastructure alternatives, including the elements of the process, the emerging multicasting solutions, the issues involved in creating company channels on the Web, and potential webcasting applications
3) The remaining chapters focus on selecting appropriate webcasting business strategies for using push technologies

Chapters describing webcasting development tools, webcasting services, webcasting early adopters, and their webcasting implementations are also included.

The report consists of 13 chapters:

1) Executive Summary
2) Anatomy of Webcasting
3) Multicasting Solutions
4) The Search for E-commerce Solutions
5) The Web Information Push Alternative
6) From Web Pages to Channels
7) Creating Enterprise Channels on the Web

8) Major Push Applications
9) Webcasting and Push Business Strategies
10) Webcasting and Push Browser Capabilities
11) Webcasting and Push Services
12) Webcasting Case Studies
13) Conclusions

Chapter 1: Executive Summary underscores the idea that webcasting as an emerging alternative is mostly untested, although it is expected to improve E-commerce on the Web. The chapter also suggests that webcasting promoters and publishers must evaluate the real need for this technology in their specific enterprise environments and select the most appropriate development tools or services to implement such programs.

The specific elements that create a webcasting operation are covered in *Chapter 2: Anatomy of Webcasting.* Webcasting alternatives, such as pure push, selective pull, and distributed push/pull solutions are also discussed. What specific characteristics offer webcasting subscribers different levels of services? The chapter answers this question and also indicates the importance and problems associated with interactive multimedia information content in competitive webcasting applications.

Chapter 3: Multicasting Solutions focuses on the emerging multicasting technology, which is increasingly seen as a webcasting infrastructure for the future. The chapter discusses the mechanics and protocols of multicasting and the increasing availability of networking routers and switches with built-in multicasting capabilities.

Chapter 4: The Search for E-commerce Solutions outlines the growth of intranets, extranets, and the Internet as a new infrastructure for E-commerce. It also examines the effect of information overload, and the need to develop alternative and more effective methods of capturing the attention and controlling the interaction of the users in those networking environments.

Developing the user subscription business model as a Web information distribution alternative is discussed in *Chapter 5: The Web Information Push Alternative.* The chapter also compares the various forms of Internet data transmission, including unicasting, broadcasting, multicasting, and narrowcasting solutions. Videoconferencing and collaborative computing are also discussed. In addition, revenue-creating potential and disadvantages of webcasting as a business undertaking are detailed.

Chapter 6: From Web Pages to Channels compares the user-controlled webcasting channels and selection of content with the arbitrary nature of conventional broadcasting media. It also discusses the developing digital alternatives, such as digital TV services, and the need to compete with traditional broadcasting solutions in content and presentation quality.

Chapter 7: Creating Enterprise Channels on the Web discusses issues associated with creating company channels on the Web. These include the identification and analysis of special target audiences and the assessment of their webcasting content needs. Subsets of these issues may include alerts or notifications, and associated services such as real-time chat, multiuser conferencing, and interactive advertising. Chapter 7 also examines using multimedia elements such as animation and streamed audio and video in webcasting. Emerging streaming media services are also explored.

In *Chapter 8: Major Webcasting and Push Applications,* several webcasting and push applications are discussed. Commercially profitable applications include software implementation and maintenance, financial services, trading support systems, competitive intelligence, collaborative applications, and multiuser conferencing. Webcasting and push potential in interactive advertising, travel, legal information updating, streaming of live events, and various strategic marketing concepts are also explored.

Chapter 9: Webcasting and Push Business Strategies is a guide to implementing webcasting applications. It provides specific suggestions about procedures and activities that lead to establishing and operating a webcasting organization. This advice applies equally to intranet and extranet implementation of push technology as it does to the establishment of webcasting channels for marketing products and services on the Internet. The chapter outlines specific choices that must be made with regard to push components, bandwidth availability, multimedia content, intrusiveness, and client software features. This chapter also highlights the development of other digital broadcasting alternatives and future competitive threats to webcasting solutions.

Chapter 10: Webcasting and Push Browser Capabilities assesses the most popular webcasting development tools, reviewing products offered by several new ventures. The chapter also includes Microsoft's and Netscape Communications' recent entry into the webcasting market. The companies have "legitimized" push technology by including built-in webcasting client tools in their latest Web browser products.

Webcasting services are discussed in *Chapter 11: Webcasting and Push Services*. The group of entrepreneurial service providers is increasing quite rapidly. Still, other ventures are organized around proprietary software of specific Web information channels.

Chapter 12: Webcasting Case Studies details the webcasting implementations of 24 companies, most of which are early adopters of push technology. Some represent examples of pilot projects that are expanding to larger company environments. In short, these case studies represent a selection of webcasting application categories, ranging from software distribution, hardware support, financial services, product marketing, and trading to project management.

The statements contained in *Chapter 13: Conclusions* summarize how webcasting and push technologies are used to overcome information overload and provide new marketing initiatives for wired corporations. Webcasting is emerging as an attractive means of enhancing E-commerce, but not all enterprises offer products or services that can benefit from push technology applications.

The report also contains a glossary that provides explanations of webcasting and push terms.

Chapter 1

Executive Summary

The combination of intranets, extranets, and the Internet has developed a rapidly growing global networking infrastructure that is conducive to E-commerce. Companies of all sizes are establishing a Web presence to promote company products and services and generate revenue.

At the same time, rapid growth of commercial Web sites and increased user interaction is responsible for a tremendous information overload that is growing incessantly. Web publishers and merchants vie for the attention of Internet users. Within intranets and extranets, capturing the attention of key employees, business partners, and customers to expedite company policies, introduce new products, and provide competitive customer services is equally critical.

Webcasting, which is essentially broadcasting over the Web using the Internet protocol (IP), and push technologies, which are a function of webcasting, are the latest mechanisms used to target potential customers and better serve existing customers. The webcasting concept is new, and enabling tools and services are only now becoming available. Because of its newness, caution should be exercised when selecting products and services to implement webcasting applications.

How Webcasting and Push Technology Differ

Webcasting is appropriate for a wide range of events, both companywide and public. Webcasting and push technologies are often confused, however, because the terms are often used interchangeably. However, they are different technologies with different applications (see Table 1.1). Push technologies, such as PointCast, involve the periodic transmission of flat information, such as text and graphics. Push is passive from a user's perspective. Once scheduled, the information arrives periodically without user intervention. To hear or watch a webcast, by contrast, users must actively tune-in to the Web page where the content is available. Webcasting can be thought of as tuning-in to a TV station.

Table 1.1 Webcasting Versus Push

	Webcasting	Push
Active or Passive?	Active; users tune in	Passive; users receive pushed information automatically
Content Type	Multimedia broadcasts, either audio or video	Text and graphics are most frequently pushed
Transmission	Live or on demand	Prescheduled
Example Application	Press conference, training session, or keynote speech	Hourly stock quotes or daily sales reports

The Simplicity of Push Technology

The mechanics of push technology are relatively simple: Using Web channels or Web services, the user provides the webcasting service provider an information profile that includes demographics and content preferences. The subscriber also outlines when and how the information should be delivered.

When the PC user connects with the Internet or intranet according to the schedule, the Web channel downloads the information. The Web channel server collates any information relating to the specific user profile and downloads it to the subscriber desktop. When the transfer is complete, the subscriber is notified that the materials are available for evaluation or downloading. Figure 1.1 illustrates this process.

Figure 1.1 Push Process Concept

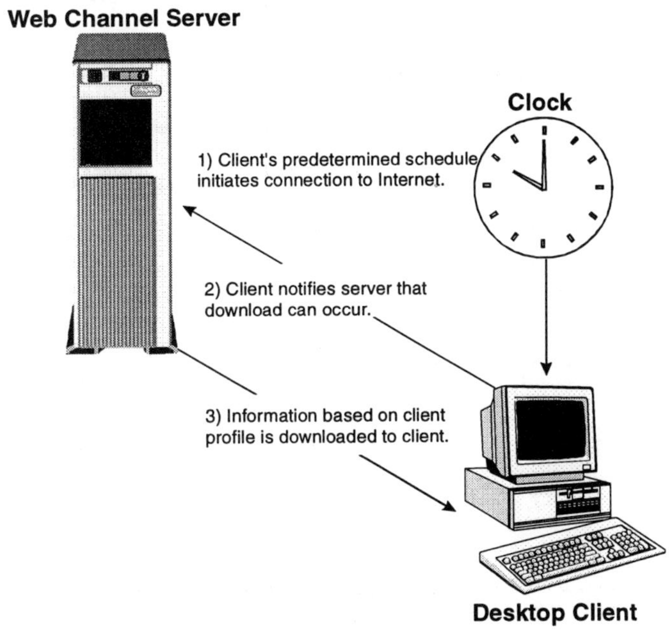

Why Push Technology?

Push technology was developed to alleviate two major issues facing users of the Internet: the overwhelming information overload resulting from the sheer volume and the dynamic nature of content on the Internet, and inadequate bandwidth (most users have low-capacity Internet connections). Originally designed to make interaction with the Internet easier and more productive, push technology is now being quickly introduced into intranets and other networking environments.

In taming the information overload, push products and services narrow the focus and expand the domain of information searches for the user. Users originally searched the Web to find productive hyperlinks and to monitor Web sites and information sources. Search engines such as Yahoo! and AltaVista improved the situation, but push technology exploits Web technology further.

The bandwidth issue relates to the fact that the majority of Internet users will remain connected with 28.8-Kbps modems, which have very limited capacity for multimedia content delivery. On average, users are willing to wait approximately 15 seconds for a Web page to download, which means the size of such data is limited to less than 45 kilobytes. Conversely, push technology delivers large multimedia files through an unattended connection during a time when the user is otherwise occupied. As a result, multimedia content including audio, graphics, animation, and video can be transmitted and accessed by users from local sources without undue delays.

A Whole New Marketplace

Personalized push services represent a new marketplace, which has emerged since late 1996. The widespread availability of these services follows the introduction of the initial PointCast service in May 1996, which became an instant success.

Push technology is a logical development as the next Internet communications vehicle. It follows the use of E-mail for textual information, file transfer protocol (FTP) for file transfer, and the Web for browsing and linking large amounts of textual and multimedia content.

The introduction of the Web and free browsers is largely responsible for the recent growth of the Internet. Its multimedia capabilities made the Internet very appealing and more accessible to the non-technical public. As a result, the Web has become the most powerful tool for navigating and retrieving information through the Internet.

The Web rapidly progressed from a collection of static pages to dynamic multimedia sites. Unfortunately, its limitations, including inadequate bandwidth, poor demographics, insufficient user tracking, and distracting advertising, are creating barriers between content producers and marketers and their intended audiences.

The Inevitable Trend

When Internet users first interact with the Web, many are truly overwhelmed by the plethora of available choices. However, they continue surfing to discover what the next hyperlink will present. As time progresses, users become frustrated by the endless switching from one Web site to another. When users reach this point, they often turn to search engines to locate more precisely defined information. Once this information has been located, users can bookmark the site so they can return to it on a regular basis. Bookmarks save time and simplify linking with frequently accessed Web sites.

Push technology is the next logical step in this evolution of convenience. Why bother looking at favorite Web sites to discover if anything new has been posted since the last visit. It is much more convenient to state that when a specific piece of information is available, it should be pushed to the user.

The Problems with Push Technology

Despite its goal to make the Internet and intranets more productive by the elimination of waiting for audio, video, and graphic downloads, the push technology concept is not devoid of criticism. Push technology may save time in searching and retrieving information, but it also may create storage shortages and other problems that will require user attention when allowed to continue unchecked. While webcasting alerts subscribers that relevant information has been located, push technologies take the liberty of downloading full articles and associated graphics to the subscriber's hard drive. As a result, even a limited search selection can rapidly consume hard disk space – particularly when multimedia content is involved.

The primary problem with push technology is excessive bandwidth use, which can occur when thousands of users download files simultaneously – a definite possibility in large organizations. Considerable network traffic congestion can ensue as a result.

A more persistent issue with push technology is one of culture. As a concept, push technology does not always appeal to company information systems (IS) managers because it is considered intrusive, interrupting with E-mail messages, scrolling ticker tapes, system beeps, animated icons, flashes, or screen savers designed to capture the user's attention. Unfortunately, these interruptions are often too frequent, impeding productivity. Although these interrupts can be disabled, push technology then loses its designed impact.

A Narrowcasting Solution

Webcasting in the traditional broadcast media is the transmission of specific information to a particular group of subscribers using the Internet protocol. Several webcasting alternatives can be implemented on the Web, but with different levels of effectiveness in using networking resources. Webcasting promoters and developers must differentiate between these alternatives and make the proper selection to create a viable solution.

Amy Cortese wrote in *Business Week* magazine, "The ability to narrowcast is transforming the [Internet] into a personal broadcast system." According to Eric Schmidt, CEO of Novell, "The combination of broadcast and personalization is really a new world."

Unlike TV, the Internet facilitates narrowcasting, the transmission of specific data and information to a very specific group of subscribers. The delivery of this information, however, can be implemented in several ways, including broadcasting, collaborative implementation, conferencing, multicasting, or unicasting (see Table 1.2).

Table 1.2 Narrowcasting Solutions Defined

Broadcasting	Transmission of information to every user on a network
Collaborative implementation	Synchronous or asynchronous multimedia applications that allow multiparty interaction
Conferencing	Interactive communications session among more than two users that are geographically separated
Multicasting	Transmission of content to a selected group of subscribers only once and forwarded by routers and switches saving bandwidth
Unicasting	Transmission of content from Web site to each user separately

Narrowcasting solutions distribute information to users without their immediate action, but narrowcasting methods differ in efficiency and bandwidth requirements.

For example, unicasting wastes bandwidth, because it requires that the same information be repeatedly transmitted from the same Web channel to each subscriber. Broadcasting is also wasteful, because it transmits to every user on the network. To be effective, it requires a way to identify those specific individuals who should receive it. For example, the subject line should be definitive. Multicasting is very selective, but requires hardware and software adjustments, such as adding special features or adding updated routing programs to the existing network infrastructure. Multiuser conferencing and collaborative computing are real-time implementations and, as such, are time-sensitive, high-bandwidth applications that require priority protocols and additional hardware.

While these narrowcasting alternatives can theoretically accomplish the webcasting objective – to deliver relevant internal and external business information to employee desktops without employees' actually requesting it – all of these methods must be matched with suitable applications and implemented in networking environments with adequate bandwidth capacities to deliver the information in the most efficient manner.

Converting Web Pages to Channels

A Web channel functions as an independent Web server with specific information. Existing Web pages with suitable content can be indexed on Web servers designated as specific Web channels. While the webcasting process is similar to conventional broadcasting, significant differences in its development and operation can be identified.

Traditional radio and TV broadcasting is based on and restricted to politically and socially acceptable information. If viewers want adult entertainment transmitted to their home, for example, they must pay a premium to obtain it. However, any Web subscriber can select one or more webcasting services to monitor and deliver any information, politically correct or not. As a result, Web channels may represent a collection of information and data with content pre-determined by the user. Not all the information acquired for a particular user will meet the stated specifications, but users maintain control of the information they receive.

In the intranet environment, creating an effective webcasting service is a matter of developing specific company news and policy information to distribute to specific groups of employees. Also important is webcasting information from company databases to employees to provide pertinent information while they are working on related projects.

In local area networks (LANs) and wide area networks (WANs), the ability to store and transmit multimedia content, including text, audio, animation, graphics, and video elements, must also be considered. As a result, developing company channels with full multimedia webcasting capabilities is important to obtain all the benefits of push technology. Without full multimedia capabilities, push technology is not as attractive or as useful for training purposes. In addition, push technology that lacks multimedia capabilities is no longer competitive as an E-commerce network.

The Promise of Multicasting

Multicasting is an emerging webcasting alternative that addresses the inefficiencies inherent in the basic transmission control protocol/Internet protocol (TCP/IP) when it is used for distributing the same information to large groups of users. Multicasting fills these gaps by activating special features or adding updated routing programs to existing network infrastructures.

Multicasting is a precise webcasting solution that allows for the transmission of information originating from a Web channel source, distributing it to multiple, designated recipients scattered throughout a particular network. This process is accomplished by enabling routers and switches in a network to forward a multicast message only to those designated multicast subscribers. This approach saves bandwidth when compared with the unicasting method, which requires transmitting content to each user separately.

Multicasting requires routers, switches, and end users to be multicast-enabled. However, the most recently developed networking equipment already includes multicast protocol capabilities. Activation involves turning such facilities on or adding a software driver.

Multicasting is the technology of the future in webcasting and E-commerce. Multicasting tools and services are now entering the market to make this solution readily available to Web merchants and publishers.

Are Enterprise Web Channels Really Necessary?

Intranets and extranets may adequately meet information needs when they consist of relatively small number of Web sites or exist in small enterprises. In large multinational companies, however, the number of Web sites can be large, and managing the daily changes is nearly impossible.

Consequently, push technology is an efficient way to distribute company information. In fact, many of the latest push technology development tools are improvements on the PointCast model, which is primarily targeted at intranets.

To maximize their effectiveness as an information resource, enterprise Web channels can be set up to represent specific company functions and links to company databases, archives, data warehousing systems, pertinent chat groups, and conferencing systems. This practice is relatively easy, because company LANs and WANs provide high-bandwidth capacity, allowing straightforward installation of multimedia content and real-time videoconferencing applications.

While creating company Web channels and acquiring the webcasting technologies are considered relatively easy, garnering user acceptance and developing the operational discipline to make it work can be problematic because users may have established alternative ways of acquiring information. In addition, some businesses may not be suitable for webcasting. As a result, determining in advance whether the nature of a business and daily habits of its workers are such that webcasting can be introduced with a reasonable expectation of success is advisable.

Where Webcasting Will Be Most Effective

Webcasting is ideal for some applications. For example, webcasting in an intranet and extranet environment is viewed as a growing medium for selective company communications, competitive intelligence, legal advice, collaborative computing, Web-based training (see Figure 1.2), and multiuser conferencing. These internal company functions can benefit from webcasting to specific groups of employees. In fact, distributing and maintaining software for company IT workers is viewed by analysts as the one webcasting application that can result in immediate and measurable benefits.

Figure 1.2 Web-based Training Market

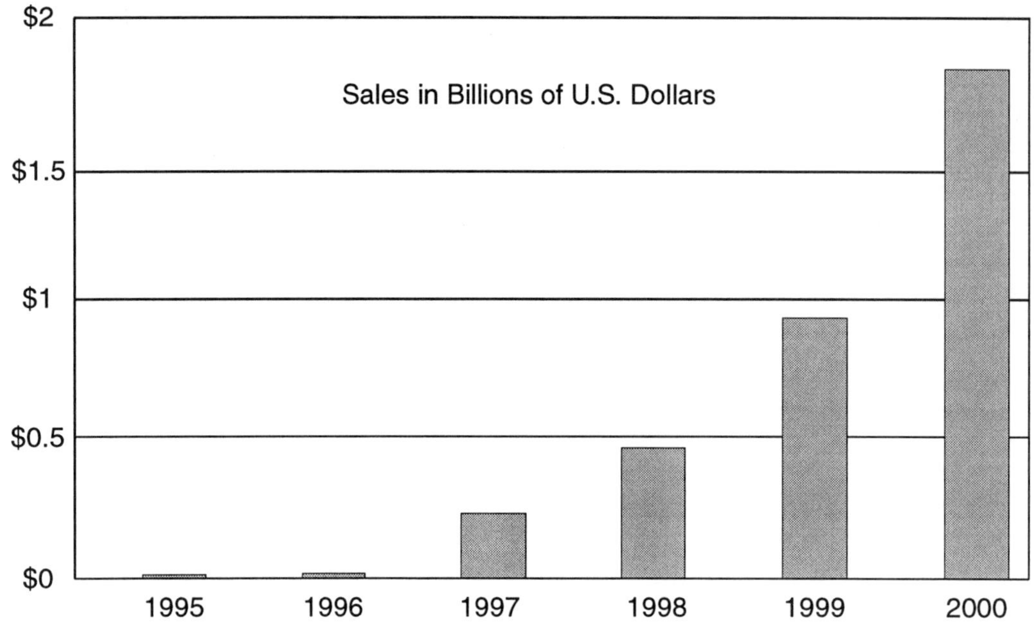

Note: Figures for 1997 through 2000 are projections.

Source: International Data Corp.

Company software products can be readily downloaded to specific users in the background mode, saving them time. In addition, new software versions, updates, bug announcements, patches, and similar information can be pushed to users as soon as they are available. These tasks can be accomplished for considerably less than distributing CDs or published materials using conventional methods.

Resulting Changes in E-commerce

Webcasting's value in E-commerce depends on the type of products or services offered. In general, online merchants must offer some added value to their physical counterparts to make webcasting a success. Although online buyers are primarily interested in making a purchase faster, not necessarily less expensively, they also use the Web to compare prices and services to make a well-informed purchase. The easier it is to make a decision using the Web, the more attractive this option will become. As a result, Web sites offering house mortgages, loans, and cars with easily understood comparisons are attractive services to many users.

For the same reason, Web sites offering books, music, or videos must offer additional incentives, such as special interest chat rooms. Figure 1.3 illustrates the relationship between Web sites offering different products and their need to provide special online incentives.

Figure 1.3 Most Probable Web Marketing Sites

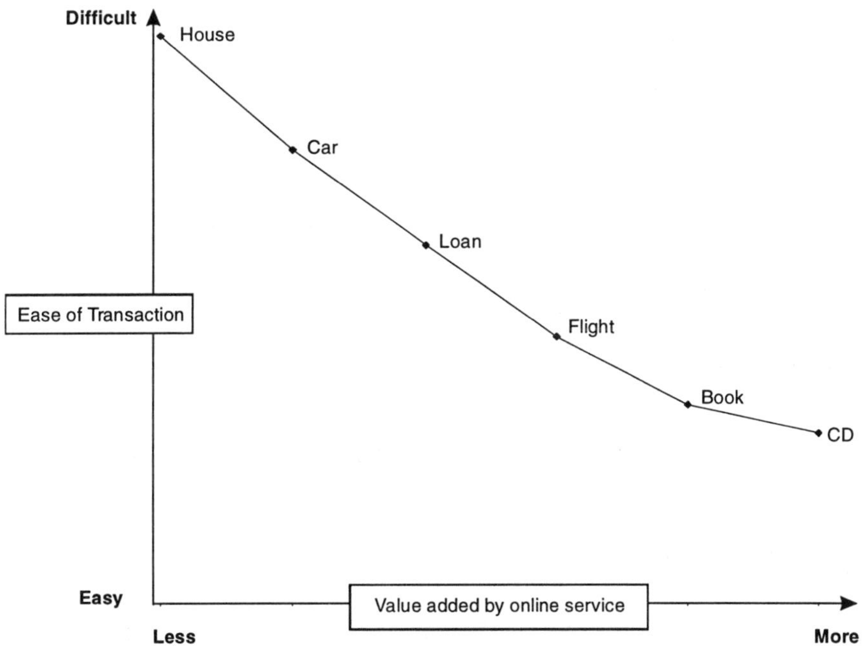

Source: Microsoft

According to Forrester Research, online insurance is expected to become a rapidly growing market, estimated to reach more than $1 billion by the year 2001, from relatively insignificant sales in 1997 (see Figure 1.4).

Figure 1.4 Prospects for Insurance Markets on the Web

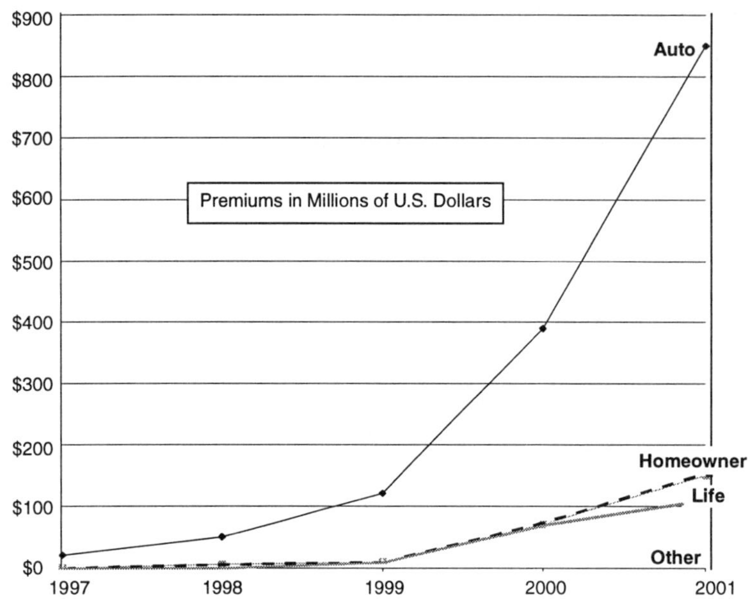

Source: Forrester Research

Online travel is particularly suitable for webcasting. The industry, which is estimated to grow from $1.52 billion in 1998 to more than $7.4 billion by the year 2001, promises to be a lucrative market (see Figure 1.5).

Figure 1.5 Projections of Online Travel Markets

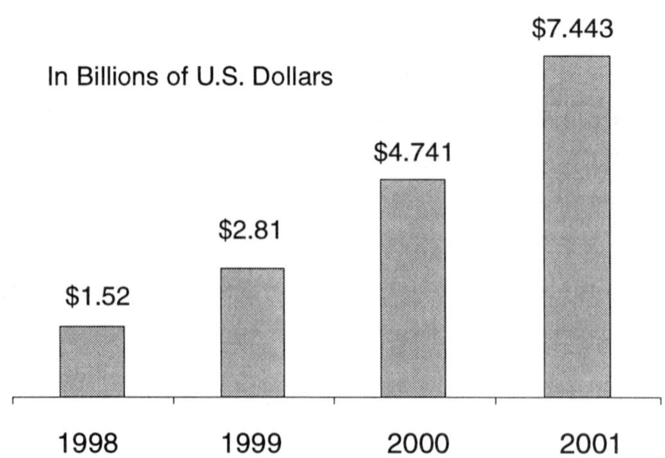

Source: Forrester Research

Interactive advertising is another online market for which the industry holds great expectations; although it will remain a relatively small percentage of the total amount spent on advertising, it is expected to reach $4.5 billion by the year 2000 (see Figure 1.6).

Figure 1.6 Online Advertising Revenue Projections

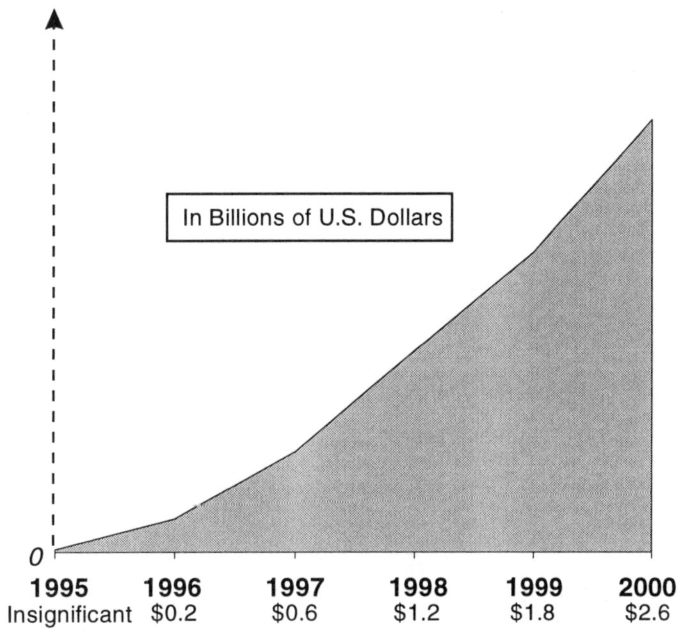

Source: Jupiter Communications

Creating a Smart Push Organization

Implementing webcasting within an intranet for marketing products and services to consumers requires a business strategy. The organization must consider the targeted user categories, select push technologies to meet those requirements, facilitate multimedia traffic, and determine user preferences and potential operating problems.

An extensive webcasting project team should carefully consider a special Web server that is dedicated to one or more specialized webcasting channels. It should combine real-time information, such as industry news, competitive developments, and stock prices, with company content from legacy databases, which may often account for at least 75% of all information to be pushed. Separate Web channels should be considered for continually updating major company functions, such as sales, marketing, finance, and human resources.

Figure 1.7 illustrates such a webcasting installation based on an Incisa push technology server.

Figure 1.7 Example of an Enterprise Smart Push Installation

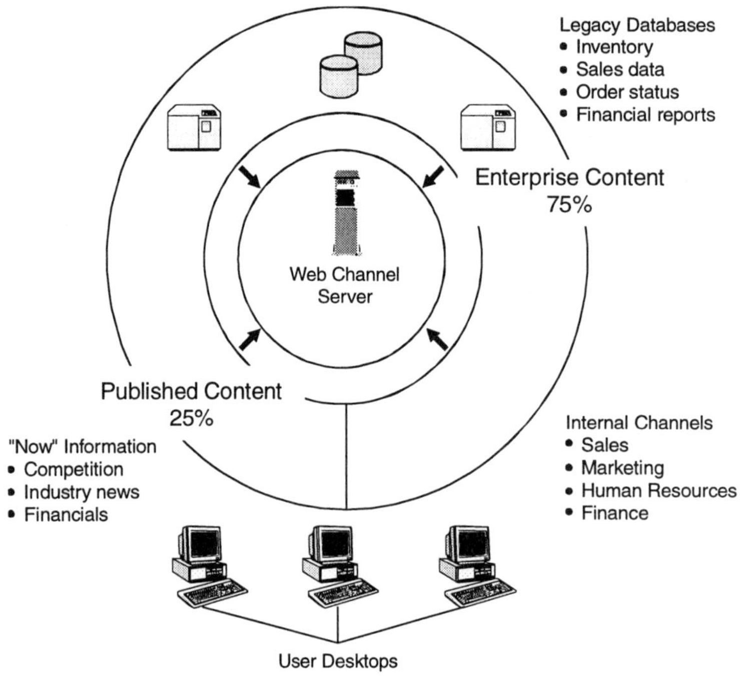

Source: Wayparol Communications

An organization considering webcasting should also remain informed about the latest tools and services. Particular attention should be given to the development of digital broadcasting alternatives and their benefits for performing webcasting functions, which are discussed in detail in *Chapter 9: Webcasting Business Strategies*.

Immature Webcasting Products and Services

The webcasting market is emerging rapidly. It consists of two groups of vendors: those supplying webcasting development tools and those supplying webcasting services. Marimba is among the most advertised webcasting tools; PointCast began as a webcasting service, but is now promoting webcasting tools. Most services are being offered by small ventures or start-up firms; many groups are specifically developing push technology server or client products, but have relatively little marketing or capital resources with which to take advantage of this opportunity.

Webcasting products differ widely from one another and standards are only now being developed. Consequently, directly comparing their performance and usefulness is difficult. The best course of action is to obtain sample product versions from the vendors and test them online with the webcasting content and environments in which they are intended to operate. Table 1.3 lists some webcasting companies and their services.

Table 1.3 Webcasting Companies

Company	Service
America Online	AOL offers Driveway, an offline component that downloads content from AOL and the Internet for AOL customers
BackWeb	Sells software tools so content providers and companies can create their own Webcast channels
Berkeley Systems	Its After Dark Online delivers content from *Sports Illustrated* and others
IFusion	This startup has a service similar to PointCast, but it can manage more TV-like animation and video
Marimba	Founded by former members of Sun's Java development team, Marimba's Castanet software can send programs and applets in addition to content
Microsoft	The company includes webcasting features in its IE 4.0 browser
Netscape	Offers the Netcaster tool in its Communicator 4.0 browser
PointCast	The webcasting pioneer; content from partners, including CNN, *The New York Times,* and *Wired* magazine is displayed with advertisements on a screen saver
Wayfarer	Its software is intended for use by companies that want to Webcast enterprise information over their intranets

Source: Business Week

Most client products are free to users, but the Web channel server products may vary in price, costing up to $50,000 per installation, depending on the number of subscribers. Webcasting products for intranets dominate the market because they eliminate advertising and other distracting materials.

Webcasting services are growing rapidly and most service providers offer predetermined Web channels as brokers for third-party Web publishers and content producers. Many services include advertising that is responsive to subscriber profiles and interaction with Web channels. Some services offer channel branding capabilities for sponsors or advertisers of products associated with selected channel contents. Pricing for these services varies widely, is often negotiable, and is consequently very difficult to directly compare.

In the absence of well-known participants, this nascent webcasting industry is very unstable. In fact, some companies existed only briefly before discontinuing their operations. Others were acquired or merged with other businesses. For example, companies such as iFusion, Individual, and Metz resigned from the industry; Lanacom was acquired by BackWeb Technologies. Extreme caution is advised when making product and service selections for company webcasting operations. Users should take advantage of free trials to evaluate products.

Who Are the Early Adopters?

Most Fortune 1,000 multinational organizations are early adopters of webcasting technology. They represent companies from various industries and their initial webcasting projects may include different applications, although few have comprehensive mission-critical systems in place.

Financial services, which depend on the most current information, are naturally among the leading and oldest users of push technology. Financial service information providers, who supply the professional institutional investment community with constantly changing data and information, are probably the most experienced users of push technology. If there are any valuable lessons to be learned about the benefits and drawbacks of webcasting, this is the area where they should be found.

Chapter 2

Anatomy of Webcasting

The emerging webcasting industry consists of three major segments of activity feeding upon each other. Figure 2.1 illustrates this interdependence.

Figure 2.1 The Push Food Chain

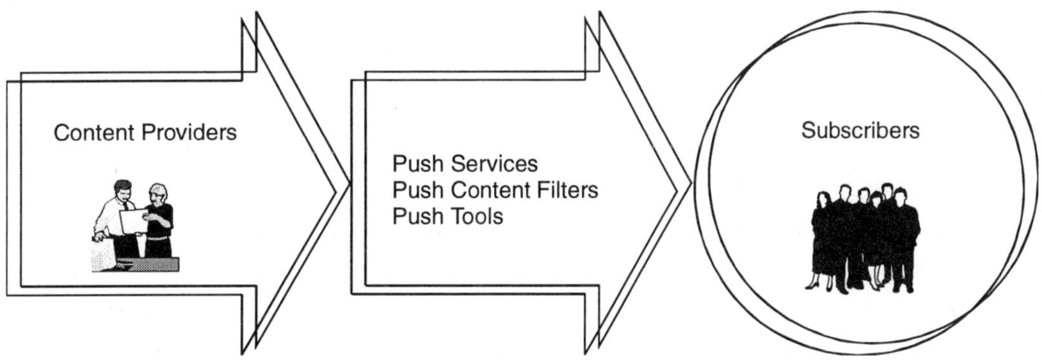

Webcasting content producers own and control information sources. They include news organizations, publishers, research companies, Web sites with specific information, and various software vendors. In addition, a growing segment of push content brokers and technology providers is emerging. This segment offers the tools, search agents, and services to acquire and transmit specific content to end users.

Internet users who install client software or are equipped with push browsers are the ultimate consumers of push generated information and represent two distinct push subscription categories, which are consumers in the home and corporate workers.

Webcasting Alternatives

Technically, webcasting using push technology is not truly a push application, but appears as one to users. Most push processes are in fact more appropriately termed automated pull processes because most require a subscription and an information request profile from the user before any information is transmitted.

The client software also initiates the pull based on a time schedule predetermined by the user, and the webcasting server responds with only the information to match the request profile. Figure 2.2 illustrates how the basic pull technology is almost identical to the automated pull, which is also known as push.

Figure 2.2 Pull and Push Technologies Compared

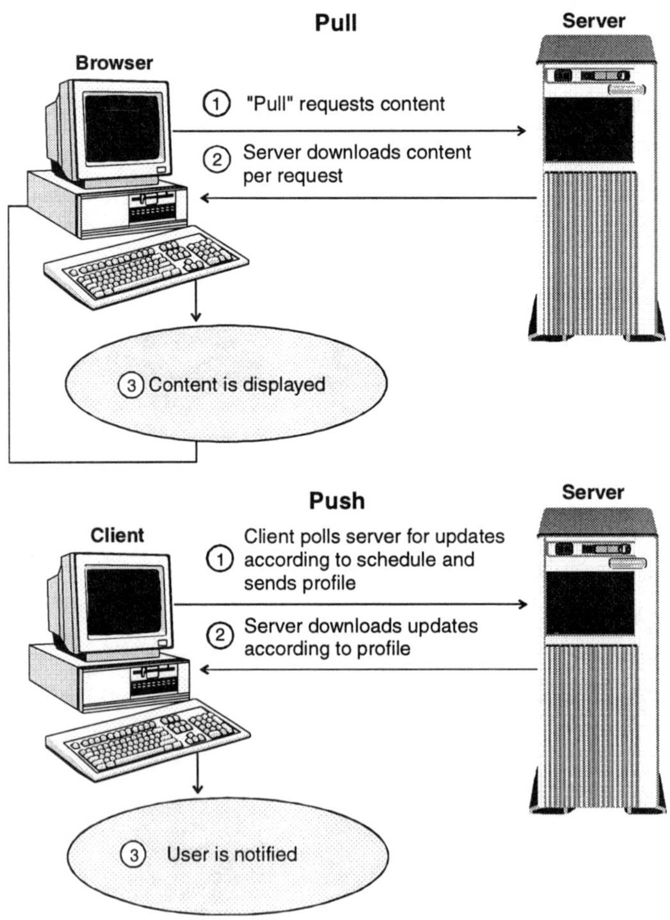

Several push technologies differ according to how the information is acquired from the originating channels or producers. These technologies fall into three major categories: the pure push, selective pull, and distributed push/pull.

Regardless of the actual mechanism involved, the approaches have the same objective: to cut through the clutter of information overload, deliver the most timely news and information, and save time and energy of manually searching large numbers of Web sites.

The Pure Push

The pure push category involves a direct connection to a push server. The connection remains open until it is disconnected by the subscriber. Until then, it continuously transmits information on user-selected topics. This connection could be wired or wireless.

This type of service is considered a pure push application because the user receives information from the push service server or transmitter until it is switched off. AirMedia Live NewsCatcher and Wayfarer's INCISA are representative of pure push technologies.

In a digital wireless network, the client application is a combination of a radio receiver and a software program. The push service transmits digital content over the airwaves in near-realtime to anyone with a suitable receiver. When information is received from a wireless push service, no Internet connection is necessary; this method does, however, require specialized hardware and a subscription to a particular service. If the receiver is operated within reach of such a wireless network, the user may also receive E-mail or use it as a notification medium. Figure 2.3 illustrates a pure push service using wireless transmission.

Figure 2.3 Pure Push Service

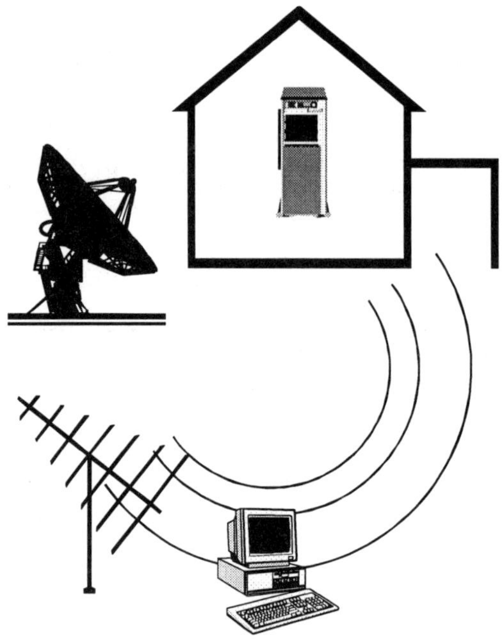

A true push scheme beams content over the airwaves to anyone with a receiver.

The Selective Pull

The selective pull is the most common push concept popularized by the PointCast Network. The push service vendor makes arrangements with selected Web channel producers and Web sites. The channels are centralized on an array of servers – a server farm – operated by the push service, which controls search agents and advertising materials on the channels. Subscribers connect to the central Web site through the Internet and receive notification or brief headlines about updated information. However, subscribers selectively request the updated materials, which are then downloaded from the server farm. This push concept is illustrated in Figure 2.4.

Figure 2.4 Selective Pull Service

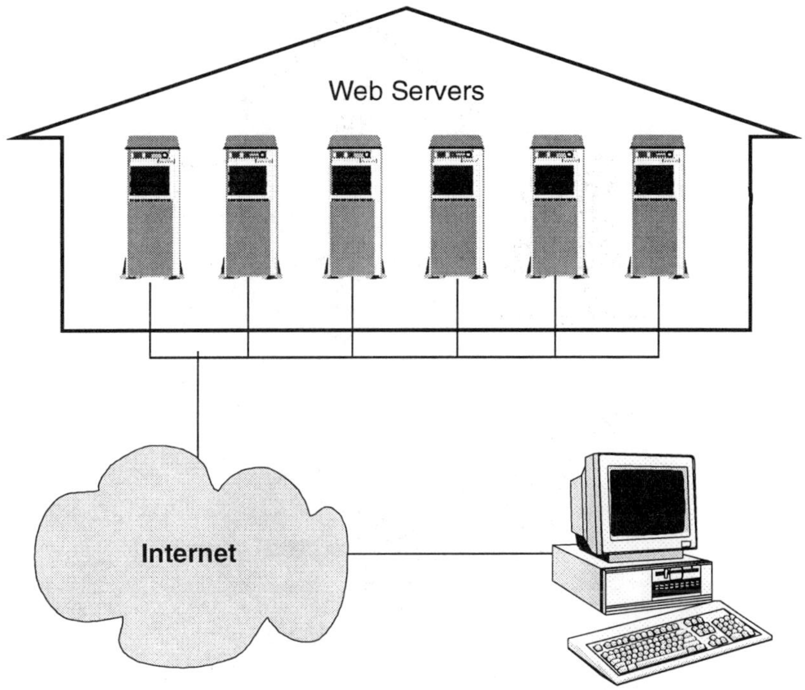

PointCast popularized the selective pull approach, which centralizes the content on the push company's server farm. With selective pull, a client requests updates and central servers send them.

The Distributed Push/Pull

The distributed push/pull alternative is yet another variant of push service technology. With this approach, push services maintain a central directory of Web channels and inform subscribers about what updates have taken place on which channels. Upon connecting with the Internet, clients learn where the updates have been made, however, they must pull any content directly from the channel where the update was made.

In fact, most push services and development tools provide only headlines or brief summaries of updated information, which are delivered through proprietary clients. The subscribers or users of such tools ultimately link directly with the Web site or channels to obtain the full story or additional news and details. Figure 2.5 illustrates distributed push/pull.

Figure 2.5 Distributed Push/Pull Alternative

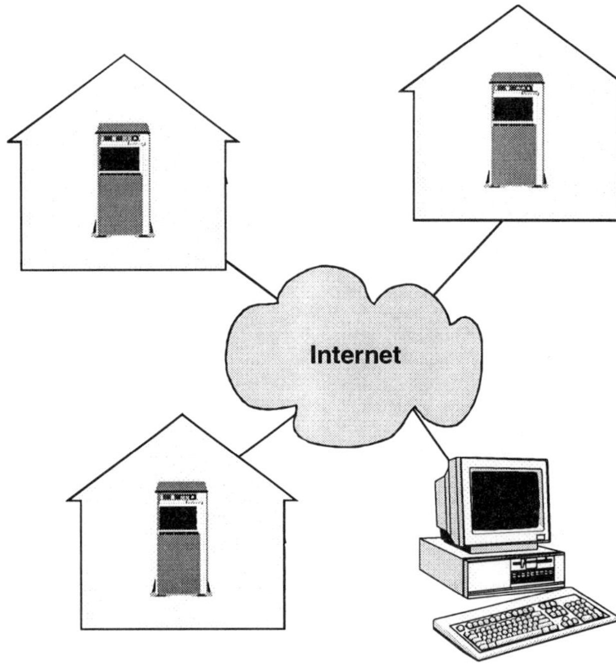

BackWeb and HeadLiner keep a central index of channels, but do not push that information to clients. Castanet, NETdelivery, and Intermind all push updates locating information to their clients from a central index. In distributed push/pull, a client locates information from central servers, but pulls content directly from originating channel partners.

Webcasting Content Delivery

The most common method for providing push service on an intranet or the Internet is a turnkey solution that includes a push server, a client, and development tools. This delivery method typically uses a proprietary protocol and is more expensive than other methods because it may require special connections and branding of its channels. In addition, this method locks the user into channel selections made by the service and carries its brand name on displays.

An extension to a Web server is a less expensive method of providing push services because no special push server is required and feedback and demographics can be collected on an external server. Such extensions operate within the user browser and do not require a special client.

The simplest webcasting delivery method is using client agents that retrieve information from Web sites and channels. With this method, a server is not necessary except for updating client information and user demographics. In this case, the subscriber can also maintain an anonymous relationship with the push vendor and undertake all the costs associated with agent implementation and customization.

Push Client Features

All webcasting applications have a common basic set of features and capabilities (see Table 2.1), which include the user's ability to create an information profile, client's ability to connect, inform the Web channel of its presence, and receive information for the subscriber. In addition to these basic features, the latest push systems provide additional user options, including messaging, security, and intelligent use of bandwidth connectivity controls.

Table 2.1 Summary of Push Client Features

Client Feature	Description
Connectivity	Ability to connect with the Internet through analog, integrated services digital network (ISDN), LANs, and online services
Flexibility	Ability to schedule connections and control associated computing resources
Customization	Ability to select topics and items from Web channels
Persistence	Ability to interrupt data transfers and resume them when connections become available
Bandwidth	Bandwidth optimization features are available on client and server sides
Integration	Ability to combine existing controls with new or updated materials
Notification	Ability to alert a user to the arrival of new information on selected channels
Security	Ability to ensure content is received only by intended client
Protocols	Availability of appropriate protocols to provide reliable transmissions to all types of platforms

Subscriber Connectivity

Users connect to the Internet or intranets in a number of ways: Internet service providers (ISPs), indirect online service providers such as America Online (AOL) or CompuServe, and company LANs. Analog or integrated services digital network (ISDN) modems may be used in addition to dedicated, high-speed, company lines.

Push client applications must be able to recognize all the possible connection types and establish a seamless link with the Internet without any effort on the part of the user. Examples of seamless connections include those established with minimal or no user interaction, such as unattended notifications or midnight downloading. This type of connectivity is becoming increasingly important as large data packages are being transferred to client desktops.

When more than one connection method is possible, a mechanism with which the subscriber can select and prioritize the required connection should be available. In more sophisticated push client applications, a feature may detect the existing configurations without user input.

User Flexibility

A successful push application allows the user to remain in control of the PC. The objective is to allow the user to organize the Internet-PC interaction so it collects the push information without interfering with data processing activities at the desktop.

For maximum flexibility, the push service or Web publisher should provide users the ability to regulate the actual connection times, length of connections, and volume of information acceptable for downloading during any specific period.

Client control over the type of information being transferred – for example its size, storage location, segments to be saved, and replacements of existing files – is becoming an increasingly important feature. This flexibility is particularly important because a growing percentage of remote and mobile users who can benefit from push technology do not maintain permanent connections.

Customization Profile

A push service should allow users to customize their information profiles and delivery parameters of the providers.

In addition, the subscriber must be able to select specific channels from a content provider. Some push technologies provide only high-level selectivity by channel, which may still require the user to search through downloaded information. Ideally, the subscriber should be able to fine tune their selections, indicating precise topics.

Clearly, the most convenient push services allow the subscriber to specify the topics of interest in considerable detail. This convenience relieves the user from the tedious task of searching through large volumes of data files.

Channel publishers should be able to divide their content materials into categories for easy user identification and selection. Equally important is the ability to specify when, how, and the duration for which the content will be displayed. Most importantly, the providers must have the ability to target the information to specific user audiences defined by subscriber profiles. These features are critical because they allow providers to accurately target audiences that are most likely to provide a return on investment (ROI) through advertising or content information sales.

Information Transfer Persistence

Persistence of information transfers is an important feature of a push service client software, particularly for those used in company networking environments where many other activities are performed on the desktop. The term refers to the ability to stop a data transfer at any particular point because the connection is required for a more important task.

The persistence feature is critical for delivering the large files typical of rich multimedia content. Push applications that include special file transfer capabilities or client/server (C/S) interactivity can save the transfer information on the client desktop when the connection is interrupted. With this feature, the push client continues from the point of interruption when the connection is reestablished.

Bandwidth Efficiency

Some push technology products minimize bandwidth use at the push server and client sides. On the client side, bandwidth use is reduced by downloading push files from the server when the desktop is not otherwise operating and is idle. Bandwidth can also be conserved by sending only the necessary data to update existing elements on the client site, thereby minimizing the updating process.

Some push tools use specific file abstracting methods that compare similar files – even if their names have changed. With such a process, identical file elements are recorded and reused, as necessary, which prevents downloading additional copies of the same materials and limiting content duplication.

Bandwidth can also be conserved by eliminating graphics or images in headlines or transmitting only thumbnail images or small representative icons with an option to magnify the image. This method may not always be practical, however, because its effectiveness depends, to a large degree, on the original Web channel design. Fortunately, channel providers seeking the widest distribution of their content will provide these types of bandwidth-saving alternatives.

New Content Integration

Client software's ability to transfer and integrate new or updated content materials with existing content already on the desktop is an ideal push application feature. Such an application automatically determines what information or parts of it from selected channels should be downloaded, what the information should replace, and where it should be stored. This capability replaces the need to download and install files.

Client Notification

Push client software must be able to notify a user when new information exists or has arrived at the designated Web channels. Although these notifications can differ widely depending on the push service involved, they include simple windows and dialog boxes, task bar icons, ticker tape animation, and may also contain audio and video elements. These alerts are generally designed for desktop delivery, but some services also provide notification for wireless notebooks, personal digital assistants (PDAs), pagers, and various forms of E-mail.

The type of alert also depends on the importance and category of information being transferred. The client alert should be configured to enhance the process and facilitate its use by the subscriber. Otherwise, the push service may not be a competitive offering. The user application determines the form of alert best suited to a particular operation.

Push Security

Push subscribers must ensure that any information pushed to their system does not contain any viruses or other elements that might corrupt user operations. As a result, subscribers should be concerned about the integrity and authorship of any information being pushed. Java transfers cause some concern because of security problems and should be considered when selecting a push service. Java reportedly has gaps in its firewalls, but this concern is being addressed by Java software developers.

Another aspect of push security pertains to subscriber content selections. It is often critical – particularly in the competitive financial business environments – that selected information is received only by the intended subscriber. In addition, the subscriber profile should never be released to third parties without user consent.

When push technology is used on an intranet behind the security of a firewall, security does not present such a pressing concern. However, if direct Internet access is allowed for some users, the security of push materials delivered from outside of the company must be assured.

Client Protocol Issues

Some of these features – persistent file transfers, efficient bandwidth use techniques, and certain environmental security measures – require special proprietary protocols for operation.

Many company firewalls are configured to block standard Internet protocols (such as TCP/IP) to prevent unauthorized access. In addition, push vendors have developed proprietary protocols that may prove difficult when transferring data across firewalls. Consequently, added programming efforts may be required to implement them. Users should check their specific firewalls to determine which protocols are safe.

Most push applications use hypertext transport protocol (HTTP) because it can pass through firewalls outside of a company environment. HTTP is a convenient protocol because browsers are based on it; however, any real-time interaction features are difficult to create because it was not designed for the task.

Content Webcasters

This group of push services includes content publishers whose primary business is to publish information and associate their specific brand names with certain types of content. Content webcasters such as PointCast develop and brand their own channels or networks on which they push their own or third-party content. In addition, they offer a variety of specialized channels that are supported by specific advertisers as revenue producing streams.

Content webcasters create content partnerships with content providers by licensing the use of such information or agreeing to pay a percentage of advertising revenues.

Content materials are not necessarily branded with the content webcaster's brand. However, the brand of the push service itself is clearly that of the content webcaster service. For example, PointCast is a webcaster's brand, but is not necessarily the original brand of the content being pushed. As a result, if a particular newspaper licenses its content to such a push service, for example, it will gain revenue from the relationship. However, the basic brand being promoted by the service is that of the content webcaster and not of the original content provider. For this reason, the primary customer relationship develops between the content webcasting service and its subscribers. This approach is considered a low-risk and low-return method of expanding their target audiences.

Content providers seeking to develop direct relationships with their audiences must find other forms of providing their content directly to users – particularly in companies striving to construct intranet channels or business-to-business relationships. The alternative is for the company to build its own webcasting channels using webcasting technology tools that provide direct control over their channels and their content. Such push technology tools include Web extenders, automated pull, push/pull webcasting, and software development and implementation.

Web Extenders

Web extenders exploit the Web server and browser model, creating additional layers on top of it to extend parts of the Web sites or channels directly to the user desktop. In effect, this approach uses the existing Web as a push infrastructure. Intermind and InCommon are two typical examples of Web extender tools.

Because the Web was not designed as a broadcasting medium, this approach presents several limitations. For example, it is primarily limited to only content available on the Web. More importantly, this solution has very few facilities for targeting specific content to specific subscribers; each user must be registered separately to receive each portion of a Web site.

Other disadvantages include the lack of facilities to target specific hardware and software profiles and assign content providers for expiration at specific times. In addition, personalized content cannot be developed on-the-fly for individual users, and off-line interactions cannot be reported.

The Automated Pull Technology

Automated pull technology is a client-side technology designed to let subscriber desktops automatically pull Web pages at specific time intervals. This approach has been introduced in Microsoft's Internet Explorer (IE) 4.0 and Netscape's Communicator 4.0.

Microsoft's proposed standard for channel definition format (CDF) enables a client to download broadcast content from any CDF-compliant Web site. As a result, thousands of Web sites can become channels with basic webcasting functions. Unfortunately, CDF offers webcasting that is not segmented or personalized; it does not provide channel control over user profiles, scheduling, content customization, or intelligent delivery of information or feedback. CDF is, however, useful for organizations seeking to broadcast similar content in a pull fashion.

Microsoft IE 4.0 offers webcasting and provides users automatic delivery and off-site access to Web channels. CDF makes transforming any Web server into a push channel without additional programming or technology possible. It creates push channels that are in effect automated pull from the clients because users must initiate the information download. It is an open, scalable solution that works with HTTP and proxy servers, HTML Web sites, and any Web authoring tools. It also scales up to multicasting push solutions, which is important for multimedia content delivery.

The webcasting facility allows an existing Web site to be pushed without any modifications or reauthoring. The actual push, or automated pull, is performed by a user searching the site on a scheduled basis. Content developers can optimize and personalize the experience by creating a channel that indexes content on an existing Web site. With this approach, the channel would be created using CDF standard file format for indexing and pushing the content on the Internet.

The Netcaster of Netscape Communications is another browser-based example of an automated pull solution. Netcaster allows any channel to be anchored to the desktop, converting it into a webtop. This webtop is designed as a cross-platform network interface rather than a proprietary Windows-only interface, such as IE 4.0. Any channel can become a webtop, and the contents are based on HTML. Content providers can envelope desktops that have been controlled by an operating system (OS).

The Netcaster also includes a Netscape Channel Finder, the user interface for accessing channels over the Internet. Channel Finder is dynamically served from the Netscape Web site, enabling users to subscribe to a number of channels from the Netcaster interface.

Netcaster can be implemented using existing open standards of HTML, Java and JavaScript; Microsoft CDF is proprietary. Netcaster matches CDF functions by allowing content developers to use JavaScript to specify Netcasting parameters, but is not based on CDF standards. Analysts speculate that it is probably the desktop most likely to influence the structure and success of push technology.

Push/Pull Webcasting

Push/pull webcasting is the cooperative C/S application solution that simultaneously provides shared control to content providers and subscribers. This architecture brings broader and deeper capabilities to webcasting than other alternatives. The push/pull business mode provides the widest range of benefits to both channel owners and subscribers.

These functional benefits include valuable feedback reporting, extensive customization, integration with back-end enterprise environments, and user notification technology. The push/pull approach is unlimited in the flexibility it provides webcasters, and it effectively delivers large files. It is also suitable for delivering software upgrades, perhaps more conveniently than specialized push technology, such as Marimba, because users have a way of selecting the software upgrades they would like to receive.

Push/pull webcasting also offers channel providers a way to specify delivery of any content on a personalized basis. It also excels in automation because of its cooperative architecture and is designed to facilitate the delivery of any content category.

Software Implementation Webcasting

Software implementation webcasting is the C/S technology and development environment designed for building applications that are delivered across the Internet and intranets. While not a Web-based approach, software development webcasting gives more control to channel producers. It does, however, have other limitations.

For example, this concept is best exemplified by Marimba technology. Because channel products must develop the content and applications with tools of that technology, the flexibility of the content that can be broadcast and development tools that can be used are limited. This approach is also more expensive because significant programming is required. This solution also offers limited control to users, who must start or launch applications to view newly delivered content. It is not as convenient, from the user point of view, as the push/pull webcasting approach.

Webcasting Concepts in Videoconferencing

Because videoconferencing includes transmitting multimedia content to one or more designated participants, certain elements of webcasting must be identified – particularly when the conferencing is taking place without the video. All conferencing operations are basically one of three types:

1) One-to-one conferencing

2) One-to-many conferencing

3) Many-to-many conferencing

Of these operations, one-to-many conferencing is very similar to webcasting via the Web using IP protocols. Table 2.2 summarizes the basic differences between the three categories. Figure 2.6 illustrates the concepts.

Table 2.2 Forms of Videoconferencing

Form	Description
One-to-one or Point-to-point	This form involves two sites that can send and receive audio and video signals
One-to-many or Multicasting	In this form, one Web video server is broadcasting audio and video signals while all others are receiving
Many-to-many or Multipoint	All sites can send and receive audio and video signals – the most complex form of group collaboration

Figure 2.6 Forms of Conferencing

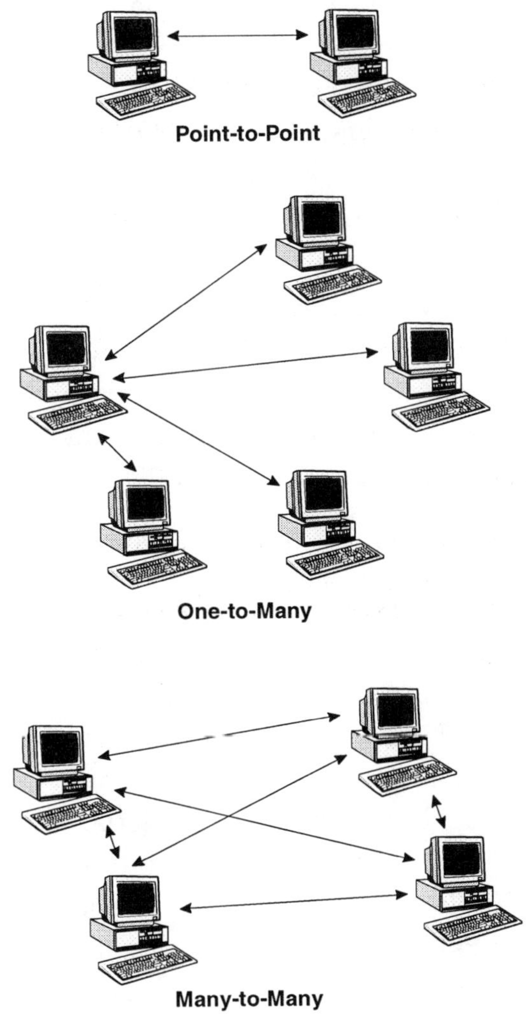

One-to-One Operation

One-to-one or point-to-point conferencing connects two sites, each of which is able to send and receive content. This type of operation requires a permanent connection between the two points to provide a real-time transmission and operates effectively over LANs, WANs, and ISDN connections – particularly when traffic is sparse. Transmission quality may deteriorate during peak periods because desktop videoconferencing over analog telephone lines and the Internet is still an emerging technology and the quality of such transmissions has room for improvement.

One-to-Many Distribution

One-to-many distribution is also known as the multicasting communications mode. Multicasting consists of a broadcasting Web video server site, targeting multiple client sites as recipients. In this form of conferencing, one site actively transmits messages or instructions while all others passively receive. Microsoft is developing specifications to allow Windows 95 users to exploit this approach in groupware networking applications.

Microsoft is collaborating with DirectTV, a division of General Motors Corporation (GM), and Hughes Electronics to design a system that will allow PCs to receive the video programming normally received with home-TV satellite dishes. The Microsoft initiative also includes a new category of multimedia services, which has yet to emerge. Unlike cable modems, the new system is primarily designed for multicasting. One component of such services is the "multimedia magazines."

Direct PC is a multicast service that delivers Motion Picture Experts Group (MPEG)-compressed streaming video over Hughes Ku-band Galaxy satellites. It is designed for business Internet users who require distributed video services from a central server. Hughes Network Systems' Direct PC operation is collaborating with Starlight Networks and Hewlett-Packard (HP) to give Direct PC users access to real-time video services on the Web through a Netscape browser. Broadcast channels of the Galaxy satellite system can provide up to 12 megabits per second (Mbps) of bandwidth for a combination of video and data, which is received by an end node consisting of a 24" antenna and the HP server with 12-Mbps receiver cards. This arrangement appeals to companies with distributed operations seeking to provide Web pages and Internet services with embedded real-time or store-and-forward video and data. Starlight Software manages the streaming video channels on the LANs that link clients to the server. As many as 100 PC clients can be supported, but each requires Starlight client software. Direct PC is intended to be used with other Internet links, including leased lines, ISDN and dial-up analog lines.

Many-to-Many Enterprise

The many-to-many enterprise, or multipoint, is the ultimate in collaborative groupware applications, but bandwidth limitations on individual connections between participants and a multiuser control unit determine whether such videoconferencing can take place.

International telecommunications (telecom) carriers, such as AT&T, MCI, and Sprint, offer multiparty videoconferencing services. To initiate such a group conference, all participants must connect to a videoconferencing bridge managed by the carrier. Any existing videoconferencing equipment that adheres to international standards is adequate for this purpose.

When several sites are connected, the images on the screen change automatically to reflect the speaker. In addition, these services may offer clipboard and document sharing with annotation in realtime. The cost of such services include communication costs from each participating site to the multiuser control unit (MCU) location, which handles transmissions from hardware with different protocols, and bridging charges for each connection. When companies use such services frequently, acquiring MCU systems for in-house bridging facilities may be more cost effective, although they remain relatively expensive and complex systems to implement.

When compared with webcasting as such, this form of content distribution is more complex because it performs in realtime and includes audio and video transmissions. The MCU hardware performs all transmission management and tracks all participants and their immediate requests for connections and transmission of voice or images, text, and graphics. Certainly, multiuser, real-time videoconferencing is the ultimate content distribution method and offers lessons for managing multimedia, multiprotocol, and multiuser transmission in other webcasting or push technology applications.

Powerful User Interaction Potential

Cyberspace customers and their time are scarce resources, and Web advertisers must compete for them. Some Internet businesses began offering rewards to consumers conducting business with them. Industry observers believe that user interaction will increase significantly when payments, discounts, and rewards become an everyday expectation with regard to the Web.

Web businesses must give customers incentives to do business on the Internet. From the customer point of view, there is no reason to use the Internet if online shopping is not easier or less expensive than ordering through a toll-free number. Without these incentives, only a small segment of the population will continue shopping in this manner; the concept of E-commerce cannot be expanded on such unrealistic expectations.

As a result, some airlines offer lower fares and other services discount their fees for those who use the Web to obtain their products. These discounts are possible because the significantly lower cost of doing business on the Internet provides a wide enough margin to give a portion of the savings to the customer.

Another incentive to attract online buyers is to make certain products and services available exclusively on the Web. Some companies are also introducing frequent Web buyer incentives comparable to airline frequent flyer programs. Webcasting provides a cost-effective means of tracking, notifying recipients, and implementing such promotions.

Increased user interaction is also expected by providing free Internet access to customers – a particular advantage in financial services where online customers are frequent Web site users. Businesses pay $5 or more for direct marketing leads of such a prospect.

Webcasting is also a means to collect very precise demographics about the users who qualify themselves every time they interact with any Web site or channel. Sale of such information is expected, but access to such information is likely to be more restricted than direct mail lists and telemarketing campaign information. For example, Web businesses are now facing regulatory propositions that require customer consent before using their information. With the Web, consent is not enough; customers must be rewarded for providing this information with payments or special discounts.

Indeed, the different facets of E-commerce create electronic business environments quite different from those of conventional marketing.

Digital Broadcasting: The Technology of the Future

In the final analysis, digital content distribution is truly the technology of the future. Digital broadcasting can certainly make improvements relating to demographics and tracking user response by adopting techniques from the well-established broadcast radio and TV industries.

Webcasting enhances the conventional broadcasting business model with features such as interactivity that are unavailable in radio and TV. Interaction and customization further improve the efficiency of marketing and selling to selected groups of customers. In the same manner, the ability to broadcast to selected groups of employees in an enterprise is one of the main benefits of webcasting.

Consumers of Web-based Information

To begin using a webcasting service, a subscriber must download the selected webcasting software into the desktop. This client software is generally free to the user, although some specialized webcasting services charge a monthly fee.

Once the webcasting software is installed, the user is asked to answer a profile questionnaire. The form allows the user to specify what information he or she wishes to receive, including global news or headlines from newspapers, weather reports, developments in specific industries, press releases of particular companies, or selected stock quotes.

The completed user profile is submitted to the webcasting service provider, where it is stored in a database. When the user connects to the Internet, the webcasting software automatically dials the service Web site to determine if any updates exist in the designated channels. This automatic contact between the user desktop and the selected webcasting information sources takes place at intervals defined by the user. When a change is discovered, the webcasting system automatically notifies the user.

In intranets, the webcasting system is often resident on its own server within the company networking environment. Updated information from all the channels selected is then automatically downloaded to the company server and relayed to individual employees – a simple method for reducing network traffic and conserving bandwidth between the outside webcasting sources and individual company users. Because businesses often maintain permanent Internet connections, they can receive nearly continual updates from the webcasting service.

Future webcasting client screens are expected to consist of a display with several channel buttons that will include news, company information, entertainment, sports, and productivity channels providing spreadsheets and word processing programs.

Providers of Web-based Content

Two categories of Web-based content providers have been identified: the original Web site developers that may be companies or merchants and publishers with specific information channels targeted at specific audiences; and the Web channel brokers that provide webcasting services, supported by advertisers through special access fees.

Software agents at the webcasting service site search the specified channels of Web sites for changes, similar to the way search engines comb the Web. When the agent software discovers changes in the specified channels or Web sites, it automatically retrieves that information and sends it to users who requested it.

These webcasting services are designed to operate on wired networks, but some can provide news and stock alerts or E-mail notifications to pagers and portable notebook computers.

Targeting Special Interests

Webcasting is an ideal promotion and delivery vehicle for special interests, because an initial group of subscribers have already expressed interest in a particular topic. As a result, brokers who are compiling various webcasting channels can determine which specialties to address, and compete on the basis of providing the most comprehensive information, products, and services within that specialty.

Even within each specialty channel, such as travel or investments, content providers can target individual subscribers according to their daily access to specific data. Within a Web channel, specific, more detailed interests and preferences can be identified to customize the content to each individual subscriber. This function cannot be performed on a cost-effective basis in any other way. The nearest vehicle to target the marketing potential on the Web is direct mail marketing, but it lacks the interactivity and immediacy of webcasting.

Webcasting provides an immediate conduit to conduct business with subscribers while they are responding to the push messages or are evaluating the information. Many advertising experts believe it is that point in time when a prospect is most likely to be convinced to purchase a product or a service being promoted. Webcasting and push technology offer the means to exploit that critical point.

Efficiently Distributing Data Packets

When properly implemented, webcasting distributes basic data packets more efficiently than other methods on the Web – an important feature within company networks, such as intranets, where network traffic is reducing network performance.

In addition, webcasting does not occupy the networking infrastructure by sending messages and content to all users of a particular network – an inefficient method originally used by Web publishers when relatively few Web sites and smaller numbers of Internet users consumed system resources.

Webcasting involves distributing content to only those users who indicate interest in specific Web channels or topics. In addition, users are able to schedule distribution times outside of the peak traffic periods, which relieves network overloads. The other factor that reduces the traffic on the network is webcasting's ability to provide only headlines or brief alerts to users.

Replicating Data Traffic from a Single Source

The multicast solution for webcasting is particularly useful because it provides for distributing the same content from a single source to many users, replicating across the routers and switches in a network. Replication is also an effective way to conserve bandwidth because the content is not repeated as it is sent to users.

The multicasting approach to Web channel content distribution is emerging as an important solution for a variety of applications, including webcasting company policy and financial data to designated recipients. It requires additional software investments, but networking equipment vendors are incorporating the solutions into their most recent product releases. Consequently, multicasting can now be implemented by simply activating the proper segments of the operating systems of those products.

Audio and Video on the Internet

Efficiently webcasting multimedia content on the Internet depends on the bandwidth of the connections and the sources of audio and video content. These can vary from multimedia databases to company video studios and outside radio and TV broadcasts.

The problem with audio and video for webcasting is that it must be in digital form or readily convertible from analog to digital format. To circumvent this problem, many organizations now use hierarchical database management systems with various levels of audio and video content in digital format or are readily convertible with encoding equipment.

Audio and video on the Internet present a number of issues that must be considered to produce an acceptable quality of webcasting communications. For example, people with suitable voices and appearance must be selected, and the proper equipment for recording, editing, encoding, and webcasting the content over the Internet must be purchased.

Digital Video Production

The hardware and software for digital video is being developed and new products are appearing regularly. Keeping abreast of these developments and ensuring that the products conform to predominant standards and are compatible with other pieces of equipment involved in encoding and transmitting on the Internet is critical.

Preparing original digital video begins with a story board. Stock footage and new footage are then edited to provide the final content, but current hardware and software tools allow a number of sequences to be tested in a cost-effective way. For example, inserting graphics and incorporating two-dimensional (2-D) and three-dimensional (3-D) animation can be performed on PCs, which are less expensive than specialized workstations.

Video inputs for such a production come from sources that provide varying quality of output. Because the quality of the final digital content depends on the quality of the original input, the original input should be recorded and generated on the best quality equipment.

Once a model of the final video is developed, it is used to create the actual video. The minimum software features for producing broadcast quality output are 24-bit color manipulation capability, anti-phasing, subpixel positioning, and text generation – features that are required to improve image quality and compete with conventional TV and cable broadcasting.

Digital video is also compressed for webcasting and real-time videoconferencing. Ensuring that the compression techniques used in transmission products are compatible with those in subscribers' desktops is critical.

Digital Audio Production

In creating original audio, use of the best possible microphones yields the highest-quality audio. Eliminating background noise is paramount to producing quality audio. Wired microphones and directional boom microphones produce superior results.

Setting correct input levels for creating the original sound files is critical. Other factors that influence audio production include the quality of recording equipment, selecting clear source materials, noise, equalization, compression, and normalization. Producing quality audio is clearly a function for professional audio engineers; if such expertise is unavailable in-house, outsourcing the project is a viable alternative.

Audio transmission across the Internet will suffer in quality from the inevitable delays and latencies. Audio is actually more sensitive than video to loss of pixels or delays during transmission. The eye cannot always discover losses in color or shapes within a rapidly changing video sequence. However, lack of continuity in speech or a musical selection will be noticed immediately. Consequently, more attention must be given to selecting and transmitting audio content for quality reception at the other end.

Radio and TV Broadcasting Sources

Webcasting content can come from any source if it is in a digital format. The news and specific subject interviews and documentaries continuously developed for radio and TV broadcasts are particularly desirable content materials for webcasting. These sources are in a state of perpetual change, which makes them very attractive for Web channels, where changes in content attract users to the site.

Many radio and TV stations now have a presence on the Web. Specific Web sites are online versions of their conventional broadcasting services. The advantage is that these Web sites can be reached from anywhere in the world and are not inhibited by the limited range of radio and TV stations.

Webcasting services or brokers can set up intelligent agents that monitor a number of radio and TV Web sites for content changes, which occur continually because of the nature of news content carried by those broadcasts. As a result, these Web sites are a ready source of changing content that can be used for pushing specific channels to selected users.

However, because radio and TV broadcasts consist of audio and video content, webcasting such materials requires significant bandwidth for real-time delivery. Many networks – particularly those of Internet users – cannot handle such content with broadcast quality and present only small windows of video at a fraction of the full video frame speed.

Alternatively, push technologies can be used to download segments of such broadcasts in the background mode for later viewing. In such instances, the video is downloaded to the user storage disk. This method does, however, consume hard disk capacity to store digital video. The most recent innovation involves streaming media solutions, which retain the immediacy impact of delivering news broadcasts but compromise on image size and quality.

Multiple Encoding Requirements

When multiple audio and video sources are involved for providing webcasting content, multiple encoding systems or services must be used to handle the multimedia content materials. Such features are often included in multimedia authoring and webcasting development tools.

As a result, these tools include various encoding and decoding algorithms and automatically switch to the appropriate algorithm when handling multimedia content. This feature is particularly important in the latest Internet videoconferencing products, where the software involved must be able to communicate with end-user platforms that have different videoconferencing encoding systems. The most recent versions of videoconferencing software can manage multiple coder/decoders (codecs).

Even as videoconferencing standards are promoted and implemented, however, the possibility of an odd audio and video source remains. In such cases, obtaining conversion software to create a compatible version of the source or create a new compatible version of the same content are the only alternatives.

Webcasting: The New Form of Multimedia

Webcasting is seen by some users as a new form of multimedia. The new aspects include selecting the channels to be monitored by specialized agents and user notifications, which in themselves may be small animated graphics and running ticker tapes that create a semblance of new multimedia forms.

Actually, webcasting simply assembles existing and established multimedia content in a new way. Text, graphics, animation, audio, and video now include additional hyperlinks to link the user with the original sources of information they represent.

Instant Updating Capabilities

One of the most attractive and appealing features of webcasting is the availability of updating capabilities of the services and push technology development tools. Higher frequencies are offered online for updating some of the publication channels because new information is normally collected during the preparation period. This information must wait until the actual publication of the newspaper or magazine, while it is immediately available to anyone who can access that publisher's Web site.

Despite webcasting's many advantages, producers and users can misuse the updating capabilities of webcasting channels. For example, even a change in a headline will be reported as a new change, while in fact no substantial change has occurred. Web channel producers occasionally use this technique to increase the exposure of their channels to users.

On the other hand, users may request updating that is too frequent for the channels selected. As a result, their desktop storage will be consumed with redundant information and the user will waste time evaluating the contents. Consequently, instant updating capabilities must be used with caution.

Conclusion

Webcasting is represented by three basic solution categories: the pure push, the selective pull, and the distributed push/pull models. (Pure push is seldom possible unless it is based on wireless Web channel distribution technologies.) These alternatives are used by three groups of webcasting participants:

1. Web channel content producers and publishers who own the information and products that they want to distribute or sell over the Internet or intranets.

2. A separate group of brokers, services, and tool vendors facilitate the implementation of webcasting by providing the services and the software to develop Web channels. This group represents a rapidly growing segment of Web-related businesses that expects to capture a significant market share. Most of these ventures are relatively small, unprofitable, and subject to mergers and acquisitions. Companies considering developing webcasting channels or services should screen these product vendors very carefully to make sure their products and customer support will last long enough to establish a profitable webcasting operation.

3. The clients or users who subscribe to the webcasting services and buy products and services promoted on the Internet. The clients are offered free access to the webcasting service by simply downloading a client interface. However, they must provide a profile of their interests and preferences before receiving any content. Webcasting clients also vary depending on bandwidth connectivity, flexibility, customization choices, persistence of information transfer, bandwidth efficiency, new content integration, user notification, and available security measures. User interfaces vary widely from one offering to another, although all provide the basic means of Web channel selection, user profiling, and notification.

Webcasting channel content comes from a variety of sources. To further E-commerce, webcasting must provide real-time, interactive multimedia to compete with alternative digital TV solutions that are also going to be compatible with Web channel content distribution across the Internet.

To attract users to conduct business via the Web, monetary incentives such as discounts are needed. The goal of online vendors is to offer goods and services more conveniently and less expensively than conventional catalog buying. For this reason, webcasting is seen as more likely to succeed in the next few years in intranet and extranet environments, where the audiences are more predictable and more influenced by the webcasting organizations.

Chapter 3

Multicasting Solutions

Multicasting delivers high-bandwidth applications without overloading networks. As a result, it is ideal for distributing multimedia content across intranets and the Internet. Multicasting makes implementing webcasting, push technology, and video server applications possible, without concern about traffic bottlenecks.

Multicasting benefits any organization where large numbers of individuals must receive the same information. At the same time, it is a suitable solution for communicating real-time information to large audiences, including sales trends, product introductions, and press conferences, because it sends the same information only once to multiple recipients – an efficient way of saving bandwidth and maintaining scalability of the service.

Multicasting does, however, require some changes in the networking infrastructure and desktops, including ensuring hardware and software are multicast enabled, selecting special routing protocols, setting up switching, and securing intranets. If multicasting is implemented on company LANs, any WANs involved in enterprise communications must also meet these criteria.

Multicasting is not suited for all forms of Web traffic. For example, it is not recommended for Internet telephony, individual Web access, file access, and video-on-demand (VOD) applications.

Multicasting Advantages

IP multicasting enhances a company network by enabling a wide variety of applications, improving productivity and competitiveness of an enterprise.

Consequently, it is suited for making pure push technology a proposition for efficiency.

Multicasting is an ideal infrastructure for collaborative high bandwidth applications, such as multiuser videoconferencing and whiteboarding, in which many-to-many traffic flows are the norm. In addition, multicasting enables one-to-many traffic flows, such as webcasting push applications, video servers, and software distribution. Higher-level protocols for IP multicasting provide the real-time transmission and reliability that are particularly important in videoconferencing applications.

Multicasting also provides better opportunities to address predictable network audiences, manage networking growth and expansion costs, and minimize network loading and response times.

Probably the most significant and immediate advantage of multicasting is reducing bandwidth requirements. The webcasting server is not required to transmit as many sequential or concurrent packets and, consequently, is available for other tasks. An alternative way of saving costs is to use a less expensive server for performing the webcasting functions.

How Multicasting Works

Without multicasting, a Web channel or site sends information as unicast packets, replicating many identical data streams and wasting bandwidth. A Web channel, however, can broadcast the information effectively.

IP multicasting enables Web servers to transmit only one stream of data to multiple recipients using specific protocols on hosts and desktops and in routers and network switches.

Multicasting can be implemented in steps because it can operate without enabling every router at the outset. It is implemented in pockets that are linked by tunneling encapsulated multicast traffic in a unicast mode. Figure 3.1 illustrates the multicasting island principle.

Figure 3.1 Multicast Island Concept

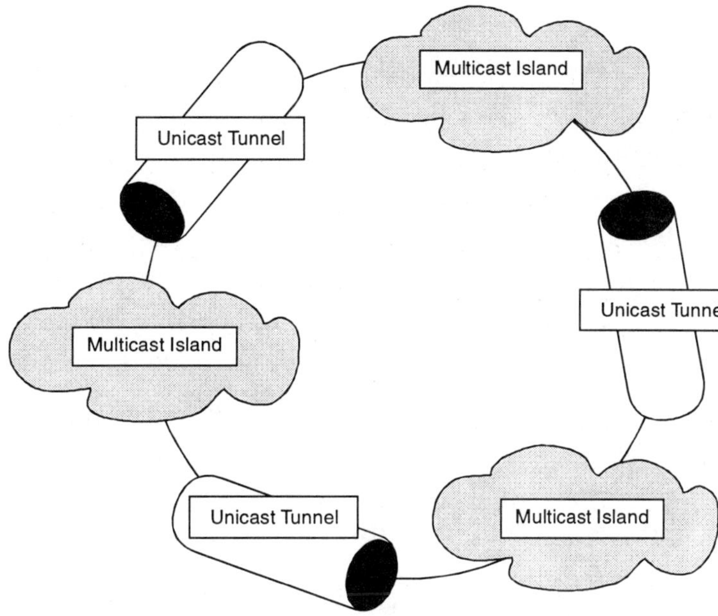

To transmit a multicast stream, a Web server must have a TCP/IP protocol stack that supports IP multicast, the Internet group management protocol (IGMP), a multicast-enabled application, and a network interface that can filter multicast traffic.

Multicast routers require IGMP and additional multicast routing protocols, such as multicast open shortest path first (MOSPF), distance vector multicast routing protocol (DVMRP), or protocol-independent multicast (PIM). They must also be configured to initiate tunneling when necessary.

Multicast filtering switches in networks require IGMP filtering to forward packets to network segments only where multicast-enabled desktops exist.

A network filtering switch that is not multicast enabled will broadcast traffic to all attached segments. Routers that are not multicast enabled, however, will pass unicast traffic with multicast encapsulated in it until it reaches the next multicast-enabled segment of the network.

In addition, the application itself must be modified; the webcasting information must be written originally or redesigned to take advantage of IP multicasting.

Virtually all of the latest operating systems – Windows 95, Windows NT, and latest versions of UNIX – can accommodate IP multicast and IGMP. The most recent adapters and network drivers also include IP multicasting capabilities, and a large number of network equipment products are ready to operate in multicast mode. They merely must be activated when multicast operations are being implemented.

When users with IGMP capabilities send a request to participate in an IP multicast group, it is received by a Web server running the multicast application, which then adds the user to its subscriber list. As a result, only users who want to participate will receive multicast content from that channel. The concept of a network with IP multicasting in some of its components is illustrated in Figure 3.2.

Figure 3.2 Multicasting Network Concept

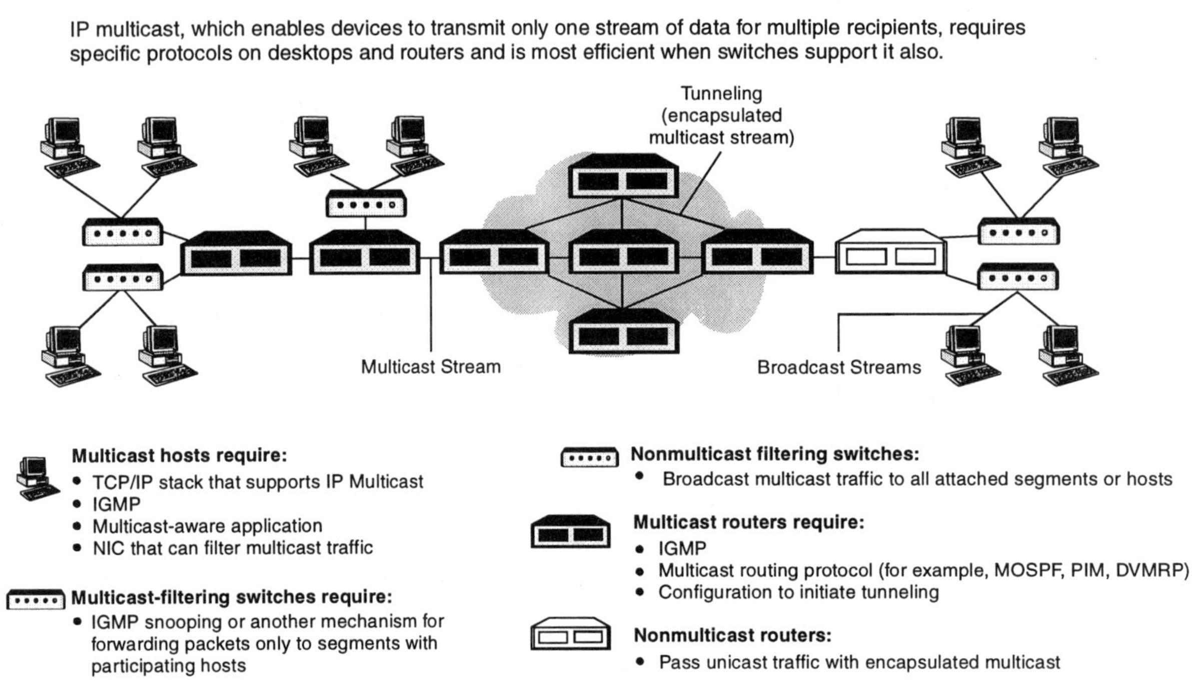

TCP's Inefficiency for Multicasting

The different tasks that multicast applications perform require several multicasting transport protocols. Most unicast or one-to-one interactions on the Internet run under the TCP, which provides reliable data delivery via a point-to-point IP connection.

However, using TCP for one-to-many webcasting distribution is inefficient because every recipient requires a separate TCP connection to the Web channel. Consequently, webcasting across such a network results in redundant use of network and server resources and rapid performance deterioration.

The User Datagram Protocol

IP multicasting applications run over user datagram protocol (UDP), which provides the most effective method of packet delivery – with the option of error detection – to specified destinations. UDP does not guarantee 100% delivery of every packet in an application, however. This lack of guaranteed delivery may suffice for audio and video distributions where occasional missing pixels can be tolerated, but it is inadequate for real-time videoconferencing and software distribution applications.

Because UDP is a minimal service, the specialized transport functions in a multicast transmission must be provided by additional layers of protocol. All IP multicast applications run on top of UDP. They use protocols such as RTP, RTCP, reservation protocol (RSVP), and real-time streaming protocol (RTSP), that are becoming widely available.

IP Multicast Protocol

IP multicast is an Internet Engineering Task Force (IETF) standard network protocol designed specifically for one-to-many communications and has been adopted by the majority of TCP/IP stack and router vendors. IP multicast uses IP addresses that provide for group communications, representing a selected subset of all the clients.

IP multicast requires each host in a multicast group to have a TCP/IP stack supporting IP multicast; it also requires that all routers in a network support it. The scope of an IP multicast packet transmission may be controlled by its time-to-live (TTL) value, which provides a regional limit on propagation of packets through internetworking routers.

IP multicast is best suited to implementing the publisher/subscriber business model where the user does not need to know the sender's address to establish a connection to receive delivery. It is the basis for push technology, which is viewed by multicasting proponents as the next generation of applications that will revolutionize the Internet.

IP multicast is unreliable, however, because it is merely a routing protocol that directs how routers forward each packet; it has no mechanism to recover from network service failures. To increase multicasting reliability, several higher level transport protocols ensure reliable communications over IP multicast networks, including protocols such as DVMRP, PIM, and others forwarding a multicast to potential destinations.

Internet applications require more reliable communications because between 5% and 50% of data packets are lost on the Internet and intranets. TCP/IP provides reliability in one-to-one communications by recovering lost packets for IP. However, IP multicast protocol itself is not reliable because it does not yet have the equivalent of TCP/IP functions. As such, it is usable only by audio and video streaming where some level of packet loss is tolerable to a certain degree.

Internet Group Management Protocol

IGMP determines participation in a multicast group. Routers and desktops of a network must run it and one of several IP multicast protocols to participate. IGMP enables users to register for multicast sessions and permits the multicast groups to manage dynamically in a distribution fashion.

These multicast groups are dynamic; clients enter and leave at any time. Groups cease to exist on a network when no members are present. In addition, these groups are scalable as more clients join a multicast.

When a client joins a group as a subscriber, an IGMP message indicating that another client wants to receive data distributed to that group is sent to the local router. A client then sets up the IP process and network card to receive the multicast on the group address. When a client leaves a group, the router stops sending data to it and frees bandwidth on that segment. Table 3.1 summarizes the various protocols that make multicasting possible.

Table 3.1 Summary of Multicasting Protocols

Protocol	Description and Application
USP	Provides best efforts delivery of a packet to a specified destination with the option of error detection.
IP Multicast	IETF standard protocol (RFC 1112), which is very efficient, but unreliable becuase it is merely a routing protocol.
IGMP	Determines participation of a client as a subscriber in a multicast group of users.
DVMRP	Uses reverse path forwarding algorithm to determine multicasting paths at a router in a network.
MOSPF	Extension of open shortest path first unicast protocol for multicasting at router level.
PIM-Dense	Similar to DVMRP, but works with any unicast protocol. Best used when few channels distribute to many clients.
PIM-Sparse	Designed for numerous multipoint transmissions targeted at relatively small numbers of subscribers.
Reliable Multicast Transport Protocol (RMTP)	Developed by Bell Laboratories. Optimized for asymmetric networks.
Multicast File Transfer Protocol (MFTP)	Designed for distribution of large multimedia files and content.
Reliable Multicast Protocol (RMP)	Uses ring-based algorithm and guarantees delivery.
Scalable Reliable Multicast (SRM)	Provides best efforts reliable multicast for up to thousands of users.

Multicast Routing Protocols

Multicast routing protocols and routers perform the bulk of the multicast-enabled work on a network. The objective of these protocols is to create an optimum multicast delivery path through the network. These routing protocols use a variety of algorithms to achieve the most efficient routing and operate with major routers whose manufacturers have included multicasting capabilities. Multicasting on these routers is enabled by adding memory capacity and updating software.

An efficient multicast delivery path ensures that the multicast content travels along the shortest available path only to those clients who want to receive it.

Routers receive multicast content and send it to network nodes where other routers of network segments with subscribers wait for information. Routers exclude branches where no members exist and include new branches when a new multicast client joins the group of subscribers. This routing is accomplished with DVMRP, MOSPF, and PIM.

Distance Vector Multicast Routing Protocol

DVMRP is implemented by a program on routers in a network. It maintains topological knowledge using the distance vector routing protocol with which a multicast forwarding algorithm is implemented.

DVMRP is based on the reverse path forwarding technique, which requires the router to send a received packet to all paths except the one leading back to its source. If a router on any path does not want to receive a particular multicast, it can return a message. This feature stops multicast content from going to areas without subscribers.

Periodically, DVMRP resends multicast packets to all the paths to discover if any new subscribers have joined the group in locations not currently served by the multicast. As a result, time lags between a new subscriber registering for webcasting and actually receiving his or her first transmission because the router performs the periodic "flooding" of all paths that always lead away from it.

Initial DVMRP implementations did not include the path pruning feature. The protocol also suffers from scaling limitations because of its necessity to perform the flooding operation. DVMRP has been used to develop the MBone across the Internet and consists of unicast tunnels between DVMRP-enabled platforms. DVMRP is an IETF standard described in detail in request for comment (RFC) 1075 (see *http://ds.internic.net/ds/rfc-index.html/*).

Multicast Open Shortest Path First Routing Protocol

MOSPF is an extension to the open shortest path first (OSPF) unicast routing protocol that allows it to support IP multicast. The basic OSPF protocol enables each router in a network to identify all available paths and calculate routes from itself to all possible desktops. MOSPF includes multicast information in OSPF path data, which indicates where multicast clients exist on a LAN.

MOSPF develops a decision tree for each source and group connection and computes the paths for active channels transmitting to them. This decision tree is cached in router memory and recomputes whenever changes in the paths occur or when the cache times out.

This routing protocol operates only with OSPF internetworks and is best suited to networks with only a few channels transmitting at any particular time. MOSPF does not perform optimally with many active channels or numerous unstable paths.

Protocol Independent Multicast

PIM operates with all unicast routing protocols but supports two different categories of multipoint traffic patterns known as dense and sparse. These patterns were developed by the IETF interdomain multicast routing (IDMR) working group and can support both modes simultaneously for various channels and user combinations. Routers use this protocol to indicate whether other routers need to receive multicast traffic for a particular group of subscribers.

The PIM-dense mode is based on reverse path forwarding algorithm and closely resembles DVMRP. However, PIM-dense does not require a particular unicast transport protocol and functions with any unicast protocol. It is suitable particularly for environments with few channels and many clients, the high and relatively constant multicast traffic volume and the relatively close together webcasting channels and clients, as in an intranet.

The PIM-sparse mode is designed for environments with numerous multipoint data transmissions reaching a relatively small number of LAN segments. Sparse mode is also used when subscribers are scattered throughout the network or when bandwidth is limited.

This technique works by defining a distribution tree around a focal router – the core router – and the rendezvous point to which all webcasters send their content and at which clients are registered. Multicast traffic for the whole group is sent and received over the same distribution tree, regardless of the source channel. Once data is transmitted, routers along the path optimize it automatically.

This routing protocol assumes that multicast traffic is not wanted unless it is requested – an approach best suited for small groups of subscribers separated by WAN links and transmitting intermittent traffic. A shared tree of this type results in savings for webcasting applications with many active channels distributing content to small groups of selected subscribers.

Multicasting on LANs and WANs

On company LANs, multicasting can be optimized through the use of multicast filtering switches. In basic mode of operation, a switch floods a broadcast or multicast data packet to all its ports. An IP multicast-enabled switch sets up filters and sends multicast traffic automatically only to participating users. The switches receive information about these ports from IGMP. In effect, a multicast-enabled switch operates similarly to an IP multicast router, except that it operates in the local area.

Many ISPs are introducing IP multicasting services for WANs, and many offer IP tunnels to the MBone virtual network layered on top of the Internet. MBone is expected to remain a multicasting transitional strategy alternative until IP multicast becomes widely available for WANs. The tunneling capability of MBone is important at this stage because packets are dropped if multicast traffic is transmitted to devices that do not support it.

In addition to the Internet, wide area multicasting can be implemented on top of WANs that support it, including asynchronous transfer mode (ATM), frame relay (FR), switched multimegabit data service (SMDS), satellites, dial-up asynchronous, and ISDN.

Multicast File Distribution

Multicast file distribution is a one-to-many application that can involve thousands of users and requires reliable delivery. Unlike collaborative computing, multiuser conferencing, and real-time data feed distribution, however, it is not a time-sensitive application.

Efficient methods for retransmitting lost packets and improving reliability can be implemented. For example, file transfer receivers can request retransmission when prompted by the Web channel after a time lapse. This delay can reduce a sudden burst of many-to-one retransmission requests to the originating channel.

A reliable MFTP that employs such a concept has already been developed by StarBurst Communications in collaboration with Cisco Systems and has been submitted to IETF for consideration as a standard baseline.

The MBone Initiative

Multicasting technology is still in the developmental stages, but the most widely known and used multicast-enabled network is the Internet MBone, a virtual network consisting of Internet sectors known as multicast islands. In areas of the Internet that are not multicast enabled, multicast transmissions travel in the form of unicasts using the tunneling principle. The multicast packets are hidden inside unicast packets until they reach a router that understands the multicast packets and can process them as multicast data streams.

Most of the software running multicasting on the MBone is for high-end UNIX workstations, including Digital, Silicon Graphics, Inc. (SGI), and Sun Microsystems, Inc. In addition, multicasting video streams require a minimum of 128-Kbps bandwidth of ISDN – the most effective telecommunications (telecom) link is a T-1 or better. The MBone consumes a large amount of bandwidth and requires a heavy-duty UNIX workstation and a T-1 line to provide for multimedia traffic. A 56-Kbps line is adequate if only audio distribution is involved.

The MBone originated with an audiocast on the Internet from the IETF meeting in San Diego in 1992, which included only 20 sites. Two years later at the IETF meeting in Seattle, more than 560 hosts in 15 countries were able to receive an audio and video channel and interact with the proceedings on the audio links. Since then, MBone has been used to demonstrate its capabilities by distributing data from an experimental robot at the bottom of the Sea of Cortez of the northwestern coast of Mexico.

An estimated 3,000 interconnected networks on the Internet comprise the MBone system. Many of the major backbone providers also offer some form of

MBone connectivity. MBone's value is important particularly for audio and video streaming, push applications, electronic software distribution, international player games, and multipoint videoconferencing. Unquestionably, multicasting is required to deliver multimedia content to individual households.

How MBone Works

The MBone network is possible because many UNIX workstations have built-in audio and processing power to decompress and display videos in Windows – the basic platform for conferencing application programs and for packeting real-time content for Internet transmission.

The MBone is a virtual network layered on top of the Internet supporting routing of IP multicast packets. The tunnel end points are typically workstation category platforms with operating systems that support IP multicasting.

The MBone topology is a combination of mesh and star patterns and is constantly under construction and development. No single provider offers MBone networks; users connecting should contact an Internet service provider (ISP) involved in the endeavor. Some of the major ISPs providing access to MBone include SERFnet, PSInet, SDSCnet, and UNINETT. If locating such an ISP is difficult, a tunnel to another point on the MBone can be constructed.

Internet Multicasting Channels

A new Web channel dedicated to the multicasting of movies and news and the handling of voluminous file transfers and software distributions is developing. It is a product of the Internet Protocol Multicast Initiative (IPMI) and is a development out of the MBone portion of the Internet.

IPMI replicates a core of MBone routers to accomplish this objective. Other efforts to develop a multicast service of this type are also recognized. One was announced in 1997 by MCI called Realnetwork, which is running over MCI's Internet backbone.

IP Multicast Initiative

IPMI is a multivendor, cooperative effort designed to address the issues of overcrowding on the Internet. Its charter is to speed the migration of native IP multicast by providing a set of marketing and educational services that promote the implementation of standards-based IP multicast products and solutions.

IP multicast promoted by IPMI is an open, IETF standard that enables efficient bandwidth use for webcasting applications. Unlike traditional unicast, which creates individual point-to-point data streams between the Web channel and each receiver, or broadcasts sending streams to everyone on the network, multicasts transmit a single stream accessible by any recipient desiring the information.

The IPMI includes more than 50 company members, among which are leading hardware and software companies such as AT&T; BackWeb Technologies; Bay Networks; Bolt, Beranek, & Newman (BBN) Corporation; Cabletron; Cisco Systems; Digital; FORE Systems; Hewlett-Packard (HP); IBM; Intel; Lucent Technologies; MCI; Microsoft; NASA; Netscape Communications; Novell; Progressive Networks; and Silicon Graphics, Inc. (SGI). Stardust Technologies of Campbell, California, has been chosen as the managing member firm to coordinate the effort. More details can be obtained at *http://www.ipmulticast.com/*.

The ISP Role in Multicasting

Wide implementation of the IP multicasting technology would result in more efficient use of bandwidth on the Internet and other IP networks. To achieve this objective, however, ISPs must be convinced that upgrading their infrastructures to support multicasting is worth the expense.

ISPs' failure to support multicasting remains a roadblock to its universal implementation. Nevertheless, industry observers believe that IP multicasting capabilities will become a competitive necessity for most ISPs in the short-term future.

Concerns About Multicasting

Multicasting reliability is a general concern because there is no guarantee the IP multicast data transmitted to subscribers will actually be received.

However, IT managers are voicing many other concerns about the use of multicasting technology.

The two leading concerns regard the relative scarcity of multicasting application software and the lack of understanding of multicasting effects on the network. In each case, 54% of IT managers interviewed by IPMI voiced those concerns.

Other concerns about multicasting include the need for company network upgrading (26%), limited bandwidth at remote sites (26%), lack of security (24%), limited administrative tools (22%), and new business partners with which employees are unfamiliar (16%).

More minor concerns include limited ISP implementation or multicasting capabilities, multiple multimedia standards in use, and the impact of push technology.

Toward More Reliable IP Multicasting

The multicasting technology is still developing and its reliability remains in question as a result. Industry analysts believe that it must improve substantially before IP multicast can be used to distribute real-time, mission-critical business information to thousands of users.

Nevertheless, more than 50% of IT managers surveyed by IPMI in mid-1997 believe IP multicasting will create new business opportunities for their companies. The 1997 IPMI multicast use study reveals that 60% of IT managers surveyed consider audio and video distribution and webcasting as the most likely multicasting applications. These applications are followed by collaboration and conferencing (38%), push technology and information delivery (30%), and file transfer applications (12%). Figure 3.3 shows the IT managers' interest in multicast technology solutions.

Figure 3.3 1997 Multicast Use Study Results

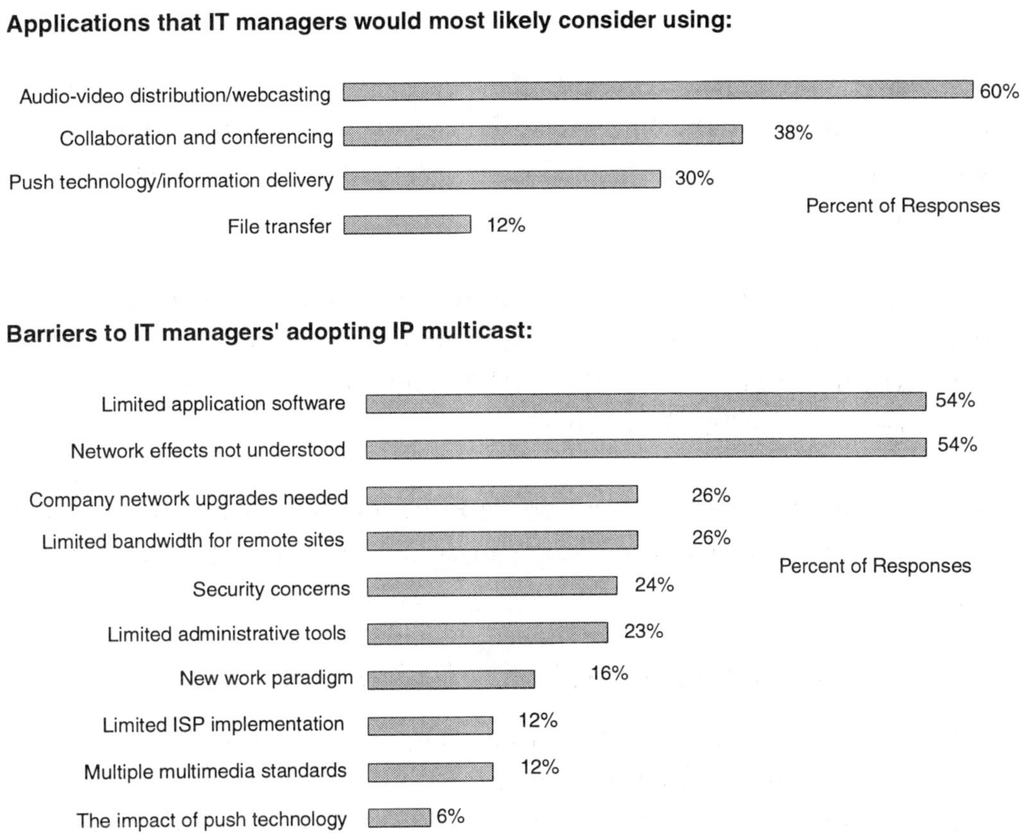

Source: IP Multicast Initiative

Developing Reliable Multicast Protocols

Reliable multicast protocols are needed to provide optimal communications and performance for each category of application and network. RMP, SRM, and RMTP have been developed to provide this capability. They are built on the IETF standard IP multicast protocol, which is efficient, but unreliable.

Lucent Technologies of Murray Hill, New Jersey, has formed a partnership with GlobalCast Communications of Fremont, California, to create a unified platform for reliable multicasting. It is designed specifically to increase the performance of time-sensitive transmissions over private intranets, extranets, and the Internet.

The partnership is based on Bell Laboratories RMTP, which is integrated with the RMP developed by GlobalCast. If this partnership can develop a unified concept, it will eliminate the need for different multicast protocols for push applications, file transfers, media streaming, and live event information feeds. For more details, point to *http://www.gcast.com/reliablemulticast.html/*.

Reliable multicasting is also seen as a means to mirror heavily used Web sites where latency issues appear when reproducing Web channels involves gigabytes and terabytes of content. Leading ISPs would prefer to reproduce enormous amounts of data in that method, but must be assured that simultaneous and accurate transmission of data can occur.

Reliable Multicast Protocol

RMP provides guaranteed multicast communications using a ring-based algorithm that passes a token to guarantee delivery. It creates a list of destinations and informs the originating channel that is in the group of subscribers and what it has received.

RMP is best suited for environments where a few members of the group require high guarantees of delivery and quality of service (QoS). Replication Web servers in LAN environments or file transfer in low-loss networks are organized using RMP. This ring-based protocol is the only one to achieve a level of commercial viability for mission-critical applications; it can scale 100 to 200 nodes without deterioration in performance.

Scalable Reliable Multicast

SRM protocol provides reliable multicast communications but requires receivers to be responsible for recovering lost packets by noticing missing numbers in packet sequences.

Because SRM does not maintain a membership list, the channel provider does not know who is in the group or whether the content was received as intended. It is best suited for streaming applications, including high-quality audio and video multicasting and real-time financial and news feeds. It can scale up to thousands of subscriber nodes.

SRM is a scalable protocol because it does not maintain membership information. However, SRM's high performance leads to low stability of the multicast, and high-session stability comes at a price of lower performance.

Reliable Multicast Transport Protocol

RMTP provides reliable multicast communications optimized for asymmetrical networks. It is a tree-based protocol that tallies acknowledgments midpoint in the network. It provides performance for satellite and cable connectivity, which require high bandwidth to transmit but receive a limited data stream in return. It is most effective for delivering files, software, and real-time data.

Tree-based protocols have the most effective scalability, but require considerable network management effort in construction and maintenance of the structure. RMTP also scales to thousands of subscribers.

Multicasting Tools and Services

As multicasting is better understood and becomes more common, new products and services appear on the market to facilitate its implementation and provide some means of control.

Percept Software of Palo Alto, California, an IP multicast startup, developed a software tool to provide audio and video content webcasters with detailed information about audience demographics and reception quality.

Percept's StreamWatch measures use patterns of multimedia broadcasts and multicasts over intranets and the Internet. It tracks the numbers and identities of users, times of tuning in, and individual reception quality. This information allows channel providers to bill viewing time to specific multicasts and helps content providers set advertising rates. The system also assists network operators in monitoring trouble spots on the multicast tree, which could indicate a need to give attention to specific routers on the network.

StreamWatch obtains its data from multicast data streams that use the real-time transport protocol (RTTP) for audio and video transmissions. It was originally developed for an IP/TV multicast product, but it works with other IP Multicast standard protocols. The tool is not considered a threat to privacy because it checks information regarding the viewing of a multicast transmission and not the content itself. It is priced at $995 per copy, and more details can be obtained by calling the vendor at 01/415-845-5200.

Multicast Services Using Satellites

Satellite services such as the 140-nation Intelsat are considered ideal for delivering multicast services worldwide. Satellite-based networks can also serve as overlays to the land-based Internet.

Satellite network operators such as Intelsat, Iridium, Globalstar, and Teledesic are being courted by IPMI to deliver multicast services. As of mid-1997, satellite operators remained reluctant to become involved in multicasting because they objected to the costs and potential risks of upgrading their networks with new routers, switches, operating systems, and other multicast software. The major objection of satellite services to date is the fear of destabilizing their networks and unknown revenue-making potential of multicasting services.

However, Telecom Finland is offering satellite multicast services. BBN, MCI, and UUNet are also conducting trials of such services. IP multicasting via satellite is considered a main factor in making universal application of push technology a reality.

Satellite services continue to question network delays affecting the Internet, however. NASA and Cisco Systems are conducting research to reduce high latency on satellite networks using a variety of new approaches. One solution being tested is the elimination of the TCP/IP slow start procedure which requires repeated acknowledgment to be sent to data suppliers. One proposed solution is to increase message size from 512 bytes to 4,096 bytes after the initial acknowledgment.

Conclusion

The multicasting communications mode consists of a broadcasting Web video server site targeting multiple client sites. In this form of videoconferencing, one site transmits messages or instructions actively while all others receive passively.

To provide a reliable multicasting service, these conditions must be satisfied:

- Clients must have a means of determining when a multicast of particular interest will take place
- They must also be able to indicate their desire to receive a multicast, and the network must be able to route multicast data efficiently to clients who want to receive it

In short, a price must be paid to reap the benefits of multicasting.

The effort to enable reliable universal multicasting requires implementing multicast-enabled routers and specialized protocols. Major router manufacturers are adding multicasting capabilities to their products; older routers can be upgraded with additional software and memory.

Several multicast routing protocols use algorithms to achieve transmission efficiency. This approach ensures that multicast data travels only to those clients who want to receive it along the shortest route.

Introducing multicasting in relatively small intranets and expanding it to limited, associated extranets is the easiest implementation approach. The Internet, which constitutes the much larger networking environment, will be the last to acquire full multicasting capabilities. However, telecom equipment vendors are creating more uniform platforms for reliable multicasting.

Chapter 4

The Search for E-commerce Solutions

Since the advent of the Web and rapid increase in commercial Web sites, a frantic search for the most effective E-commerce solutions has been underway. This quest is fueled by projections of rapid growth in Internet-related revenues. According to a forecast by the Economic Strategy Institute of Washington D.C., these revenues are expected to reach about $140 billion by the year 2005. Figure 4.1 illustrates this astronomical growth.

Figure 4.1 Projected Explosion in Internet Revenues

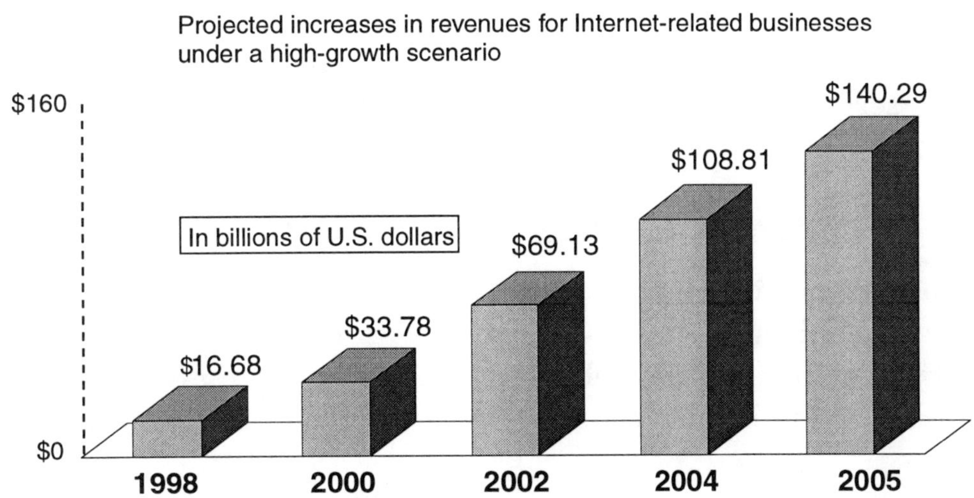

Source: Network World/Economic Strategy Institute

Initial E-commerce concepts included passive Web sites that were intended to attract a large number of users. The exceptions have been a few instances where Internet and Web client navigation tools have been given away free of charge.

Another variant of businesses on the Internet is the search engines or service Web sites supported by advertising, many of which did not meet user expectations. However, several search engines and services have developed significant support and account for a large part of Web advertising revenues. In comparison with the advertising revenues of the traditional print and broadcast media, however, this portion is minuscule. Hundreds of other Web sites based on this concept failed to develop either a mass user following or any significant advertising revenues.

The online services business model, where subscriptions and special fees for access to prime areas comprise the revenue streams, represent another attempt at conducting business on the Internet. However, the number of such services has decreased dramatically.

The lessons learned thus far suggest that major advertisers and promoters of products and services on the Web are reverting to more conventional approaches that can be combined with the special features of cyberspace. Industry experts now consider the traditional broadcasting business model with individual customization the most likely to succeed.

A large number of ventures are introducing a variety of push technology products and services to facilitate this form of company communications and E-commerce.

Intranets, Extranets, and the Internet

Intranets, extranets, and the Internet are critical facilities that play an increasingly strategic information delivery role in business communications. The enterprise's ability to effectively use its networking resources can make a significant difference in the struggle for customers, market share, and profitability.

The actual amount of information available to company workers has increased explosively to a level at which an information overload is imminent. This deluge of information creates increasing clutter and chaos for company managers and results in wasted time and effort as users search for information. Consequently, companies are ready for solutions ensuring that employees receive the information they need in a timely manner.

By definition, intranets are internal company networks based on open Web standards. They use the same software, network equipment, and computer languages as the Internet, but they exist only within an organization. Because these private networks operate behind firewalls, the information and data contained on intranets is limited to company databases.

Extranets provide secure connectivity between the enterprise intranets and those of its business partners, materials suppliers, financial services, and customers. Access to those external intranets may be limited by an agreement with the collaborating parties. If an intranet presents an information deluge, additional access to outside intranets will only aggravate this problem. Connectivity with the Internet beyond the safety of intranets and extranets contributes to the information overload.

Consequently, tremendous pressure is brought to bear control of those vast information resources and acquire and deliver the right information to the appropriate people when they need it.

E-commerce Defined

Various forms of E-commerce are already in operation, including product and services marketing and sales. The E-commerce ideal is the ability to acquire new customers, deliver the product, and collect payments entirely through electronic transactions.

Information, software, music, movies, videos, and certain audio products are ideal for electronic promotion and sales. Product categories such as electronic components, clothes, books, automobiles, and appliances are also promoted through electronic advertising and can be ordered and paid for via electronic media. However, most products of this type require locating the goods and shipping them to customers by conventional delivery methods.

In business environments, electronic data interchange (EDI) between major manufacturers and numerous suppliers is also considered an example of E-commerce. While EDI eliminates significant amounts of paperwork, it reflects only the transmission of goods through conventional means.

E-commerce solutions have been implemented for some time in the financial services industry, where information and transmitting funds are basic activities. However, those solutions were mainly based on expensive and proprietary networks that are not necessarily suitable for mass marketing and sales of other products and services.

The development of the Internet and the Web drastically changed the perception of E-commerce. More than 500,000 commercial Web sites now compete for attention from more than 40 million users all over the world. As a result, a desperate rush among businesses to capture a market share of this rapidly growing market is developing. Figure 4.2 illustrates the projected growth in company and small business clients connected to the Internet through the year 2000.

Figure 4.2 Growth in Number of Clients on the Web

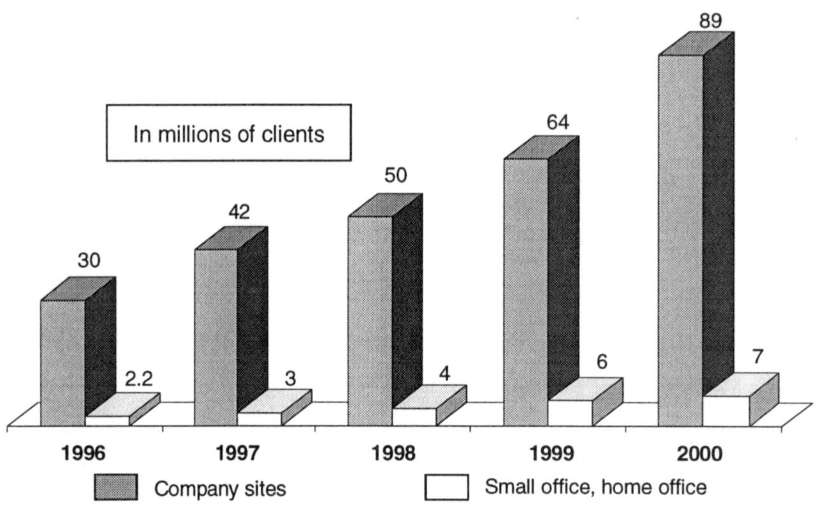

Source: The Gartner Group

The Quest for Web Site Revenues

Initial commercial Web sites were posted by many businesses and corporations with unrealistic expectations of conducting E-commerce. With the exception of some browser suppliers and search services, this initial phase of Web marketing and promotions was largely a disappointment to most sponsors because content providers faced a number of challenges that were not apparent during the initial stages of Web development. Initially, Web sites were relatively few, and the majority of users were Internet hackers and aficionados, which resulted in the rapid growth in popularity of many Web sites. This growth captured the imagination of the media, which forecast lucrative new markets based on the Internet.

A few Internet and Web tools distribution sites recorded massive user interaction and began selling advertising to generate revenues. This approach works well with Web sites such as browsers and search engines because users must use those sites to navigate the Web. They spend considerable time at those sites when using Internet services, and they must return to those sites to use the Web again.

To generate Web site revenues and encourage user traffic, a large number of businesses developed other Web sites with similar search capabilities. These efforts are driven by a number of projections from research services suggesting that business-to-business sales on the Web will surpass sales to consumers and may reach as much as $120 billion by the year 2000 (see Figure 4.3). Unfortunately, very few existing Web sites are producing any significant income. Consequently, many are abandoned or eliminated after a brief period of unprofitable operations.

Figure 4.3 Projected Web Sales by the Year 2000

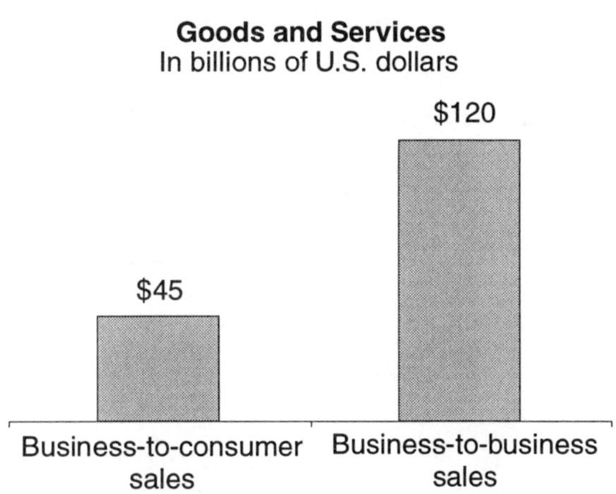

Business-to consumer sales via the Web are now greater than business-to-business sales. Market research firm Input projects that the ratio will shift by the year 2000.

Source: Input

Surfing and Browsing Inefficiencies

As the number of Web sites multiplied exponentially, attracting traffic to any particular Web site became very difficult. Specific content publishers resorted to conventional media advertising to direct Internet users to their sites. At the same time, Internet users experienced increasing frustration trying to locate useful content on the Web.

The initial expectation that "if you build it, they will come" was not fulfilled. Too many Web sites compete for user attention to make this expectation realistic. Even if the 500,000 Web sites and the 40 million Internet users estimates are valid, this averages only 80 users per site – not enough to generate sufficient revenues. Only a small percentage of well-promoted Web sites attract a significant number of visitors.

As a result of a large number of Web sites, Internet users are often frustrated when searching for specific data, products, or services. Very often, the returns of search engines indicate hundreds of thousands of hits; examining and evaluating each one is impractical at best. Even search engines with intelligent rating systems often create an avalanche of abstracts and reviews. Browsing through such a mass of data is extremely time consuming.

Introducing multimedia content into Web pages was expected to improve search and evaluation productivity, but this expectation was not realized. The prolonged downloading time required for images and graphics only adds to user frustration.

Information Overload

The proliferation of Web sites and the development of internal intranets increased the information and reduced worker productivity.

Many companies use intranets to publish their memoranda and working directives because they are less expensive and more efficient than traditional publishing and distribution methods. However, these companies inadvertently contribute to the information overload resulting from the Internet. Additional content is also being generated by Web sites operated by business partners, suppliers, and customers connected to intranets through extranets.

The situation is not improving; the number of Web sites and Internet users continues to increase at a rapid rate. Projections of millions of Web sites operating by the year 2000 and as many as 200 million Internet users is not uncommon. In addition, network computers (NCs) and Web access through TV sets, PDAs and other mobile devices promise to further aggravate the information overload.

Conserve Bandwidth

LANs and WANs have always suffered from inadequate bandwidth to accommodate the growing network traffic, even before the massive advent of the Internet, the Web, and intranets. Network administrators tried to keep pace with escalating demand by increasing the bandwidth of the backbones and network segments; within a few years, 10-Mbps LANs were enhanced to 100-Mbps capacities and are now being restructured with 1-Gbps backbones to manage the traffic.

These hardware and software solutions alleviate the networking bottlenecks to a point. A more efficient, less expensive way to improve networking throughout is to reduce the unnecessary and unwanted traffic generated by Internet and intranet users searching for information. For example, intranet bandwidth can be conserved if users are not required to download, evaluate, and discard data and information.

The same can be said of unwanted and unnecessary advertising associated with many Web sites and Internet tools; particularly the multimedia content Web publishers often believe is necessary to capture user attention. In fact, most advertising consumes an inordinate amount of bandwidth relative to the value of information transmitted.

Disadvantages of Search and Metasearch Sites

The major disadvantage of search services is advertising, which distracts the user, reduces the bandwidth, and slows Web interaction. However, search engines such as Yahoo!, Lycos, and InfoSeek are largely dependent on advertising for their revenues.

Search engines such as AltaVista provide the basic search software for intranets, eliminating advertising and other distracting content. However, this type of solution carries a price: Network administrators must pay for the software, its maintenance, and operations. However, such search facilities within an intranet do not preclude the use of the free search services if employees continue to maintain Internet access.

Metasearch engines seemingly improve the search process by simultaneously launching several different search services. Some also eliminate the advertising and duplicate Web sites that are often identified. Metasearch sites do, however, produce large quantities of hits and, as a result, are only as effective as their relevancy ranking mechanisms and output selection tables.

Customized Content Delivery Dilemma

Intranets and the Internet are facilitating universal access to information. This access is responsible for the emergence of new business models that offer services without interruption – particularly in the realm of financial services where business transactions depend on information and are executed through data transfers.

Customers are demanding to conduct business their way– the way that is most convenient for them. The Web plays a major role in meeting these demands, and companies are realizing that they must provide such electronic means of conducting business to remain competitive. This realization results in the increasing integration of business and IT strategies.

In the final analysis, content customization makes the delivery of such information possible and push technology is the mechanism of implementation. Push technology is applicable to a wide range of sales and marketing activities of an organization and will become critical in business-to-business customer service operations.

Similarly, push technology is also applicable in the consumer markets – particularly as the number of specific Web sites offering products and services to consumers increases – and will become mandatory for success when digital TV with Web access becomes widespread. Such a development will increase the number of Internet users and Web sites dramatically, and better ways of handling the massive information overload will become even more important.

Controlled Information Delivery

An intranet can be used as the infrastructure to deliver relevant company information to employees. The most effective way to distribute such information is for managers to act as individual publishers. As such, they are best positioned to select and deliver the most relevant information to those who can make informed decisions based on it.

Because managers control content selection and delivery, such a distribution arrangement eliminates wasted time and effort. After all, managers should be the most knowledgeable about who needs to know what information.

Targeted Advertising

The ultimate Web marketing site is able to discern user preferences and activity characteristics and catalog and maintain them for business and promotional use. Once this information is collected and verified, it can be segmented for promotions based on specific areas of interest.

Designing a system that will provide highly targeted notifications and announcements, designed to attract specific users, is the best way to implement this invaluable information.

Growth in Interactive Advertising

Despite relatively meager sales, advertising on Web sites remains the most promising way of making money in cyberspace. At the same time, the congestion and growing traffic results in long waiting times to view a Web page. While advertising is desirable, manually searching the Web is not a sustainable business model for the long term.

The advertising banners associated with many Web search engines and service home pages are, in fact, direct hyperlinks to the company home pages. In theory, users can click on the advertisement and immediately view the home page of the product.

Unfortunately, the multimedia content of many advertisements on the Web makes downloading very slow. Many users simply avoid clicking on these hyperlinks because of the time required to download them.

For business users, Internet advertising is often seen as an unwanted, distracting feature. Web sites with advertising are either filtered out or may be outright banned from reception on intranets. As a result, many vendors are developing push technology tools and services that will selectively deliver specific messages of information only to those who request it.

Linking Brands to Consumers

Software applications can track demographics. For example, when users click on a hyperlink behind a headline or an advertising banner, that information is registered. If this type of demographic preference data is collected and stored, Internet user groups linked by their common interest in a particular brand or product line can be compiled.

In fact, the Internet and appropriate accounting programs can provide a Web site with a very precise level of detail about user preferences and desires. Conventional TV and print advertising cannot reach that level of detail.

Once Internet users are identified and linked to specific brands or product lines, successful Web sites encourage repeat visitors. Because users do not necessarily bookmark every site they visit, a means of notifying them about updated information relating to their favorite brands or products is needed.

User Targeting Factors

Software that develops background files on individual customers and visitors makes Web site business more effective. This software consists of intelligent agents that operate in passive or aggressive modes, acquiring marketing data about individual users or groups of customers.

The passive approach involves recording individual behavior of visitors and customers. The objective is to learn their buying habits and tastes to target new products and service advertising. Such a system makes recommendations to the users specifically tailored to individual tastes.

A more aggressive approach involves periodic surveys where users are asked to answer specific questions indicating their preferences on a variety of topics related to the advertiser's products and services. Groups of customers can then be categorized by similar tastes, creating community marketing. In this case, users benefit from collective opinions and evaluations about specific products.

Targeted Keyword Advertising

One form of targeting the end user is associated with using keywords in search engines. In this type of interactive advertising, the Web site displays the results of the search with selected advertisements related to the keywords used in the most recent search.

Search key words may not always reflect the true interest of the user because they are often used in specific search procedures to reach Web sites or locate information that is not truly representative of the final objective. As a result, keyword advertising is not a precise indicator of user interests.

Pinpointing Target Audiences

With traditional marketing using print media, advertisers, publishers, retailers, and marketing firms can predict who is receiving the printed materials with a relatively high degree of certainty. Audited circulation data enables advertisers to justify using specific advertising vehicles. These demographics are available on a periodic basis, corresponding to the frequency of the periodical involved.

Most E-commerce is being conducted by the same advertisers. The medium is different, but their objectives are the same: To pinpoint target audiences. Many Web sites target a broad universe of Internet users to sell advertising space on their Web pages.

As a result, a growing number of software applications monitor Web site use and prepare demographics reports. Until the Web sites can document their traffic with more details than only the number of hits in a specified period, justifying advertising sales on these Web sites will be very difficult. In the same way, organizations promoting and selling products directly to consumers or business clients must acquire meaningful statistics about their cybersales to decide whether it is a profitable venture.

Controlling Information Distribution Reach

Advertisers and large media companies do not like the passive, user-controlled searching, browsing, and access to information over the Web. They want to control exactly who will see their information and when; push technology is a way to develop and maintain such control.

More importantly, distributing company data and information within intranet environments must be controlled precisely to provide a meaningful and productivity – enhancing communications system.

Webcasting is the next wave of Web marketing. Because the Web has potential as a broadcasting medium, advertisers can expect top-down control of content streams. As a result, webcasting is perceived as a strategic cyberspace marketing tool; it provides a precise way of controlling information distribution within any targeted group.

Push technology makes analyzing single consumer markets in realtime possible. Once this information is recorded and associated consumers are identified, automating the content customization and presentation is possible.

Advertisers do not want users to determine how and when they access Web content. They do, however, want precise, real-time demographics about users preferences that can influence their purchase decisions. Such demographics also provide accurate estimates of the numbers of potential buyers for products and services.

Determining Distribution Frequency

With conventional print or radio and TV media, the frequency of distribution of advertising or promotional messages is determined at the outset, depending on the frequency of publication or a particular program, and remains fixed and predictable.

E-commerce offers an unusual opportunity for advertising and marketing, albeit to a relatively small population of approximately 40 million users worldwide, because Web sites and virtual storefronts are open and operating continually.

The user – not the publisher – determines when and how often the Web site is being accessed. To keep users returning, Web site operators must update the site regularly.

Most Web sites are divided into information categories. Each of those categories can be seen as a separate channel of information that is updated independently of other channels.

Although it is a valuable concept, information categories do not guarantee that a user will return to the site because notification that updated information is available is not given.

Obtaining a commitment from Internet users to visit a particular Web site regularly represents the ultimate solution to this problem and can be achieved if the user registers the client address with Web sites that provide automatic notification of the user when new content of interest is available.

Web site developers entice users to register their address by offering a free service or information. As part of such registration, the user should also indicate specific information categories of interest and the frequency with which such notification should be made.

Measuring User Response

Operators must provide user-response statistics to justify advertising fees for posting messages at particular Web sites. User response metrics at Web sites are often limited to the number of hits in a given period. This information is adequate only to compare the popularity of one site against another. More precise metrics are needed before interactive advertising and E-commerce can reach their full potential.

Data pertaining to user access – to the Web site as a whole, as well as to click-through rates for advertisements displayed during interaction with the site – is invaluable. The actual purchase is the ultimate statistic being sought.

Advertising may not exist on intranets, but statistics on user response are equally as important to company managers. When company directives and information are being disseminated through the network, managers must be able to ascertain not only that the information reached all the workers, but also that it was accessed and viewed by them.

The situation can be complex when only certain employees are allowed to access one set of documents and other groups are provided with different information. Security measures that provide different degrees of access to company Web sites address this problem.

Reporting on User Interaction in Cyberspace

Network managers require frequent reports on network traffic to identify bottlenecks and assess the need for more appropriate facilities. Simultaneous use of intranets, extranets, and the Internet create considerable system demands. Software products to accumulate the statistics and develop management reports detailing traffic between the users and specific Web sites are required to perform this task efficiently.

This type of monitoring is particularly important in preventing employee access to unauthorized Web sites. Many organizations also limit access to outside Web sites that contain consumer advertising.

The Quest for a Total Solution

Organizations are striving to increase their effectiveness by improving information flow between employees using the Web. To meet this goal, they must gather numerous information sources and customize the information for delivery. The key to enhancing organizational productivity is in matching the available information to employee requirements.

A total solution must enable convenient access to relevant company content from any source, including databases, data warehouses, reports, E-mail, help desks, and terminal applications.

The ideal integrated company communications solution would also conserve bandwidth of the available networks by notifying users with only brief headlines or summaries about the availability of new information. Such headlines of summaries would also be hyperlinks to the full reports or information and Web sites.

The total integrated solution also requires the ability to customize the information in realtime. This customization may exist at several levels, based on department, group, or individual profiles. Individuals should also be able to select a specific method of notification, such as ticker tape, screen saver, E-mail, or pager.

Additional features of such a total solution should also include company customization reflecting the business identity. It should also leverage existing company systems with minimum programming development, provide easy updating, keep network security standards in place, and minimize intranet bandwidth use.

The Interactive Broadcasting Medium Is Born

The search for more effective E-commerce solutions on the Internet led to the webcasting concept. It initially appeared in the form of PointCast Network, which targeted consumers using PCs. PointCast was an application of the first push technology on the Internet.

The user is not involved in searching and is notified about updates in selected channel categories as soon as they occur. PointCast access is free to the user, but the news is interlaced with advertising related to the categories selected by the user.

While PointCast provides a solution to many of the problems associated with information delivery, it also creates some of its own. Depending on the requested frequency of searches and the number of updates requested, the system downloads significant amounts of information onto the desktop, devouring system resources. In addition, several simultaneous PointCast updates create traffic bottlenecks and overload storage capacity.

While PointCast is clearly not a perfect solution, it represents a new delivery medium full of promise to E-commerce promoters. Because of its earning potential, numerous ventures developed more refined versions of push technology tools and services targeted at the intranet.

Conclusion

To develop meaningful E-commerce, implementing customized interactive solutions targeting Internet users is necessary. Doing so requires an ability to link user preferences with relevant advertisements customized to maximize user acceptance and action. Collecting extensive statistics to measure user response and determine interaction frequencies is critical to achieving this goal.

In addition, control over employee intranet use and the ability to prepare reports on network use are needed. Bandwidth conservation must also be considered.

These problems created a whole new set of solutions in the form of webcasting and push technology products and services. The push alternative is seen as the next Web-based paradigm and is destined to encourage the expansion of E-commerce.

Chapter 5

The Web Information Push Alternative

The Push Alternative

Webcasting's objective is to introduce the user subscription concept into electronic communications. With this model, users receive desired content on a regular basis and content producers receive precise demographics on Web use. For marketing operations, the webcasting approach is clearly superior to the conventional Web-based promotions where users search for specific data and information.

While newspapers deliver content daily, magazines weekly or monthly, and direct marketers on a seasonal basis or according to product introduction schedules, the Web can deliver information with even greater frequency, but subscribers must request specific options.

The User Subscription Model

Indiscriminate broadcasting on the Web is feasible, but wastes bandwidth and user time. The indiscriminate broadcasting approach raises the question: To whom should such webcasting be directed? Web site operations are interested in the largest possible audiences, but they also want to qualify all who access the site as potential buyers.

Subscribing to a webcasting service is similar to a subscription to many specialized trade magazines: Subscribers are required to complete a form providing specific information about their work, equipment used, preferred product brands, travel plans, and possibly even memberships in clubs or organizations and subscriptions to competing publications.

Similar to trade magazine subscribers, webcasting clients receive free access to webcasting sites once they register their profiles and indicate their preferences. Unlike the trade publications, however, most webcasting services are not specialized and provide a range of information categories from which selections must be made.

The webcasting subscription model is relatively simple: Users register for a service and specify the categories they wish to receive. They also specify the frequency of updating and a method of delivery. Special client software is required to subscribe to a webcasting service, but it is easily downloaded free of charge from the Web site of the service provider.

On the client side, webcasting is relatively straightforward; behind the scenes, however, it is a more complex business that requires sophisticated agent software programs that monitor information sources and Web sites on behalf of subscribers, relieving the need to search for information. The price users pay for this convenience is targeted advertising, which they must tolerate as they read updated headlines or download pages.

User Interests and Needs to the Forefront

Webcasting eliminates the barriers between businesses and customers by giving control of the process to both sides. The clients of a webcasting service are given an opportunity to unobtrusively receive only the information they want. They also have the option to change their preferences and make a new selection at any time. Similarly, clients can terminate their involvement with a webcasting service without cost.

While the client feels a high degree of control in a webcasting service environment, businesses also enjoy a cost-effective way to reach a well-defined subscription base. The service becomes more reliable and predictable as clients interact with information providers and advertisers.

Personalizing Web interaction is considered one of the most critical requirements for building customer loyalty and encouraging repeat visits to the site. However, localized, interest-specific, and demographics-related content depends on identifying user interests and needs.

Mass Distribution of Real-time Information

One of the biggest Web advantages is the complete platform independence and ease of access. This ability suggests that real-time interactive communication with millions of individual prospects and customers is possible. Unfortunately, no universal delivery vehicle for multimedia content is available – a fundamental limitation. As a result, marketers cannot deliver multimedia information to individual users.

Many methods have been used to determine precisely how people are visiting a Web site, who they are, and how often they return. This information is important particularly because promoters and corporations want to deliver their content to individuals in a systematic way, ensuring timely delivery of late-breaking news, special sale offers, and other important announcements.

Many Web site content providers use E-mail to notify Internet users of updated information or new products. However, E-mail can only be used if the users originally register at a Web site and submit a valid E-mail address. Mass E-mail notification is limited to a specific browser or E-mail system and does not provide a universal solution for mass distribution to Internet users.

Mission-critical, real-time information is often distributed to large numbers of employees. As a result, new vendors developing software for handling mass distribution of real-time information in a cost-effective and controlled manner are not targeting the business sector.

Eliminating Keyword Searching Inefficiencies

Most Internet and intranet users use search engines and services to find information or data when they do not have a specific universal resource locator (URL) address. These search engines were effective when only a small number of Web sites were on the Internet.

However, once the Web was commercialized and Web sites proliferated, the simple search engine became less efficient. Keyword searching – the most common approach – now returns large numbers of results. Metasearch engines and Web sites that simultaneously launch several search engines return even more information. In either case, evaluating all of the information is impossible – even when search engines use relevancy measures. A new group of search engines and services use intelligent agents, and more sophisticated artificial intelligence case reasoning approaches.

In the final analysis, some form of keyword or key phrase entry is required to initiate the search. As the number of Web sites increases, those searches can become quite lengthy; features that limit the amount of time or the number of results the user is willing to accept are now available. However, this type of approach does not guarantee that the most relevant sources have been accessed.

Unicasting

Most Web applications are based on a unicast distribution model: The same information is copied repeatedly for each recipient on the LAN or WAN. Unicasting is also defined as the distribution of or downloading of information without user interaction.

This method wastes bandwidth and costs money. As the number of users increases, so do the distribution costs. As the number of users increases, traffic bottlenecks. The solution is an increased capacity of mirrored Web sites. These alternatives require an additional investment and special coordination to guarantee that all updates to the sites are synchronized.

Unicasting costs escalate as Web site use increases. Therefore, when the number of users is predictable within intranets and the frequency of distributing data and information is high, the unicasting model may not be the most effective solution.

Webcasting as Broadcasting

Broadcasting in the traditional sense means distributing data or information to many users or viewers simultaneously, as in the case of TV. Conventional broadcasting avoids transmission bottlenecks because there are no wired connections between the broadcaster and the user; conventional broadcasting also does not involve direct user interaction.

With cable TV, each user has a dedicated private cable, solving the problem of transmission ranges and amplifying broadcast signals for local distribution by cable. With wireless or cable broadcasting, however, users are not competing for the same transmission resources at any point and traffic bottlenecks do not occur. The number of users can be increased exponentially simply by the creation of additional receiver stations.

Webcasting on a network wastes bandwidth because it sends information to the whole network, regardless of whether the data is wanted, requiring each user to process the information.

Multicasting

When the same information is being transmitted to only a select group of clients on the overall network, unicasting and broadcasting both waste bandwidth. An alternative information distribution method is multicasting. Rather than endlessly duplicating data, information is sent out only once to multiple recipients. However, only end users with receivers at multicasting-enabled end nodes will receive the information.

Multicasting is particularly useful with multimedia applications on the networks because they require considerable bandwidth. Multicasting is ideal for communicating real-time information to large audiences. It is also useful in supporting interaction such as multiuser videoconferencing using audio, video, and whiteboarding systems. In addition, multicasting is ideal for narrowcasting streaming video or for company software distribution.

Multicasting saves bandwidth and can be used with any network that carries an IP. It has been in operation since the late 1980s and is now supported by all major internetworking vendors. Figure 5.1 illustrates the general concept of multicasting.

Figure 5.1 General Concept of Multicasting

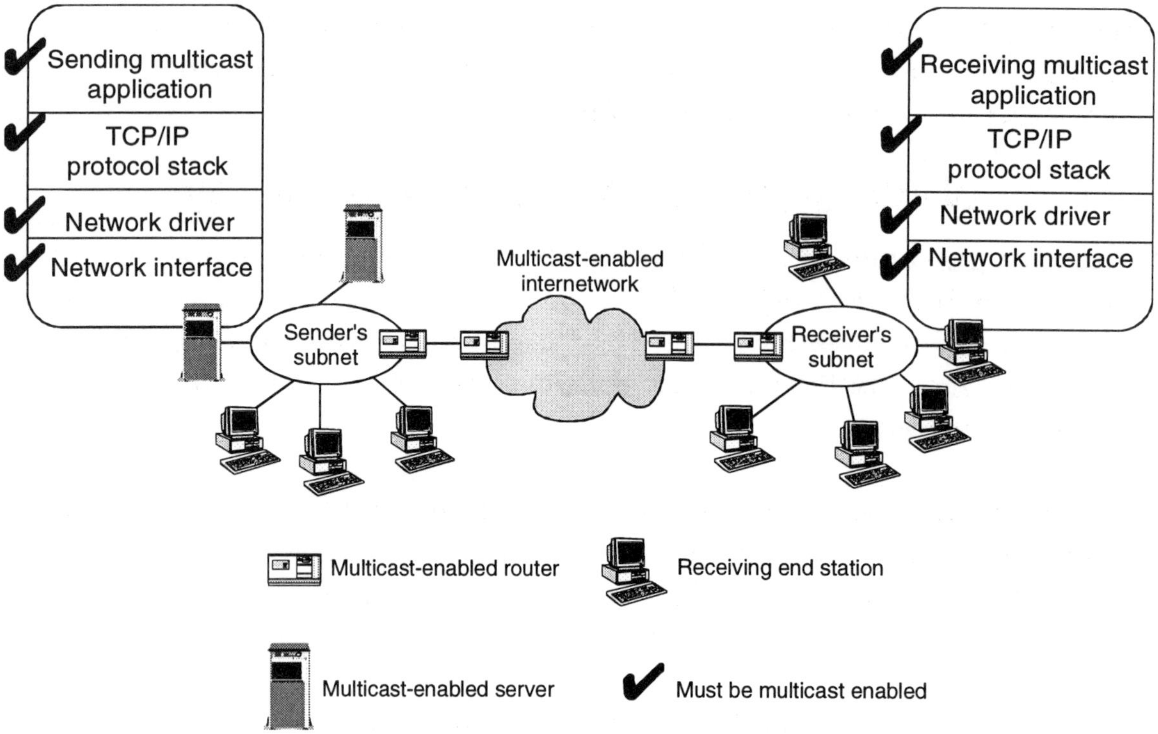

A Narrowcasting Solution

Whether unicasting, broadcasting, or multicasting – netcasting, as it is also called – distributing information along a network is a narrowcast when it is personalized and delivered only to a specific user or group of users.

Narrowcasting is defined as a signal distributed to a limited viewing audience, thus limiting the scope of a broadcast to those who have a declared interest or a special information need. In business applications, narrowcasting defines a technique for distributing only marketing messages customers want to hear.

Narrowcasting has also been referred to as real-time marketing or one-to-one marketing. In the broadcasting world, radio stations and cable TV companies narrowcast when they target programming to specific classic, sports, comedy, science fiction, weather, or news formats.

Webcasting is narrowcasting; push technology is also representative of narrowcasting. When a selection can be made from specific Web sites or channels and the information is delivered to a specific user, that information is being narrowcast. A more refined webcasting service, however, may offer not only a more detailed selection of basic channels and information categories, but also more precise searches within those channels by using sophisticated intelligent agents. This type of webcasting is also narrowcasting with greater degree of precision.

Developing Reliable Multicasting Technology

Multicasting technology is still developing. The most widely known and used multicast-enabled network is the MBone, a virtual network consisting of Internet sectors known as multicast islands. In non-multicast-enabled areas of the Internet, multicast transmissions travel as unicasts using the tunneling principle.

The MBone has been in operation since 1992 and includes more than 3,000 subnets. It is used to multicast live audio and video events and has successfully demonstrated the practicality of using multicasting for multimedia transmissions across the Internet.

Collaborative Computing

Application sharing allows a number of users to work on a single document simultaneously. Even with a point-to-point system, several workers can be stationed at each end, creating a group-to-group collaborative activity.

Groupware software is being used to enhance collaboration of workgroups throughout an enterprise. Collaborative computing increasingly integrates E-mail, voice mail, faxes, and video elements as networks facilitate access to global information. A one-to-many multicast service is necessary to accommodate multimedia traffic in collaborative work.

Whiteboarding allows the user to edit images using tools included in a videoconferencing package. Both of these functions are very useful and cost relatively little. They can be implemented without video, do not require cameras, and generate a reasonable amount of data traffic – an important factor to avoid network bottlenecks and continuously increase traffic on LANs, WANs, and the Internet.

Data compression is the traditional solution to collaborative conferencing problems and can be implemented using hardware or software solutions. The software alternative is less expensive, but is severely constrained by the power of the platforms involved. Even with high-end PCs, video images transmitted using software compression are small – usually 4" to 5" square in size – and will be jerky in display. In addition, the quality of such video will vary greatly depending on the amount of motion being transmitted and the volume of traffic on the transmission links. When smooth video is secondary to application sharing or a whiteboarding collaboration, these videoconferencing limitations are often acceptable.

Whiteboarding and file sharing are effective initial Internet or intranet groupware applications because existing 14.4-Kbps or 28.8-Kbps modems and standard telephone lines are adequate for the purpose. The software programs required are relatively low-cost packages and cameras, video boards, or ISDN connections are not needed. These systems can be readily upgraded to videoconferencing levels when video transmissions is needed.

Multiuser Videoconferencing

Multiuser videoconferencing is the ultimate collaborative groupware application, but bandwidth limitations on individual connections between participants and a multiuser control unit determine whether such videoconferencing can occur.

International telecom carriers, such as AT&T, MCI, and Sprint, offer multiparty videoconferencing services. To initiate such a group conference, participants must connect to a videoconferencing bridge managed by the carrier. Any existing videoconferencing equipment that adheres to international standards is adequate for this purpose.

The Impact of Push Technology on Revenues

Is push technology a viable choice for business applications? As a mechanism to distribute news to consumers or workers, it often does not present a desirable service. In fact, it can result in significant drain on time, worker attention, and network bandwidth. Push services cannot offer news information any more effectively than a direct CNN or MSNBC TV tuner. Businesses that depend on time-sensitive news were using live feeds, stock services, and cable TV news long before Internet became popular.

When properly implemented, however, push technology offers useful business solutions. Initial Web users are overwhelmed with information choices, but as time progresses and the novelty of the concept wears off, they start looking for more effective ways of exploiting the Web. Push technology addresses the need for immediate, up-to-date information.

Creating a Web site revenue stream through advertising products and services is not always successful. User audiences are not consistent or well-understood, although push solutions enforce user participation levels and provide a better mechanism to understand information use.

The Disadvantages of Push Technology

Ad hoc implementation of push technology software has given many network managers an unpleasant surprise. Push clients periodically download bandwidth-hungry content such as advertising, graphics, and even Shockwave movies. This became particularly pronounced when employees downloaded and started using push technology services such as PointCast Network. Consequently, many companies prohibited installing and using PointCast to reduce intolerable traffic bottlenecks.

Conclusion

Web marketing and enterprise communications are entering the next generation of operations, introducing webcasting or push technology business models. These efforts represent new attempts to justify E-commerce on the Web.

The webcasting alternative reverts to the subscription business model that is prevalent in print media and offers various delivery frequencies and a high degree of audience predictability. Alternatively, push technology offers an advantage in the form of customized information delivery frequencies.

Webcasting enables mass distribution of real-time information in unicasting, broadcasting, and multicasting modes. Of those modes, multicasting is the most effective alternative because it selectively narrowcasts information; however, it also requires network and desktops to be enabled to receive multicasting signals.

Web narrowcasting is currently at a stage where reliable multicasting standards and protocols are being developed and introduced into groupware, collaborative, and multiuser videoconferencing products, all of which can benefit from push technology applications.

Whether push technology will have a significant impact on E-commerce revenues remains to be seen. Webcasting applications are still relatively new, and early adopters' primary focus is on intranet communications and selective distribution of company data.

However, webcasting also has some disadvantages. For example, improperly chosen push technology services and excessive selections of unnecessary channels can create bottlenecks and may even flood storage capacities.

Chapter 6

From Web Pages to Channels

For the last few years, businesses have rushed to establish a Web presence in anticipation of lucrative new markets. For the most part, however, the rate of growth of those Web sites far outstripped the growth of any online business.

The rapid increase in Web sites is such that users cannot possibly hope to reach and evaluate even a fraction of them. As a result, Web content producers and marketers are turning to webcasting to ensure their Web sites develop and retain a well-defined, loyal user following.

To introduce webcasting, Web pages and sites first must be converted into channels. Internet and intranet users who express a specific set of information needs and interests are then provided with notifications of changes and updates in specific Web channels. This process provides advertisers with a more predictable group of prospects and theoretically increases the potential of conducting business on the Web.

Another reason for moving to webcasting and Web channels from the original chaotic Internet and Web exists: Earlier attempts to develop E-commerce via electronic malls, search and metasearch engines, interactive TV, and E-mail spamming failed to create a critical mass market in cyberspace. Webcasting is yet another attempt to increase E-commerce opportunities. Webcasting's best opportunity today, however, lies in multicasting within intranets and extranets rather than the Internet because these implementations are secure and controlled. Regardless of the perspective, one observation is certain: Webcasting requires a clever way of changing Web pages and sites into Web channels to keep subscribers returning.

Internet Cyberspace

The Internet is a chaotic collection of computer networks that provide access to databases and Web sites. The variety of information in these storage facilities is almost infinite. While a great amount of it is free, prime sites charge for access. In addition, some services require subscriptions for regular information delivery, similar to print publications.

A number of measures are taken by some countries and administrations to limit the storage, transmission, and delivery of unedited, uncensored materials. These measures are implemented by some online access services, but most ISPs provide unrestricted access to any Web site. As a result, Internet users can roam the Web at will and access and select any topic they desire.

Broadcast Channels

Radio and TV broadcasting offer news, information, and entertainment in the form of programs delivered according to a predetermined schedule. Broadcasting stations are considered channels of distribution that transmit content on specific frequencies according to a well-determined program.

Users with interests in a particular program can tune their radios or TV receivers to the channel of their choice. However, they must also conform to the channel's specified time schedule.

The value of broadcasting channels lies in the fact that advertisers can precisely determine the popularity of a particular program relative to another. This ability allows broadcasters to assign a specific value on programs and determine pricing for advertisers based on this value. User interest is determined by counting how many tune in to a particular channel at a particular time. Web advertisers and promoters are considering this business model as a more appropriate way to conduct business on the Web.

The Biased Traditional Media

Web-based information is not biased or restricted in the same way as traditional print and broadcast media are generally believed to be.

While some Web sites are inherently very biased, users can choose whether or not to view them. In comparison to the uncensored Web, the nature of information distributed by traditional media is significantly restricted.

In effect, the Internet user becomes an independent editor of the materials being downloaded and viewed, by clicking from one Web page to another. As a result, a more balanced perception of the news or other developments is possible.

The Convergence of Two Technologies

The webcasting concept is a combination of Internet sources and the broadcasting discipline and presents some unique advantages.

Conventional TV provides information that typically is received by millions of viewers. On the Internet, however, digital content can be targeted to specific groups or individuals. This narrowcasting capability transforms the Web into a personal broadcasting system. The convergence of customized broadcasting and the wide variety of Web sources is creating a new interactive medium that is expected to bring some order to the Web, promote E-commerce, and create a whole new software product group.

Creating the Broadcast Paradigm on the Web

Recreating the broadcast TV paradigm on the Web is difficult because of bandwidth limitations. However, real-time delivery mechanisms for the Web have entered the market, allowing Web advertisements to run as smoothly as they do on TV. Such products will make the Web more feasible as an E-commerce infrastructure.

Macromedia Flash, originally seen as an alternative to animated graphic interchange format (.GIF) files, has become a real-time element on the Web. As a result, the commercials originally developed from broadcast TV can now be digitized and displayed equally well on Web channels.

Bandwidth limitations have not completely dissipated, however. Many users are still limited by 28.8-Kbps modems. The development process continues, however, because rapid developments are being made in that arena.

Psychographics of Webcasting and Push Technology

Push technology brings an additional benefit to webcasters and its promoters: It holds the promise of providing specific information about the clients or users who receive the customized content from a Web channel.

Most Web sites today report only basic data about their activity, such as how many people visited the site during a particular period of time. Little information about more psychographic reasons, such as specific interests, frequency of visits, and returns to particular sites or topics, is available.

Creating Web channels to which users must subscribe is a way to generate better psychographics about them. Upon registration users must provide details about their addresses, E-mail, and telephone, and must indicate topics or channels of interest to them. This procedure creates a profile of the individual user, which can then be matched against targeted advertising.

This is not to say that these systems have achieved perfection, however. In fact, most push products represent only the initial versions, focusing primarily on notification and content delivery. They provide basic statistics about how many people subscribe to a specific channel and how many users may have canceled their subscriptions. Developing a way to determine why some users continue to return to specific Web channels or topics and why others do not will be the ultimate advertising application. Push technology and webcasting lend themselves to many psychographic monitoring ideas.

The Emergence of the Web Page

The appearance of the Web with universal access, ease of use, multimedia capabilities, and its rapid growth has become synonymous with the Internet. Most of the attention is focused on the Web as such, and almost anyone can create Web pages or a Web site and become an information provider. Potentially, such information could reach millions of users. To reach these users, however, their attention must be captured.

Because the Web is ubiquitous and posting Web pages has become commonplace, traditional newspaper and magazine publishers, catalog marketers, retailers, and many other marketing companies have shown an interest in the Web as a way to promote and sell their products.

Many Web pages and sites were initially developed in the form of online storefronts and shopping malls. Suppliers built their Web pages on a site and waited for users to visit and buy. Unfortunately, few Web sites enjoyed any significant or lasting success. To entice users to return to these sites, Web page sponsors embarked on various programs to attract users, including E-mail, bookmarks, offline browsers, intelligent agents, and HTML-enabled E-mail.

While the number of Web sites and pages continues to multiply, no foolproof method to indicate precisely how many people are visiting a Web site, who they are, or when and how often they return has been developed. Despite advances in Web page development, assessing the editorial and advertising content of the Web site or justifying its advertising rates is difficult.

Whether commercial Web pages will receive an ROI remains an unanswered question. Some analysts predict that this will not happen until the year 2000 at the earliest. They also suggest that more than $3 million must be invested into a Web-based venture before it will generate revenue for its operators.

Transmitting Text and Graphics

Web sites that contain text and graphics are the most common and represent the bulk of all content on the Web and the Internet as a whole. This is also true of intranets where servers contain massive databases pertaining to business clients, accounts, and employee records.

Such Web pages are readily organized into Web channels because they already exist in digital format. In fact, creating a specific Web channel for each individual user in an intranet is optimal. In such a case, the channel reflects a dynamic user profile and provides customized demographics or psychographics of the user.

To provide these detailed demographics, a mechanism for defining user interests and identifying and collecting that information into a specific Web channel is needed. This mechanism is a Web server.

Including Animation

Numerous Web sites use animation to capture and hold user attention. Many manufacturing and design organizations use animation such as virtual reality (VR) to simulate products and processes, saving money that would be spent otherwise on constructing models. Animation is a cost-effective method of testing new products and mechanisms.

Streaming animation on the Web is now possible with the latest RealNetwork products using Macromedia Flash software. Such animation can be streamed from a specific Web channel and synchronized with audio for delivering online movies. Macromedia Flash is also an effective vehicle for providing customer services and maintenance instructions for complex products and equipment. In addition, streaming animation also opens a whole area of Web training and education; specific streaming multimedia Web channels are expected to broadcast knowledge and instructions about nearly any topic in the short-term future.

Adding Audio and Video Elements

Adding audio and video elements was not practical previously because of insufficient bandwidth and incompatible network protocols. Streaming media technology now makes it practical and cost effective.

New tools make the creation of streaming media content, which can be published to either HTTP pages or Web servers, possible. With high-speed connections, such multimedia channels can support full-screen video transmission across 100-Kbps to 300-Kbps connections. The new tools can also insert audio and video advertisements automatically within a streaming media presentation. Increasing support for commercial systems that support streaming media transmissions for subscription and pay-per-view (PPV) operations are also available. These developments are conducive to the development of push technology and webcasting.

The next generation of push technology products can actually transmit audio and video feeds from radio and TV stations or special multimedia databases. The addition of audio and video content makes push technology particularly attractive in several applications. It also makes pushing audio and video clips of music, videos, and movies for promoting artists and new productions practical. Adding audio and video elements is a tremendous step toward developing E-commerce on the Web.

The Full Multimedia Web

Webcasting promoters' ultimate objective is to deliver customized, interactive multimedia content to anyone using the Internet or intranets – a potential global market currently estimated at approximately 50 million users, but expected to reach 200 million by the year 2000.

In total numbers, this 200 million represents less than 1% of the world population, which is approaching six billion. This market, however, is a relatively high-income segment and is eagerly targeted by webcasting publishers and providers. Moreover, segments of this elite population can be targeted with push technology for relatively high-priced products and services, such as foreign travel, real estate, yachts, and luxury automobiles.

Traditionally, such products and services are promoted and sold with extensive images, videos, and full multimedia support. For this reason, a full multimedia Web is required for E-commerce to reach its full potential. In addition, this multimedia content should be comparable in quality to broadcast TV and video home system (VHS) video, which are now used widely as promotional alternatives.

While streaming multimedia is now a proven technology and currently available, it is just coming to market and will not support Internet users with low-bandwidth connections. While it is a desirable cost-effective means of delivering Web content, it is still relatively limited in its availability.

The Internet as a Delivery Channel

Any network is an ideal infrastructure for transmitting information streams that result from changes taking place on its Web sites or in databases. The Internet and the Web are constantly changing and as such represent numerous channels or information streams. When a user connects and interacts with the Internet, communications channels are endlessly being established with various Web sites or databases.

A market develops when a high level of activity takes place between a group of content providers and consumers over one or more channels. The development of these channels of information is governed by market dynamics and reflects the continuous demands and search of Internet users.

Cable TV services deliver preset and limited selections from the same video channels to all subscribers, except for a small percentage of PPV customers. Push technology and webcasting introduce a whole new distribution concept by allowing customers to specify which channels are to be delivered and what particular times are convenient for them.

Consequently, channel content will become competitive and a whole new group of channel suppliers will emerge, offering diverse, real-time, focused, in-depth, and updated coverage. The selections made by clients will also trigger intense one-on-one marketing campaigns based on detailed profiles of online users.

What Is a Web Channel?

The channel metaphor is used widely in defining webcasting products and services because it is a familiar concept for explaining the push subscription and updating mechanism. It is analogous to the TV channel as a means of providing news, information, and entertainment to an individual user.

However, many push product vendors use the channel metaphor to define various forms of push technology. This practice creates a certain amount of confusion. Those planning to implement specific push products are well-advised to evaluate the definition of the channel concept of each vendor involved.

A Web channel is a Web site that is regularly accessed as a source of information; the content provider notifies users about updated information using push tool features. These tools vary depending on the product and will provide different levels of control to the user. For example, some push technologies require a special channel server that can be organized into multiple subchannels. Other solutions consider a collection of files in a single Java application, a Java applet, or HTML source directory pushed as a channel. This multiple channel conceptualization is expected to persist until push technology matures and its market consolidates. At that time, channel metaphors will likely cease to exist.

The Company Channel Idea

The company channel is a very attractive concept in principle – particularly for a company that already has a Web presence. In fact, various departments and groups within an enterprise maintain their own Web sites within intranets and engage in multiuser conferencing. This activity is taking place in digital form and in realtime.

The latest Web development and manipulation tools enable organizations to operate an internal facility designed to coordinate and archive the most important results. This archival system can lead to the development of one or more company channels on an intranet, each designed to provide multimedia content to specific companies and outside audiences.

One very promising sector for company channels is the intranet and extranet arena, which links an enterprise with its business partners, suppliers, customers, advertising agencies, financial services, and retirement plans. Each of those groups needs to be informed promptly of company policy changes, new products, designs, litigation, competition, pricing, discounts, employee status, and insurance coverage. Webcasting such information to those who need it when they need it appears to be the most cost-effective, attention-getting solution.

In fact, company channels can be set up to meet individual group requirements. Despite massive potential, intranets and extranets present a more ready opportunity for webcasting.

Quality of Service Issues

Quality of service (QoS) of Internet transmissions depends on the reliability of the message delivery system. Four levels of service categories have been identified, including best-efforts, reliable, guaranteed, and transactional services:

- Best efforts service provides an efficient transport of information, but without error correction
- Reliable service is a less efficient transport such as TCP, but offers error correction
- Guaranteed transmission indicates queuing of messages on permanent storage devices until it has been received by the user
- Transactional service involves a transaction between content producers and consumers

Any actions by all parties are committed or aborted in unison.

Digital TV Standards

Digital TV standards that have been announced by the U.S. Federal Communications Commission (FCC) have created an opportunity for development of digital TV hardware and software. Consequently, an entirely new infrastructure potential for transmitting Web-based content to large numbers of TV viewers is emerging. Early forecasts suggest that more than 50% of all households in the United States will be able to receive digital TV broadcasting by the turn of the century.

This potential represents a powerful incentive to start creating Web channels. Initially, targeted audiences will be affluent sectors to whom customized interactive advertising can be distributed. Promoters also hope this form of communications will be profitable and serve as the mainstay of E-commerce in the coming years.

ISPs such as MCI and UUNet already have begun offering interactive multimedia broadcasts over the Internet because it is a cost-effective way to deliver video over long distances. WebTV, @Home Network, and NetChannel are some of the initial ventures offering Web-based digital channel services. Clearly, the Web is being developed as a source of information that will be accessible from an increasing number of TV sets and PCs.

The Push/Pull Broadcasting Solution

Because computer users must switch their PCs on and dial up to connect with the Internet or an intranet, they are forced to perform a certain amount of pull before receiving any push content. Strictly speaking, any form of webcasting is not a pure push operation, but a combination of push/pull activity. On the user end, various levels of pull must be involved before a definite connection between the webcaster and the subscriber can be established.

The only pure push webcasting is theoretically and practically possible when Web channels are broadcast using some of the wireless distribution alternatives. Even then, it is not a pure push implementation unless the user has a special receiver that can be tuned in directly to the Web channel without any user interaction.

The webcasting model varies because of different software solutions of end-user notification and delivery functions. All subscribers must register and provide interest profiles, but not all Webcasting services respond to this information in the same way. For instance, some provide immediate delivery of the complete designated item as soon as changes are detected, while others create notifications about changes in specific Web channels; still, users must decide whether to pull the content for further evaluation.

Conclusion

The sudden rush to webcasting is a logical technological development made possible by the introduction of several push software tools for converting Web pages and sites into Web channels. However, the major driving force for implementing webcasting comes from Web publishers, content producers, and Internet merchants frustrated with low revenues from Web sites, search engines, and online advertising. The webcasting concept is a more realistic business model for the future, borrowing heavily from the experiences of conventional broadcasting.

The transition from Web sites and random Web pages to more defined, organized Web channels targeting subscribers is logical. Web channels, around which Web communities of special interest can be constructed, are seen as a solution in the face of a massive cyberspace information overload.

Web channels also offer a solid basis for user psychographics, which is expected to result in superior E-commerce. However, such demographics require an interactive multimedia webcasting environment, which is presently only possible within intranets based on LANs with adequate bandwidth capacities.

The Internet as a webcasting delivery channel with real-time, multimedia content is technically possible. However, whether it is needed and whether it can be cost effective remains questionable.

Chapter 7

Creating Enterprise Channels on the Web

Web channels are created as accumulators of specific information for distribution by webcasting solutions that may include push technology.

The push concept means different things to different company users and product vendors. The only common concept is that company data and relevant content will be delivered to a designated list of clients. How this task is performed and to what extent it becomes automatic depends on the interpretation of requirements and push products or service selected.

Many push systems are simply search agents that crawl intranets and notify users when updated data is available. The users must then engage in individual pull activity to download and evaluate such content.

To implement a complete webcasting system, push products must be given considerable attention and testing to determine whether they perform according to enterprise objectives. They should be evaluated based on several criteria:

- Availability of automatic filtering and security
- Automatic detection of new content on Web channels and sites
- User-customizable channels and interfaces
- Support for all company data types inside and outside the intranet

Ideal Push and Webcasting Characteristics

Any webcasting or push application targeting intranets must address a number of issues to provide an effective means of content distribution. The ability to recognize, separate, and deliver the correct information to the correct audience at the correct time is paramount.

Filtering, security, bandwidth, and automated operation are among the primary concerns of a company developing such an information system. Many of these issues can be resolved by selecting a technology that addresses those concerns.

The push or webcasting technology must provide a way to filter the content that is distributed throughout the company information resources. The most productive filtering should occur automatically within the distribution system. If the users become involved in filtering content, the system does not provide adequate content control. The objective should always be to reduce user interaction and inefficiency when system resources are questionable. See Table 7.1 for push technology selection factors.

Table 7.1 Push Technology Selection Factors

Feature	Description and Remarks
Filtering	The most productive information filtering takes place during the distribution process without user involvement
Security	The best push technologies provide a means for access control to sensitive and confidential materials by authenticating users and limiting their access privileges
Bandwidth	Push tools that have built-in capabilities for measuring their own impact on network performance and can adjust their operations accordingly are the preferred solutions
Automation	Automatic location and acquisition of information from various company sources with minimal involvement of programming talent is the best type of product

Security for push or webcasting systems is an extension of enterprise security policy. However, selecting a tool or service that provides levels of controlling access to sensitive and confidential materials, such as a technology that supports authentication for verifying access privileges of users to specific Web channels or type of information, is important.

Another important feature is the technology's ability to measure and manage its own impact on the performance of the network, automatically limiting its delivery activity during high utilization periods of the network. This effect can also be obtained by using products that deliver only notifications or headlines, relegating the responsibility of selecting an appropriate time for retrieval of voluminous files to users. While push is not used to create Web sites as such, flexibility of design based on the content required by users is critical.

This approach will be useful only if individual users have access to network management tools and can determine when the network is loaded lightly. As a result, products that can provide such functions automatically without involving the user are clearly more efficient.

A characteristic often overlooked by push system developers and promoters is the ease of installation and automatic operation – the ability to automatically locate and incorporate new content into predefined distribution channels. Therefore, seamless integration with various company information sources is required. Reaping this benefit without providing additional programming and monitoring for this function enhances productivity.

Real-time Chatting

The advantages of a chat channel on a company Web site are increasingly important. Chat offers the ability to provide real-time technical support, creates virtual question and answer sessions, and facilitates the creation of a community of users associated with a specific site or brand.

A growing trend toward two-dimensional (2-D) and three-dimensional (3-D) graphical chat with specialized software is emerging, but the most cost-effective way to create a company chat channel is through the use of a text-based chat server.

Whether a channel for chatting is appropriate depends on the business. Clearly, many engineering and development organizations can benefit greatly from chat channels that may pertain to groups – or communities – of employees involved in a specific project.

In complex design environments, text-based chat is not sufficient and the organization may consider 3-D technologies. Chat channel products using virtual reality modeling language (VRML), which require the creation of specialized "worlds" populated by avatars, graphical representations, and individual users, are now available.

Creating Web Content for Push Applications

Automated push systems rely on keyword matching to determine whether a file meets the criteria for inclusion in a particular channel, a user profile, or whether it must go through software known as a master filter, which selects specific topics for a user or groups of users.

Developers of Web channels and documents can improve the push systems' ability to recognize content by emphasizing indicative keywords within such documents. However, the major search engines are now designed to discard and eliminate Web pages with excessive keyword loading to limit this practice. The agents used in push systems may not necessarily have such sophistication, and the Web channel designers control the intranet environment and can design their systems for maximum performance in response to specific keywords.

This keyword emphasis is relatively easy with HTML documents: add the <!...keyword1, keyword2...> comments or use the META NAME tags with the keywords. In documents such as text files, adding a section at the top that includes all the applicable keywords may be useful. In word processing documents, adding footnotes, annotations, or summaries using built-in tools is useful. Alternatively, keywords can be typed in and hidden either in the form of very small type or they can be made the same color as page background to disappear from view on the screen.

Many push products allow customization of response or HTML-based pushed document presentation pages. Consequently, integrating a push product into existing company information structure for easy access and effective appeal is worth the effort.

Specialized Intelligent Agents

Intelligent agents already exist in cyberspace and generally operate in isolation for tasks such as filtering E-mail or retrieving information on a scheduled basis.

Intelligent agents are software programs designed to automatically collect specific types of information on the Internet or perform other services, which are available to operate on desktops, across intranets, and on the Internet. Depending on the type of intelligent agent, they may also collect data regarding user interaction frequency, time spent researching specific topics, and other demographics. Agent software performs tasks as directed by the user and exists on Web servers, enterprise networks, or individual desktops.

Intelligent agents are a practical development of artificial intelligence concepts and expert systems whose objective was to create computer programs that approximate the intelligence of a human being. Complex agent systems are used widely in industrial environments.

Search engines are specialized intelligent agents and play a key role in push technology. Individual subscribers are either given or attached to a specialized agent when they register for a Web channel. Web channel developers must focus on the types of agents they will use in setting up their webcasting operations. In some cases, selecting a particular push technology development tool resolves this issue, but it may also be enhanced by independent design or choice of more powerful intelligent agents for the task.

The future of this technology, however, is even more fascinating. Researchers at Carnegie Mellon University in Pittsburgh are trying to develop an agent OS, enabling different agents to locate each other in cyberspace and cooperate to enhance their productivity in responding to specific client requests.

Multimedia on Demand

Traditional online applications can be enhanced with push technology by providing an effective delivery mechanism for updated material. In many cases, these enhancements involve multimedia content including audio and video elements being added to an existing text-based Web site or channel.

Push technology facilitates the delivery of multimedia content on the Internet through the use of local storage and transparent content downloads in the background mode. This method eliminates waiting for graphic and multimedia content to download in realtime.

Preparing Multimedia Content for Webcasting

Most push technologies currently in use are able to distribute multimedia materials but do not have the ability to determine the content or subject of such files. As a result, much of multimedia materials desired by push service subscribers may not be recognized or referenced by the customized agents.

Web site developers and channel producers can improve potential recognition and distribution of multimedia content by embedding multimedia files within descriptive documents, creating an HTML document with an explanation of its content and proper hyperlinks, such as <EMBED>, <APPLET>, or <OBJECT> markups, for creating links to multimedia elements. This method allows an automated push system to categorize the content and inform users about their existence.

Webcasting: Another Form of Multimedia

When Web channels are being created, some of them will transmit multimedia content, including real-time audio and video. Because these channels can handle a limited number of simultaneous users, their capacity should be designed to avoid creating network bottlenecks.

Audio and video data is processed by compression software over the networks of the Web. Encoding packages manage various numbers of simultaneous users – an aspect that must be considered when Web sites and company channels for handling multimedia content are created.

Webcasting is a form of multimedia communications that combines the best features of newspapers, magazines, newsletters, radio, and TV. It also allows instant user interaction and information updating.

Multimedia Webcasting Software Requirements

Three types of software are involved in webcasting multimedia content: encoding, content storage and broadcasting, and decoding software. When company channels are created, all three software types may be involved, depending on the nature of push applications implemented.

Encoding software is required for converting multimedia materials such as audio and video cassettes, film, photographs, diagrams, and images into digital form that can be handled by computers. This software is used separately from and externally of the webcasting process, but consists of various tools for creating Web sites and Web channels with multimedia content.

Most other information, which consists of text, numbers, tables, graphics, and animation can be developed using many standard word processors and presentation software packages and is initially created in digital format and does not require conversion. Digitized multimedia data files are stored on Web servers or video servers for distribution to push service subscribers and end users.

An organization planning to create its own Web channels and push technology services must consider the hardware and software required to create and digitize original multimedia content, unless arrangements are made with service firms that specialize in those activities. The process also involves additional editing and facilities for combining various multimedia elements into desired Web channels.

Multimedia Content Encoding and Decoding

Various proprietary encoding and decoding approaches are in use. Consequently, multimedia content encoded with a particular software can only be heard and viewed on a platform that has the appropriate decoding software installed.

Multimedia content providers pay for the encoding software on a Web server, but the decoder software is often available free to users. Proprietary applications do not present a problem when Web channels are created on an intranet because the enterprise controls both the webcasting server channels and the user software installed on its desktops.

Becuase Web channels represent souces of information that may be used to push information and multimedia content to users, business partners, clients, and outside consultants, it is impossible to determine precisely what decoding software exists for receiving multimedia webcasting content materials. As a result, the webcasting organization must be prepared to distribute the appropriate decoding software to all its prospective users. This task is normally performed at registration time when subscribers indicate their needs and preferences and identify the parameters of their platforms.

As an alternative, webcasters can make their Web channels accessible to the maximum numbers of users by designing multimedia content encoded by several widely used methods. If this approach is selected, however, the webcaster should research existing users and potential subscribers to determine the predominant type of software available on their desktops.

Streaming Multimedia Characteristics

The most important characteristic of streaming multimedia presentations is audio and video quality and their performance over delivery links. In an environment with LAN bandwidth capacity, the video quality could often approach that of broadcast TV.

Video transmission over the Internet, however, does not reach TV standards. The transmission rates are only about 10 frames per second (fps), which is typical of browser video players and standard Internet modem connections.

Other streaming multimedia quality features include playback, content quality, availability, interactivity, and ease of installation and use.

Even with the latest 56-Kbps modems and digital lines, the Internet remains overwhelmed by digital video bandwidth demands. The existing Internet streaming video solutions are a compromise combining small frame size, reduced frame rate, and innovative storage for near real-time Internet video.

As a result, streaming video is usually available in small windows of 160x120 pixels resolution at as low as 6 fps or less. These measurements yield a small, jerky image, but this quality is expected to improve rapidly. Figure 7.1 illustrates the streaming video frame size relative to an average full screen size.

Figure 7.1 Streaming Video Frame Size Relative to Full Screen

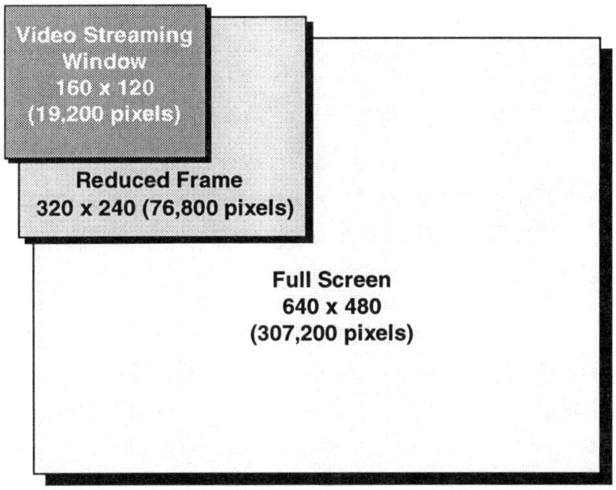

Use of Animation in Web Channels

Most animation on the Web can be created by sequences of individual .GIF graphic files. Numerous multimedia authoring tools that include animation facilities are available, and no special software is needed to receive such animation. Any Web site or channel designer with a set of multimedia authoring and development tools will automatically have the equipment necessary to create animation content for the channel.

Animation can be viewed by users connecting through a standard 14.4-Kbps modem, although it will download relatively slowly into the desktop memory or hard drive. However, such animation can be replayed at full speed once it is available on the desktop.

For smoother animation, users should have at least 28.8-Kbps modems. If such animation is pushed to users on a LAN intranet, this problem will not exist because of the LAN's higher bandwidth. Nevertheless, content providers should design animation channels with full knowledge of the networking infrastructure to obtain the best results.

Audio Streaming on the Web

Audio streaming on the Internet debuted with Progressive Networks' 1995 introduction of RealAudio software. RealAudio 3.0 on a 28.8-Kbps modem compares favorably with FM radio transmission sound. Over a high-speed connection, RealAudio approaches the fidelity of a CD player.

During the last two years, RealAudio has become a de facto standard for streaming music over the Internet and is running on an estimated 12 million desktops and thousands of Web servers. Despite rapidly emerging competition, RealAudio – the first of its kind and bundled with IE – captured an overwhelming market share of more than 85%.

RealAudio is used to transmit live events such as professional sports and network newscasts. Some small ventures are regularly streaming more than 50 channels of music onto the Web. As a result, RealAudio is worthy of webcasters' consideration because a large percentage of users are already equipped with RealAudio software or can readily download the free receiving software from the vendor.

Creating a Web Radio Channel

The Internet enables broadcasting audio signals without a radio transmitter, relay stations, or licenses. A PC, a microphone, a modem, and streaming audio software are the only requirements, making for a relatively low-cost alternative to broadcast data. At its best, Web radio quality is comparable to CD sound, but depends on the amount of traffic on the Internet.

Anyone with a Web browser enabled with streaming audio software can receive such transmissions on a multimedia PC with loudspeakers. Progressive Networks, Liquid Audio, and Xing Technology provide such free streaming audio client software that can be downloaded from their Web sites.

More than 500 Web radio stations already broadcast on the Internet, including professional broadcasters such as ABC Radio News, CBS News, and CBC Radio. A list of all Web radio stations available on the Internet can be reached at *http://www.timecast.com/*.

The Web radio does not appear to be a viable business model in itself. Web radio services such as AudioNet at *http://www.audionet.com/* and NetRadio at *http://www.netradio.net/* offer dozens of radio shows and events as selected packages. Whether these will survive is another matter.

Streaming Video Channels

Streaming video over the Internet was introduced in 1997 by Progressive Networks. The images are small and jerky, but the principle has been demonstrated to work and its quality will improve rapidly. Streaming video allows Internet users to see video clips even over dial-up telephone lines.

Streaming video channels are of particular interest to companies wishing to conduct business on the Web. Such a video channel allows the content producer to show a commercial to a prospect and provide ways to immediately order the product or service.

Streaming video products come in two major categories. Web browser plug-ins allow users to play back live video from Web channels in realtime, and are primarily designed for entertainment applications. Higher bandwidth products are designed for operation on intranets and are particularly valuable for distributing computer-based training (CBT).

Streaming video is a way to gain a competitive edge in online business environments. It provides an easy, more attractive way to distribute internal communications, reduce training expenses, and significantly enhance marketing efforts. In addition, it is very valuable in training marketing staff and resellers to service and support company products.

Implementing streaming video involves some effort, although vendors are trying to provide relatively easy software. If used with IP multicast standard, streaming video can deliver video images at speeds ranging from 100 Kbps to 1.5 Mbps and selectively stream it only to those who want to receive it. Videos can also remain stored on video servers for random access.

Although the quality of streaming video is not yet comparable to that of broadcast TV, the advantages of being able to see and read body language during a presentation still apply. Consequently, streaming video is increasingly being introduced in the financial services industry, a total information business. Table 7.2 summarizes the major streaming video products available.

Table 7.2 Summary of Streaming Multimedia Products for the Web

Product	Details and Remarks
Microsoft http://www.microsoft.com	♦ NetShow 2.0 streaming media server ♦ Works with Windows NT 95, 3.11, Mac, and UNIX ♦ Owns VXtreme, 10% Progressive Networks
Motorola http://www.mot.com/truestream	♦ TrueStream 1.2 ♦ Variable bit rate encoding production tool ♦ Server and client modules with proprietary protocol
OLIVR http://www.olivr.com	♦ OLIVR Viewer 1.0 ♦ Streaming interactive 3-D movies ♦ Plug-in tool
Progressive Networks http://www.prognet.com	♦ RealAudio and RealVideo plug-ins ♦ Bundled with Microsoft IE 4.0 ♦ RealServer 4.01 proprietary algorithm ♦ RealNetwork service with MCI
Silicon Graphics http://www.sgi.com	♦ WebForce MediaBase high-bandwidth tool ♦ Designed for CBT production on company LANs ♦ Supports RealPlayer for content broadcasting
TNC http://www.tnc.com	♦ Cheetah videoserver for up to 700 hours of content ♦ LAN encoding capability ♦ Handles up to 300 individual users
VDONet http://www.vdo.net	♦ VDOLive and VDOMaster streaming software ♦ VDOPhone videoconferencing ♦ Low and broadband products scalability ♦ Proprietary algorithms
Vivo Software http://www.vivo.com	♦ More than four million free players installed ♦ Post-production tool for streaming video ♦ Supports multiple servers on the Web
Vosaic http://www.vosaic.com	♦ Browser plug-in streaming software product
VXtreme http://www.vxtreme.com	♦ Web Theater streaming video plug-in ♦ Has 25% screen display mode for high-bandwidth content ♦ Acquired by Microsoft in late 1997
Xing Technology http://www.xingtech.com	♦ StreamWorks streaming audio product ♦ Second to market following RealAudio by six months

As streaming video becomes more popular, implementing management controls to determine which users can receive particular levels of bandwidth or multimedia content is important. Also, the bandwidth used for streaming video may have to be scheduled according to time of day to prevent unnecessary network performance deterioration.

Audio and Video Newscasting on the Web

In February 1997, Progressive Networks introduced the first Internet service to broadcast streaming audio and video directly to a PC. It is delivered using the RealPlayer 4.0, which plays both RealAudio and RealVideo and gives users a chance to select and customize a Daily Briefing from more than 50 content providers. RealPlayer 4.0 is a real-time, custom news service on the Web delivering news, sports, weather, business, and entertainment information. It features video advertising from companies such as GM, Dell, The Gap, and Sprint. RealVideo also enables interactive video advertising. Users who click on RealVideo advertisements are automatically linked to the advertiser's Web site. The Progressive Networks Web site can be reached at *http://www.real.com/*.

The Enterprise Training Channel

Training is one of the most common applications for multimedia on intranets; an increasing number of companies, including Boeing, Cisco Systems, Digital, MCI, and Oracle, are selecting streaming video solutions.

Streaming videos are particularly cost effective for company training. Some users estimated that two-day training sessions cost approximately $1,000 per person, without considering lost production time. The same training information can be broadcast on a streaming video over an intranet at a much lower cost; also, the trainees can download it when it is most convenient or most needed. In addition to improved accessibility and a decrease in training costs, streaming videos allow the trainers to select employees for specific internal news webcasting according to their performance.

Video streaming and multicasting for training is one of the most acceptable applications of webcasting technology. It is particularly appealing when used on intranets because the high bandwidth available on those networks provides better quality and performance than on the Internet. Products such as SGI WebForce and Xing Technology StreamWorks are designed with that market as a target.

Emerging Streaming Multimedia Services

In developing company webcasting channels, the emerging streaming multimedia services are also worth researching. Progressive Networks and MCI Communications announced the RealNetwork service in August 1997, which allows users to support live or on-demand video broadcasts over the Internet. It is designed to alleviate inadequate bandwidth and severe overload resulting from Internet video traffic.

RealNetwork consists of designated servers throughout the Internet backbone and supports RealAudio and RealVideo streaming technologies. RealNetwork users can broadcast live events or on-demand content, such as company management announcements, without developing their own channel infrastructures. Users are charged according to the number of video streams downloaded from such Web sites or on a per-event basis. The system can handle up to 50,000 simultaneous streams, enabling content suppliers to reach targeted audiences.

Users can also use RealNetwork services for E-commerce applications. They can broadcast 5- to 30-minute video clips that demonstrate new products or services on the Web. Initial estimates suggest that a one-hour video stream can be distributed to 25,000 viewers worldwide for only $8,000 a month. Content producers, including ABC News, Atlantic Records, and ESPN, have already joined the service.

UUNet Technologies also announced UUCast Service, which supports audio and video broadcasting. UUCast customers can distribute up to 250,000 simultaneous streams to customers of an ISP or online service. It is a multicasting network that is available on a monthly basis to content providers and business users.

Another multimedia multicasting service on the Internet is Live Event Stadium offered by Digex Communications, an ISP recently purchased by Intermedia Communications. It is available on a per-event basis to business users and content providers.

The @Home Network

The @Home network is a multicasting, streaming audio and video service over cable modems that delivers content at 128-Kbps to 256-Kbps speeds. The company is also working with more than 150 content providers to develop video channels for live events and chats, headline news, business news, sports, weather, and other categories.

@Home selected Progressive Networks for providing audio and video streaming software. However, streaming technologies are only one aspect of this service because they are not scalable and break down quickly with multimedia applications. The costs of serving thousands of 128-Kbps unicast streams would be prohibitive.

As a result, @Home relies on multicasting protocols that are built into Cisco routers and cable modems. The company multicast server converts unicast streams into multicast streams, which can be broadcast once to all authorized subscribers who are tuned in to receive it. For more information, visit *http://www.home.net/*.

Streaming Multimedia Standards

RTSP is the current streaming standard and was developed by Progressive Networks and Netscape Communications. However, Progressive is now also working with Microsoft to develop the active streaming format (ASF), which is expected to become the future streaming standard in conjunction with RTSP.

The NetChannel Concept

NetChannel is a TV-Internet service competing with the WebTV Network, which was acquired by Microsoft in 1997. NetChannel of San Francisco launched its initial set-top device in the United Kingdom, where it is using the NetStation unit that provides the link between a TV and a telephone socket. The purpose is to offer easy E-mail and Web access through a conventional TV. The specifications of this device are similar to those for network computers (NCs) developed by Oracle.

NetChannel provides Internet access using a smart card for approximately $25 monthly. The company expects significant success in United Kingdom and other European households because PC penetration there is much lower than in the United States. Only 11% of U.K. homes are estimated to have PCs capable of accessing the Internet; this percentage is nearly 40% in the United States.

NetStation is based on a 40-MHz ARM7500FE microprocessor from Cirrus Logic. It includes 8 MB of RAM, 4 MB of ROM, and a 33.6-Kbps modem for Internet access. The unit also contains a browser and a proprietary OS.

Multiuser Multimedia Conferencing

The Web can help users more effectively implement electronic document sharing. New multiuser services are being designed to allow a number of users to simultaneously view a document presentation over the Internet.

This concept is a wide area data conferencing system where a single presentation Web site operates special document conferencing software. Conference participants use their browsers to enter the conference but must register to become actively involved.

In this type of multiuser presentation, full-scale data collaboration is not involved, reducing interactive data transmissions. Participants can be connected and benefit with Internet access links of only 28.8 Kbps, although faster connections produce more immediate results.

With multiuser, multimedia conferencing, only the presenting Web site can manipulate the documents. Simultaneous audio conference is available over standard telephone lines. In addition, the virtual auditorium is very useful in situations where targeted audiences are connected to the Internet with Web browsers but do not have any specialized conferencing software. Web conferencing of this type is available from MCI Communications and ConferTech, a subsidiary of local and long-distance carrier Frontier Corporation.

Consider Channel Replication

Depending on the nature of a business, it may need to replicate its Web channels on several servers. If the webcasting or multicasting networks are established across the continent or the world, replicating the master channel server databases in various locations where local access will be faster and less congested is logical.

Channel replication – particularly with databases – can help distribute the overall system workload in a company network environment. However, it can also cause flooding of network traffic and create out-of-sync databases that offer different answers to different clients requesting the same information. Channel replication makes the difference between efficient replication and chaos.

Current replication technologies allow the distribution and exchange of data among active databases without human intervention. A process known as complete refresh can transfer the entire contents of a table to remote Web servers; quick refresh sends only changed data.

The act of replication copies data from its owner, who upgrades it to other Web servers. Whether users are random interfaces or regional subscribers to a push channel is irrelevant. The information can be replicated synchronously or asynchronously, but the original data has only a single source channel.

Recent tests of replication systems conducted by *Network Computing* magazine suggest that in situations where a master server communicates with slave servers through an intermediate server, replication technologies act as a distribution buffer. As such, this may be revealed as the most tolerant architecture in a push environment becuase it prevents overflow of end-user PC storage capacity.

Creating Remote Push Channels

Not all businesses can host their own Web channels, and many intranets or small- to medium-sized companies outsource their Web site hosting to ISPs. Those companies face the problem of creating remote push channels to announce new products and services to their customers. In many cases, however, bringing their Web sites in-house to accomplish this task is impractical.

Several push vendors have announced products to create remote channels. Because the results of user responses are often affected by additional caching and proxy servers outside of company firewalls, this operation must address adequate means of tracking user responses to Web advertising.

Three push technology vendors from California – Astound of Palo Alto, inCommon of San Mateo, and BackWeb of San Jose – have released push technology software during 1997 that meets the following requirements:

- Virtual private networks (VPNs) on the Web
- Webcasting development studio ideas
- Streaming multimedia industry trends

Virtual Private Networks on the Web

VPNs use public networks to establish WAN backbones instead of using leased lines and dial-up services. VPNs provide lower costs and greater flexibility advantages and the Internet creates additional opportunities for them. All that is needed to use VPNs are the IP protocol and a measure of security provisions. Figure 7.2 illustrates a VPN example.

Figure 7.2 An Example of a Virtual Private Network on the Web

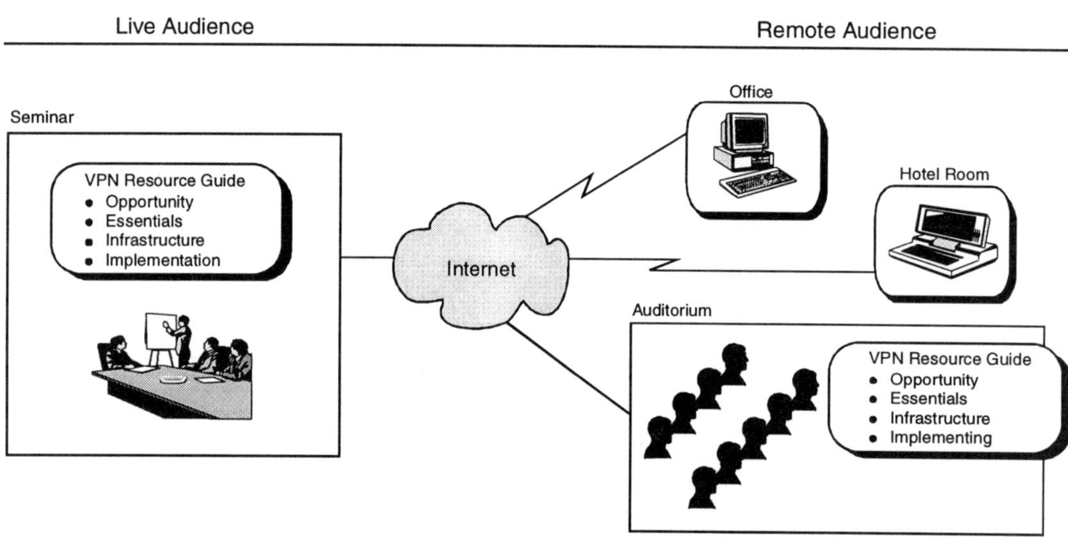

By capitalizing on the Internet's worldwide multicast capability, the VPN lets users participate in a virtual meeting or attend a training class.

Source: Ascend

VPN over the Internet is particularly advantageous where targeted users are geographically dispersed and equipped with relatively modest bandwidth connections. The greater the number of user sites and the greater the distance between them, the more likely the VPN solution will be cost effective. VPNs are able to save up to 60% more than equivalent private networks because they eliminate long-distance, leased lines between users. In addition, these networks do not pay for idle time and use less communications equipment. Global presence of the Internet also makes VPNs a practical and flexible proposition.

Many organizations leverage the Internet for business communications because it is suitable for webcasting applications where performance is not critical, IP protocols are acceptable, and the traffic is not isochronous. Remote access, enterprisewide intranets, and collaborative work are particularly well-suited for Internet VPNs. The Internet's powerful multicast capability can broadcast materials to users efficiently. This aspect of the Internet is only now being developed, but should not be overlooked when creating company communications channels on the Web.

Webcasting Development Studio Idea

Creating company Web channels for distributing information to employees or customers is a full-time occupation and requires a team of skilled operators. In one way, there is a need for networking experts who can set up the IP intranets, adequate bandwidth links, and extranet infrastructures, secure it, and connect it to the Internet. Yet perhaps more important is the actual creation of Web channels. These require accomplished content developers who can select and update the proper sources to satisfy the changing demands and preferences of subscribers.

Only a part of the push content will pertain to routine company announcements and information. The most important and valuable aspect of push service is to satisfy the information needs of company users. This in itself may be the result of push information compiled by marketing and competitive intelligence channels. Company webcasting should be a dynamic system and requires a permanent and competent staff to keep it operating effectively.

Connecting Web channels used to push applications to company legacy databases and archives are also needed. As a result, a group of specialists who know how legacy databases are organized and maintained must work with the webcasting organization.

Streaming Multimedia Industry Trends

This nascent industry is consolidating as Microsoft and Progressive Networks develop and create de facto streaming multimedia standards on IP networks.

Microsoft developed its NetShow product, but also agreed to bundle RealAudio and RealVideo client software in its IE. Progressive Servers will also be available with NetShow developer kits.

Microsoft bought 10% nonvoting stock share in Progressive Networks for an approximate price of $25 million. Microsoft also acquired VXtreme, which developed the plug-in Web Theater technology for providing streaming video on demand. This acquisition gives the company a key technology for adjusting streaming video to fit available bandwidth.

Conclusion

The Internet video market was originally distorted by the looming broadcast TV industry and its expectation to expand into interactive TV services. After a number of pilot tests, this concept is no longer being promoted, and the use of the Internet for streaming video to users and TV households is not considered a more viable alternative.

Internet video was pioneered in late 1995 by Xing Technology with VDONet, Vivo, and VXtreme. Unfortunately, most of the software supplied video solutions that were unacceptable when compared with consumer TV standards.

Several factors drive the industry and on-demand, VCR quality, streaming video on the Internet is expected by the end of the century.

PCs are becoming more powerful and will be able to acquire increasingly richer video streams from existing connections. After the turn of the century, most new TVs are expected to be IP devices with built-in Internet connectivity.

Although the bandwidth per dollar does not increase as fast as computing power of hardware, it is nevertheless a significant factor contributing to this development. The two effects create a synergistic, powerful combination. However, bandwidth could increase faster than it currently does –

particularly because of rapid developments in new telecom and compression microchips.

The race to provide TV viewers with an NC, which will immediately open high-bandwidth cable TV infrastructures to the Internet, is intensifying. When networks realize they can make a profit by giving away those devices instead of asking the consumers to pay $300 for each, the competition may increase even further. Access fees, advertising revenues, pay-per-view fees, home shopping revenues, and other profitable opportunities will more than compensate for such an investment.

Chapter 8

Major Push Applications

Numerous webcasting and push technology applications are being implemented. Some companies focus on target audiences, while others deliver content-specific material in several ways.

Although innovative and spectacular push demonstrations involving multimedia and broadcasts receive frequent media coverage, applications such as software implementation and maintenance activities may be more profitable in the short term.

Webcasting and push applications are suitable for enterprises with a developed LAN, WAN, and intranet infrastructure. Examples of conventional applications that were initially implemented on such networks include:

- Distributing internal memos and alerts
- Running acquisition of financial data feeds information
- Transmitting data to partners, suppliers, and customers via extranets
- Running acquisition of industry news articles
- Publishing press releases and company-related articles
- Distributing advertising to Web customers

As users become more familiar with the concept of intranets and the Internet, these applications can be implemented:

- Routine E-mail message deliveries
- Company and Internet information overload alternative

- Heavy competitive information research on the Web
- Access to financial information
- Notification of new technological developments

Enterprise Push Applications

Many conventional functions use push technology applications because they offer advantages, including low-cost distribution and immediate delivery of information.

More importantly, the intrusive nature of push messages offers a higher probability that this information will reach all recipients. Table 8.1 summarizes basic applications in executive communications, finance, marketing, sales, customer support, product development, and human resources, where push technology benefits are the most obvious and are easiest to implement because much of the information is already in digital form.

Table 8.1 Potential Enterprise Push Application Categories

Company Segment	Specific Application Areas
Executive Communications	♦ CEO messages to management ♦ Announcements of organizational changes ♦ Personnel appointments and promotions ♦ Special messages of appreciation ♦ Motivational messages ♦ Company and competitive stock prices

Company Segment	Specific Application Areas
Marketing	♦ Competitive intelligence ♦ New product announcements ♦ Competitive analysis findings ♦ Company press coverage ♦ Filtered news from the Internet ♦ Trade show promotions ♦ Market share information
Sales	♦ Competitive updating of the sales force ♦ Major sales and accomplishments announcements ♦ Distribution of sales policies ♦ Product inventory status updates ♦ Relevant competitive information ♦ Sales levels, statistics, and forecasts ♦ Products information and changes
Finance	♦ Company stock prices ♦ Competitive stock prices ♦ Expense reports information ♦ Finance policy announcements ♦ Departmental performance deadlines announcements ♦ Financial reporting requirements ♦ Taxation policies and updates ♦ Accounting reports and updates ♦ External market reports
Customer Support	♦ Product problem status updates ♦ New versions and product updates ♦ Notification of software upgrades ♦ Customer appreciation programs ♦ Special contests and discount announcements

Company Segment	Specific Application Areas
	♦ Maintenance service news
Product Development	♦ New product releases ♦ Notification of new product data at Web sites ♦ Announcement of technical data on the Internet ♦ Training announcements and opportunities ♦ Maintenance information and changes ♦ Web site changes ♦ Research updates on new products
Human Resources	♦ Company events announcements ♦ Emergency and safety announcements ♦ Organizational changes ♦ Training session registrations ♦ Employment opportunities ♦ Benefits plans deadlines and enrollment ♦ Employee performance recognition ♦ New employee welcomes ♦ Time card deadline reminders

Audience Targeting

Push applications focusing on particular audiences can be designed for intranet use or for Internet implementation in a business-to-consumer manner. These target audiences also influence the nature and features of push technologies. Group communications within controlled networked environments are typical for business audiences, whereas push services targeting consumers across the Internet are designed to transmit general information such as news, sports scores, and entertainment.

Web channels with multimedia content are designed to provide users with edited information from newspapers, magazines, and TV and radio stations. Content from these channels are delivered through a browser and typical push tools, and services of this type are exemplified by PointCast Network or INCISA.

Delivery Applications

Controlled content delivery is provided by push technology for delivering software programs and upgrades to company employees. In this type of service, secure, time-effective delivery is paramount. This method requires sufficient bandwidth to guarantee stable and regular delivery of large data files. BackWeb and Castanet represent this type of push technology application.

A number of push applications are designed to promote sales, public events, new products, or news stories. This type of application delivers a headline and hyperlinks to more detailed information. Users are notified by ticker tape, headlines, or E-mail. While some push tools only deliver content directly to users' PCs, Headliner and Communicator provide headlines and hyperlinks.

Distributing Time-sensitive Information

Some distributed company information is time sensitive: stock quotes, change alerts, or trouble tickets in technical support systems.

To ensure that the time-sensitive nature of this material is immediately obvious, some Web sites provide a "What's New" facility, although users must still access the site to view the changes. Timely push technology alerts improve the efficiency of the Web information system.

News Services

Internet news services are selected on the basis of content, timeliness, and ease of use and are among the most popular push applications. These news services offer a wide variety of information sources, including online versions of newspapers, radio and TV broadcasts, and many specialized trade and technical publications.

The most useful news services provide headlines and notifications using E-mail with hyperlinks that connect the user directly including a specific URL for a Web site with more detailed information. Often, news services are parts of other push applications, and many services make such channels available for sponsor and advertiser branding.

A major drawback of news services of this type, however, is that an overwhelming amount of news and information is pushed unless the subscription specifications are defined precisely.

Electronic Software Distribution

For many years, software vendors and users have been interested in electronic software distribution (ESD) as a more efficient alternative to diskettes or CDs. ESD promises to facilitate software distribution and updating – a significant problem when thousands of employees worldwide work with different hardware and software platforms. Recently, ESD technology was developed for use across various hardware and software platforms, and vendors are busy developing EDS strategies. In fact, Microsoft has set up an ESD Group within its end-user unit.

Push technology enables the delivery of software patches and updates almost immediately. In addition, vendors can inform customers about new products and new versions of previously released products, offering evaluation versions for a limited period of time. Also, software manuals can be made as HTML documents, with corrections performed page by page and sent to product users automatically.

The only disadvantage of ESD is potential bandwidth shortage. If all software vendors push fixes, patches, updates, and new products to their registered end users, existing intranet bandwidth can be consumed quite rapidly. Organizations may circumvent this situation by adding intranet servers to relieve the bandwidth on the Internet connection, but direct desktop connections may suffer bottlenecks due to individual information overloads. What is needed by companies that want to take advantage of this development is the enhancement of bandwidth to their desktop and workgroup connections before introducing ESD using push technology.

Software Implementation and Maintenance

Several industry analysts believe the real value of push technology is in delivering software applications and their upgrades. Users are more aware of the costs of implementing and upgrading desktop software as a result of the Internet, the NC initiatives, and studies of costs related to these issues.

Push technology can transfer files from Web servers to client desktops, and such software tools can be extended and adapted to deliver and upgrade desktop software. To become truly valuable in this respect, push products must include additional features that check a user platform for existing software and configuration and have the ability to modify such in-house and remote systems.

Push products of this type can function well if databases of user profiles and software licenses are maintained at the Web server side. As a result, because software implementation is a systems management function, such push technologies should be integrated with other management programs.

Push products for software implementation are being developed by vendors converging in regard to this market opportunity. Marimba, Inc. is among the first to address this market, with its Castanet product line. However, users are advised to evaluate alternative products as they become available to determine if such push products integrate well with existing or planned management tools.

Financial Services

Financial services are particularly suitable for push technology; in fact, many service organizations managing institutional and individual investors have been using it for several years. However, those services are relatively expensive, providing using dedicated networks and terminals primarily to traders and financial consultants who can afford the cost and running fees.

Several push services focus on financial news and stock-related information that are available on the Web and are consequently more affordable. Individual investors subscribe to these services because the access cost is considerably lower. To receive regular updates, investors indicate the companies and stocks that they follow or that exist in their portfolios. A push service then provides the digital feeds and continuously pushes stock trading prices, news profiles, and magazine articles about the selected companies.

Consulting Communications

One of the most lucrative areas for push technology is in consulting environments where users are geographically dispersed – particularly among management consultants and system integration organizations because many employees are equipped with PCs or portable communication devices.

The Big 6 accounting firms, for example, perform services for clients worldwide and must inform their field staff regularly about the latest changes in the tax codes and accounting practices and regulations within states and countries where they operate.

In these circumstances, push technology presents an ideal solution for providing timely knowledge to personnel without another method of easy access to updated information sources.

Trading Support Systems

One of the most useful push technology application areas is trading – particularly in finance, where the industry is driven almost exclusively by constantly changing information and the ability to make rapid decisions based on that information.

Banks, insurance companies, stockbrokers, money managers, and investment advisors are among those who can benefit the most from push technology applications. It is ideally suited to their activities because it distributes highly personalized news, stock prices, company reports, and customer portfolio performance to mobile personnel. The most immediate benefit in those environments is the ability to reach people rapidly with changes in prices, giving them a competitive advantage.

Other trading support systems are also well-suited for push applications, including metals, materials, gems, paintings, and other works of art. Commercial trading applications, such as integrated circuits or electronic components – whose prices vary widely according to supply, demand, and the introduction of new products and higher-performance models – can also benefit from push technology.

Sales Force Automation

Push technology is involved in the development of dynamic sales intelligence systems customized to provide the most effective marketing and sales support. It is implemented in conjunction with intranets and can be designed to provide updated information to the entire sales force.

Companies can establish a profile of the information needs for each salesperson and use it to deliver the correct information automatically. Salespersons can add and modify the profile and may include specific news and articles about accounts, prospects, and competitors with which they are involved.

A growing trend of software products that combine such characteristics in a single integrated platform is developing. InterActive WorkPlace of Burlington, Massachusetts, is among the pioneers of such a platform that collects and integrates customized information about accounts, prospects, products, competitors, and markets. The company delivers customized ActiveBriefings to each salesperson, providing information integrated from multiple company and commercial databases, news services, and intranet and Internet sites. Figure 8.1 illustrates the infrastructure of a system that would be required to implement this type of service.

Figure 8.1 Example of an Integrated Architecture

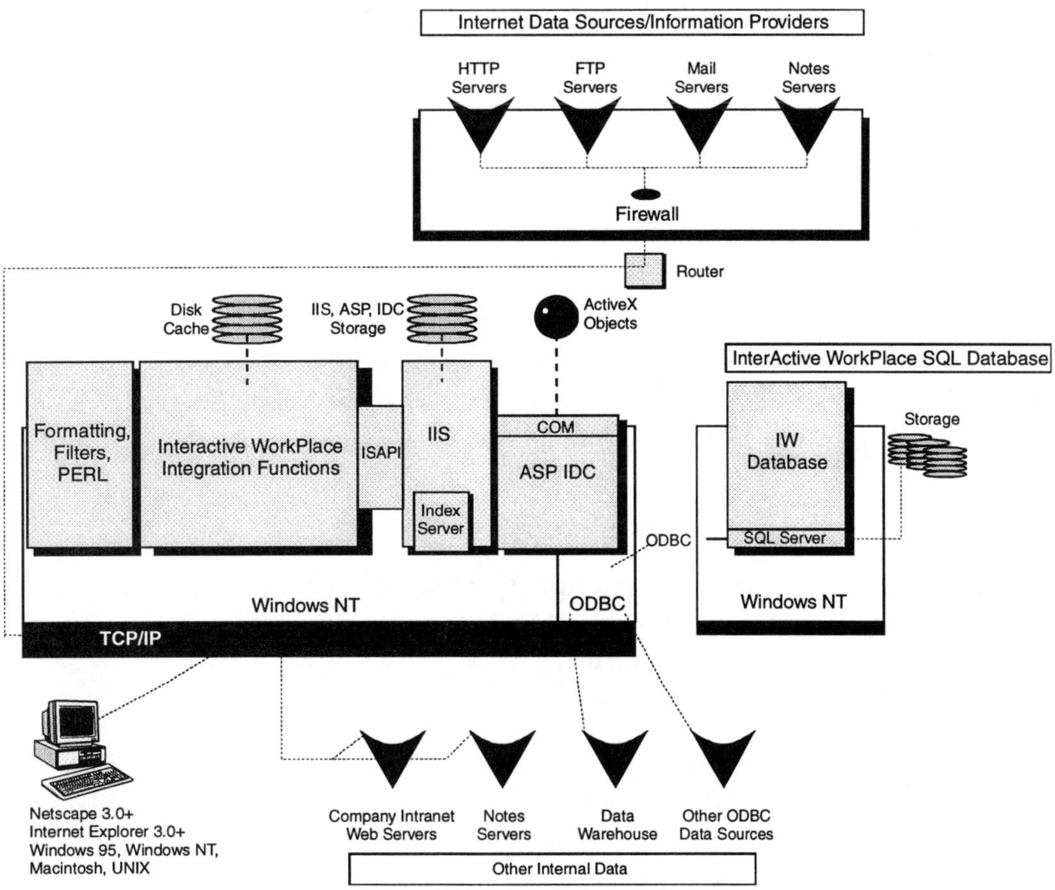

Source: InterActive WorkPlace, Inc.

Competitive Intelligence

Tracking the competition is one of the most useful push technology applications in marketing. More and more organizations create a Web presence to promote their products and services. As a result, identifying those Web site locations and setting up a competitive intelligence channel with specialized agents that monitor changes in all competitive Web sites is relatively easy. Any announcements of new products, new pricing, discounts, service offers, or other competitive aspects can be identified immediately and transmitted to the Web channel for immediate distribution to the marketing and sales department. In fact, competitive intelligence push applications can involve a group of agents dedicated to monitoring sources of competitive information, including Web sites, press releases, promotions, trade press news and evaluations, advertising, and research studies.

Strategic Marketing

Independent push Web channel services can be set up to identify and target groups of people. Highly specialized channels that contain current information about a subject are created and provide free access to users who want to provide an E-mail or postal address, telephone number, and fax information.

These channels are maintained by third parties that develop electronic digests of specific news and data. The success of such an operation depends on the sale of use of these push channels to sponsors and advertisers who can, in effect, brand those channels and acquire direct access to subscribers.

Interactive Advertising

Online advertising identifies a user profile based on Internet interaction and personalizes advertising messages, which is returned to the user immediately with the information requested or expected.

A user request for a Web page automatically triggers user profile information from a cookie repository or a marketing database. If such information does not exist with the ISP through which the user is interacting, programs can request such data from partner ISPs.

User profile information is translated into a code that describes the profile. This information is made available to an online advertising service's Web server, which contains advertisements categorized by demographic parameters. Advertisements related to the profile and the present request are then automatically selected and displayed.

Web channel product developers are also linking their Web sites to consumer profiles. Such targeting allows Web channel producers to charge premiums of 20% to 30% above conventional online advertising rates.

This type of one-on-one push advertising is more effective than customization efforts based on the use of cookies attached to user browsers. By targeting users more precisely, webcasters may not need to develop specialized Web sites for attracting specific audiences. Instead, they can use the Web site as a general-purpose marketing mechanism.

Netfomercials

Netfomercials represent a special form of interactive advertising that can be implemented using push technology; these are interactive displays that provide the viewer with hyperlinks to advertisers' Web sites automatically. By contrast, banners must be pulled by users when they download specific Web pages and may not be effective if they do not hold the users attention. On many intranets, external advertising is prohibited as a distracting influence.

For online advertisers seeking more powerful advertising concepts, 5- to 10-second animated displays – interstitials or intermercials – provide an alternative. According to Jupiter Communications, online advertisers are expected to assign 25% of their budgets to intermercials and sponsorships by the year 2001, although 50% remain allotted to banner advertising.

Push-based intermercials are expected to be commonplace on the Web by 1999. They are also expected to appeal to advertisers because they offer a high product branding potential.

Product Distribution Support

An information channel that provides customized data to support product distributors and end users is an effective application for push technology – particularly with electronic products, such as computers, peripherals, complex telephone systems, and satellite communications.

The manufacturers of such complex products establish a Web channel to distribute updated product information, including new product versions, upgrades, prices, discounts, problems, solutions, and software updates. Companies such as Compaq, Dell, and IBM are already implementing such systems for dealers, distributors, and product users.

In the automotive industry, leading push technology applications include Web channels for dealers who receive information regarding the latest models and recalls and other information about conducting business with the company. Chrysler, Ford, General Motors, and Japanese auto makers are involved in developing and implementing such Web channels as part of their marketing strategies.

Legal Information

The use of push for distributing legal information is in the emerging stages. It provides early knowledge of legislation being drafted or implemented, including patents, copyrights, trading rights, monopolies, and exclusive contracts.

Push informs employees about legislative changes that take place in other states or countries. In the insurance industry, for example, where legislation is regularly changing, push keeps employees up to date.

Collaborative Computing

Collaborative intranet and Internet tools are extremely useful because they allow groups and individuals in diverse locations to collaborate on projects that would otherwise be impractical. Adding push technology brings new features to those tools, making them even more useful.

Collaboration tools can be divided into synchronous and asynchronous applications. Synchronous tools are real-time collaboration programs that require active participation during a session. Asynchronous collaboration allows designated parties to access or receive information that has been prepared previously.

Real-time collaboration tools, including multiuser videoconferencing, often combine several related features, including background file transfers for exchanging data that may not have been presentable during actual conferencing. Even presentable information may contain material for use at a later time. The most advanced collaborative tools allow selective information distribution.

In addition, document sharing may occur in realtime, although changes made by one participant are not immediately reflected on other users' copies. As a result, tracking and individual document revisions for designated users must be performed at a later time by some form of push technology. These products and tools are very useful in sales, marketing, and customer support applications.

Asynchronous collaboration allows multiple participants to exchange information at different times. These systems also permit managers to partition and restrict access to information and notify users of any changes. In its simplest form, this type of collaboration is represented by E-mail.

Using extrapolation techniques in conjunction with Internet push technology, users can publish information in shared folders and notify other users of its availability. Users, conversely, can specify what type of information they are willing to receive.

Multicasting Applications

The idea of sending a single data stream over a network for simultaneous delivery to hundreds, thousands, or even millions of users is very appealing.

Unfortunately, actual multicasting business applications are not yet clearly understood. Industry analysts speculate that multicasting will occur sooner on intranets than over the Internet because it requires user management and specialized multicasting servers, which are easier to accomplish in a network environment.

A 1996 Internet Protocol Multicast Initiative (IPMI) study revealed that 54% of companies surveyed believe that IP multicasting will create new business opportunities by distributing large amounts of data more efficiently. Another 47% believe multicasting enhances productivity.

While multicasting is an application in its own right, it is also an enabling factor for implementing audio and video streaming, ESD, multipoint conferencing, Web site replication, and other push applications.

Multicasting company videos to individual desktops may be an attractive idea, but it requires a substantial investment. If the content is not mission-critical in some way, justifying the expense may be difficult. When interactive applications such as employee training are planned, the business case for company multicasting becomes more compelling.

Who should pay for a stream of information to a large number of workers? It is not clear how such a service should be valued and accounted for with regard to its use by individual company workers and workgroups. Billing for multicasting applications must be resolved before their use becomes commonplace.

Web Conferencing

Services designed to enable conferencing on the Web are emerging, although this type of service is not designed to compete with full-scale data collaboration applications. In addition, only the initiating Web channel or site can change and manipulate the presentation; participants are a passive audience.

Streaming Live Events

Push makes selected broadcasting or streaming of live events possible. In the business arena, organizations often sponsor sporting and entertainment events. Suppliers of products and consumables at those events use push technology and branded channels to inform product distributors about the events. Opportunities for company events to be announced and streamed to employees also exist. For example, the CEO may address employees or Wall Street analysts may receive immediate information regarding the financial performance of a company.

Promoting and Distributing Online Music

Audio streaming and push technology on the Internet create a whole new marketing and distribution environment for the music industry, which is quick to embrace new digital technologies. The Internet and the Web present a unique opportunity to bridge the gap between the artists and their fans and is changing the way music is created, marketed, distributed, and sold.

The industry is now involved in play-to-play webcasting events and is beginning to provide bundled Internet access software on music CDs. Music publishers are using push technology to inform music distributors about the latest products. However, an increasing number of artists are using the Internet to promote and distribute their music directly to their fans.

Online Travel Applications

According to a Jupiter Communications report, the online travel market was estimated at more than $800 million in 1997. It is expected to reach more than $4.5 billion by the year 2000.

Travel information is a particularly attractive online application because it is always specific, pertaining to individual needs and preferences. As a result, this industry has tremendous push potential: Thousands of travel agencies and travel consultants must be updated about price changes, discounts, special packages, and cruises.

These services are also suitable for segmentation into specific groups, including senior citizens, economic travelers, adventure, safari, cruising, retreats, and religious, historic, architectural, and folklore hobbyists and students. The list of possibilities is almost endless.

The ultimate money-making business in the online travel industry is realized in customization of those services. The objective is to acquire specific personal interests, needs, and preferences for creating unique travel experiences. Push technology is ideal for implementing such marketing programs.

Internet Webcasting Growth

Internet webcasting has grown incredibly during the last two years. By mid-1997, it included more than 700 webcasters continuously transmitting information. Although nearly 10% of them were exclusively Internet webcasters – a percentage that is rapidly increasing – the majority were and remain radio and TV stations.

Few webcasters regularly transmit live video signals on the Internet, but new video webcasters are appearing every day. The funeral of Princess Diana, for example, was webcast live by networks including ABC News, BBC, Fox News, and Globe News. The Hong Kong transition to China was also covered by webcasts. Clearly, webcasting is no longer limited to news and entertainment but also includes long-distance learning and telemedicine, for example.

Audio and Video Broadcasting

Most push applications use the channel concept to transmit content. However, push applications can also transmit audio and video feeds from content providers, such as radio and TV stations.

For example, KPIX of San Francisco, which operates TV and radio stations in the Bay area, participated in a beta project of IFusion Arrive service. It offered online versions of KPIX news programming, including live video feeds from key traffic trouble spots in that area in addition to other audio and video news items.

Music and video distributors can create Web sites with audio and video clips. These sites can be pushed to Internet users who have shown interest in specific artists or music categories.

As time progresses and the technology of multimedia transmission improves, push applications are expected to deliver the look and feel of broadcasting video.

Conclusion

Webcasting applications are being implemented in both the business and consumer markets. The main attraction of these new promotions and marketing initiatives is the ability to target individual buyers and acquire precise demographics, which lead to increasing revenues and profitable operations.

Financial services, which rely on current information, are the largest established users of various forms of push technology. In previous years, many push applications pertaining to significant company news and stock price changes were distributed through costly private networks and specialized terminals. The availability of push tools on the Web is rapidly expanding such applications to money managers and commercial traders for smaller organizations, and individual investors, who could not previously afford such services.

In the intranet environment, the most attractive push application is software distribution and online updating. Competitive intelligence, customer support, and strategic marketing are also promising.

In the consumer market, push applications using interactive advertising or various products on branded channels are being introduced. Customized travel services, music, and entertainment webcasts appear to be the most promising applications in this area. The situation is expected to change dramatically with the advent of Internet TV, which will yield an increase in consumer Web access.

Chapter 9

Webcasting and Push Business Strategies

Regardless of the webcasting and push solutions being contemplated, organizations must evaluate each push product or webcasting service with regard to their existing networking environments, proposed objectives, available skills, and budgets.

To begin the evaluation process, push products must be matched with the existing client platforms. Because push communications over intranets and the Internet may be global in scope, all client platforms involved must be considered before further planning continues. These platforms could include Web browsers, Windows 95, Windows NT, Windows 3.1, Mac, Solaris, Java, and other UNIX platforms. Identifying only those push products that will run on all platforms within the organization is necessary.

Developers have more flexibility for the server platform. They can put the channels on several platforms of choice or avail themselves of existing Web channel services and specialized Web server farms.

How to Become a Webcasting Organization

The easiest way to introduce push technology into a company is to use tools and services such as BackWeb or Marimba because their products may not require any additional functionality to meet delivery objectives.

Regardless of which push technology is used to implement the applications, the first step is to determine what content should be pushed to whom. Pushing content that users do not request wastes bandwidth. However, determining what company information is time sensitive and needs to be pushed to employees is critical.

The next step is to determine the most effective content form for users – not as straightforward an issue as it may seem. The format will differ depending on the content, and selecting the most effective presentation format is important. The type of business and environment should dictate the types of information sources to be used. These, in turn, will influence the selection of content delivery products and services.

If push applications or technologies match company requirements, the company presentation of information and data can be altered to use existing push application more effectively.

Determining Webcasting User Categories

Three major webcasting developer categories have been identified: personal and small businesses, midrange marketers and publishers, and major E-commerce practitioners and publishers. Table 9.1 summarizes these categories and their objectives.

Table 9.1 Major Webcaster User Categories

Webcasting Objective	Description of Typical Users
Personal and Small Business	♦ Individuals, consultants, and newsletter publishers ♦ Writers and small or home-based businesses ♦ Extensive E-mail users for notification of new content
Midrange Marketers and Publishers	♦ Product distributors and representatives of firms ♦ Marketing-oriented Web sites delivering information on new products, news stories, press releases, sales notices, and coupons ♦ Maintaining demographics
Major E-commerce Practitioners and Publishers	♦ Online newspaper and magazine publishers ♦ Audio and video clips on music CDs and videos ♦ E-commerce promoters ♦ Large numbers of users ♦ Interactive advertising

Determining which category webcasting developers belong to saves unnecessary expense and allows an organization to select the most appropriate push technology development tools.

Unfortunately, some organizations acquire the most sophisticated push technology tools only to discover that neither the networking infrastructure nor the existing skills can use them. In such as case, a third-party service may be the most cost-effective solution. Entering the Web channel development process under the guidance of an experienced consultant has significant value.

Push Objectives for Small Businesses

Many small businesses do not have the time, skills, or financial resources to establish their own webcasting department. They use E-mail for business communications and, often, product delivery.

Low-end webcasting developers can use simple push services or easy-to-use development tools that will result in a professional presentation to most effectively promote the product or service. Important considerations for this user category are low cost and ease of use.

Because E-mail is a common business application, the logical push solution is enhanced E-mail alerts with multimedia attachments. In addition, the PointCast Connectors channel provides free delivery to other PointCast clients. Intermind and WebCast could also meet the needs of a small organization because they provide alerts as part of the service.

Midrange Market Push Program Developers

This webcasting category differs significantly from the small business operator because most are sizable businesses that already have a Web presence. Many of these organizations have high expectations, yet their budgets and staffing skills remain relatively low for undertaking a major push effort. As a result, midrange users should consider leveraging existing Web pages with push templates, transferring existing content into push channels. Push tools and service providers now offer products that perform such tasks. Some of these products include BackWeb, Downtown, HeadLiner, and WebCast.

Midrange businesses are also interested in more sophisticated feedback about their push operations, including marketing statistics and development and training assistance. This type of activity usually involves a push server that costs between $1,000 and $25,000, depending on the size of marketing databases and number of targeted customers. However, the availability of Web servers with existing multimedia content can lower the investment in new push operations significantly.

Major Webcasting Publishers

Webcasting publishers consist of organizations that are among the early adopters of push technology and maintain a significant Web presence because they best understand the benefits of the technology. They are the major promoters of E-commerce and see push technology as a logical step in extending online business activities.

These business users want high-impact, highly customized push capabilities that will work with their extensive marketing databases. Many webcasting publishers are major publishers of newspapers, magazines, books, music, videos, movies, radio and TV content, and interactive advertising.

Audio and video channels are important in marketing the products and services of those companies. Because they also brand channels with their own logos, they use only the most sophisticated push technologies to focus on content and the overall application. This type of use includes software producers that alert large numbers of clients to new versions of their products and deliver these updates over the Internet and intranets. The BackWeb and Castanet push products are the best solutions for this type of application.

Content Branding

Content branding is a means of sponsoring a Web channel that is provided by third-party content developers to promote specific products or services. Branding is a powerful marketing feature and should be available for specific Web channels. The push application selected should provide the capability of allowing company branding on both the client and server side.

Selecting the Minimal Complement of Push Components

Push capabilities can be developed without assistance, but it may be expensive. A more economical approach is to use a software developer's kit (SDK) that provides the component building blocks for implementing push in a documented set of application programming interfaces (APIs).

Ideally, an SDK will provide a number of push components:

- Seamless company network connectivity
- Content customization profiling
- Flexible user configurations
- Persistent file transfer capability
- Efficient bandwidth use facility
- Seamless new content absorption
- Alternative client alert capability
- Acceptable company security provisions

Whether the company is planning to develop the push technology on its own or use one of the available tools, these elements are mandatory to create an acceptable system.

Building Push Communities

A very attractive strategy for content publishers is creating push communities within intranets or Internet targeted audiences. Push communities make minimizing the investment in webcasting possible while simultaneously maximizing any potential returns.

Basic push community characteristics include common effort, purpose, identity, reflection of reality, adaptability, and freedom of participation (see Table 9.2). A push community can be very successful – even if only four or five of those characteristics are present in a group. The potential for a push community could dictate the choice of push development tools with chat features or an ability to support the effort within existing groupware systems.

Table 9.2 Push Community Characteristics

Characteristic	Description and Remarks
Effort	Level of participation and collaboration required by a group of users
Purpose	The overall vision and focus of a community
Identity	Intrinsic characteristics shared by community members
Organic	Community mirrors real-life community of interest with a life of its own outside cyberspace
Adaptive	Flexibility and resilience in facing potential disruptions
Freedom	Members can join and leave without restrictions

Because the success of a push community requires a level of member participation and collaboration, the most likely push community opportunities exist among workgroups engaged in a common project or Internet users who are following specific hobbies or sports events.

The push community should also have an overall vision or mission objective around which the whole Web channel can be built. It also needs to mirror an existing real-life community with a life of its own rather than a synthetic structure designed to create a revenue stream for the promoters. In short, a push community reflects the actual relationships between communicating parties.

In addition, the push community must be flexible. Another important feature is freedom of association with such a community, which members can join or leave without restrictions.

Resolving Bandwidth Shortages

Perhaps the most important issue to consider when designing and implementing Web channels and sites for providing push content is that bandwidth is only a part of the overall company networking solution. In most instances, the endeavor will not account for the most significant applications of intranet traffic, but may impact the overall performance dramatically if bandwidth consumption is not kept under control.

The adoption of Web-based intranets and the proliferation of multimedia rich applications are already responsible for bandwidth bottlenecks. The problem is aggravated by a steady stream of increasingly higher-performance desktops, workstations, and Web servers that demand more bandwidth on intranet backbones, C/S networks, hubs, switches, and routers.

When considering a webcasting application strategy, existing network bandwidth should be assessed. Individual user bandwidth links should be increased to 10 Mbps. This level can be reached by upgrading shared LANs to switched Ethernet, which can be employed in workgroups and central network nodes. These links can be further linked with 100-Mbps Fast Ethernet to servers or other switches. Although it is an effective strategy, upgrading requires managing an aggregation of multiple, 100-Mbps switch ports. Clearly, 1,000-Mbps bandwidth is needed to provide reasonable performance for intranets.

Gigabit Ethernet is promoted as the most appropriate solution, particularly when interoperability is considered. The Gigabit Ethernet standard is the most suitable because it will ensure interoperability and 1,000-Mbps network stability. It also offers connectivity to the large installed base of Ethernet and Fast Ethernet nodes.

Figure 9.1 illustrates a potential Gigabit intranet network of this type.

Figure 9.1 A Gigabit Intranet Network Example

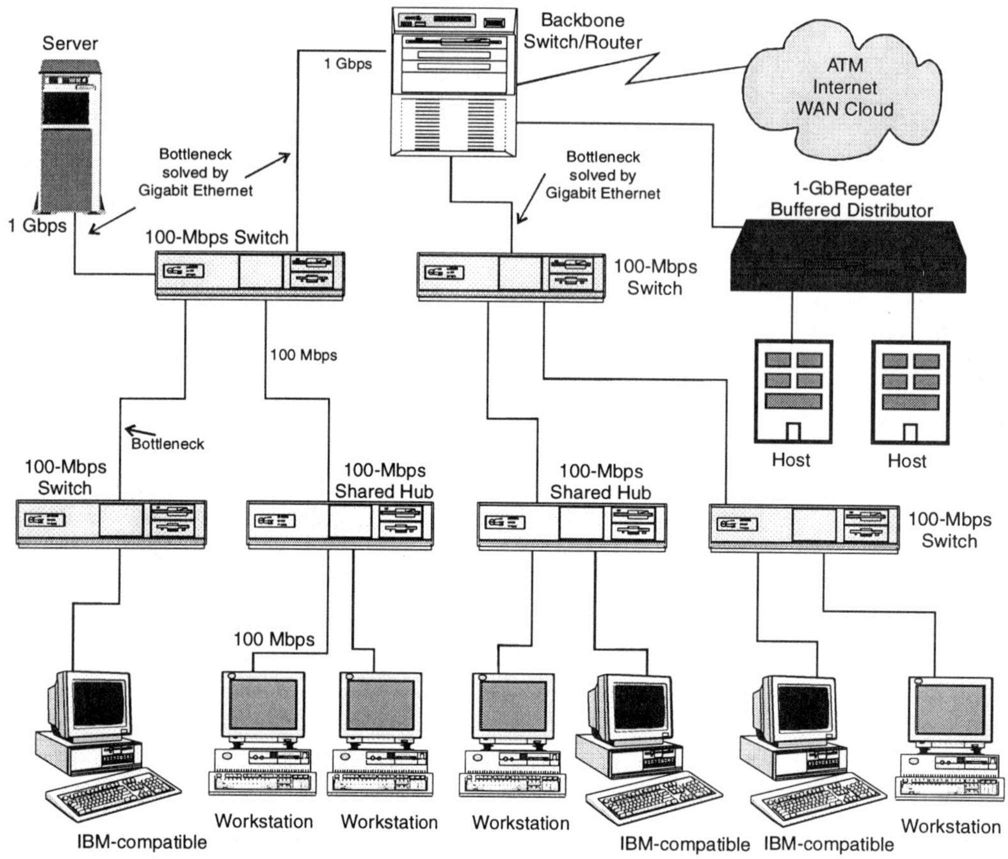

Asynchronous transfer mode (ATM) and fiber channel (FC) solutions also offer gigabit speed alternatives. ATM, however, is better suited for backbones and WAN interconnectivity applications. FC is optimized for mass storage access and is expected to be the dominant linking technology for short-distance, mass storage connectivity.

Establishing Connections

If webcasting is implemented in mission-critical applications, organizations must establish a reliable ISP connection, which is the first step in creating a reasonable business webcasting strategy.

An ISP service that offers at least two redundant paths available for backbone data transmission from each node is an appropriate choice. Each redundant path is an added layer of protection against outages and cable cuts. UUNet, for example, provides four redundant paths; ISPs, such as ANS

Communications, DataXchange Networks, and Data Research Network, each provide three redundant paths.

Diversity of local loops and long-distance circuits is also an important factor in evaluating an ISP. Diversity is the use of circuits from more than one channel; if one circuit suffers an outage, the ISP node will not be disabled completely. ISPs that operate their own facilities (for example, MCI or Sprint) ensure their routes are redundant, but do not offer diversity.

Despite redundancy and diversity, power outages can also wreak havoc with ISP nodes. As a result, organizations are advised to ensure that their ISPs have diesel generator backup at each site.

Evaluating the underlying transport system used on the ISP backbone is also important. These systems may include ATM, FR up to 45-Mbps bandwidth, and IP routing. Routed IP networks are particularly vulnerable to route flapping caused when a malfunctioning route offers unreliable service. Some ISPs protect themselves with route dampening, a process that prevents excessive oscillation when specific route service fluctuates due to malfunctions.

Determining if the ISP is connected to several network access points (NAPs) that exchange traffic is also important. At least three public NAP connections and several private peering arrangements are necessary.

Some ISPs offer performance guarantees on their backbones. These guarantees cover elements including network availability, packet loss, delay, and maximum outages. These factors are important to companies contemplating designing webcasting systems for mission-critical applications.

Push Technology on the LAN

Most businesses focus on push technology as an extension of the Internet, intranet, and Web capabilities that use TCP/IP. Most organizations are only beginning to implement intranets; however, many have extensive investments in LAN technologies. Some LAN systems include or can be converted to run on TCP/IP to become intranets, but this transition may require additional investments.

New push products can be used to implement push on LAN running protocols other than IPs. They provide a way to leverage investment on non-Internet LANs and create a future migration path to intranet technology.

NetReach from Softreach in Herndon, Virginia, provides the applications to perform this task. Its NetReach Admin Console creates channels on a file server, which specific groups can tune to using the NetReach Client software. This product can manipulate multimedia presentations and a variety of graphic and audio file formats. Alerts are displayed as screen savers or scrolling windows, and NetReach runs on virtually any LAN. Although evaluating existing networking environments before making a decision on a specific push technology is wise, products similar to NetReach can be readily upgraded to TCP/IP networks in the future.

Facilitating Multimedia Traffic

In evaluating the networking infrastructure for handling multimedia traffic, the first task should be to fine-tune the existing equipment. Network bottlenecks are caused not always by the type of equipment implemented by an enterprise, but sometimes by how it is used.

Replacing existing equipment with Gigabit Ethernet technologies may be overkill in many cases and should be avoided until doing so is absolutely necessary.

Often, the secret to effective equipment use is knowledgeable use of network management software that tracks traffic flow across an intranet. Improving the flow of traffic requires measuring and evaluating the current status.

The next step in preventing bottlenecks is to determine the proper combination of the Ethernet technologies and match it to specific applications based on bandwidth requirements. Most desktop traffic is adequately managed with 10-Mbps Ethernet. Most configuration changes are performed on the company backbone, not user segments. The key to success is selecting configurations that will be suitable investments for the next two or three years and will handle the anticipated multimedia traffic.

Also, better use of existing equipment can be made by paying better attention to industry standards. Protocols RTP and RSVP are designed to ensure that streaming data arrive at their destinations on time and in one piece. When multimedia traffic is involved, these specialized protocols should be used to the fullest extent possible.

One of the most profitable solutions for multimedia on the Internet, however, is IP multicasting because it is designed to conserve bandwidth. It is a cost-effective alternative for increasing bandwidth or upgrading to a new transport technology using existing networking infrastructures. IP multicasting and RSVP are a powerful combination.

Considering Multicasting Tools and Services

As multicasting is more widely accepted, new products and services that facilitate its implementation and provide some means of Web channel management and control appear. Percept Software and similar products are software tools that provide webcasters with detailed information about audience demographics and reception quality. Whenever multicasting is introduced, these tools can simplify webcasting.

StreamWatch tools also measure use patterns of multimedia broadcasts and multicasts over intranets and the Internet. They track numbers and identities of users, times of tuning in, and individual reception quality. Channel providers can then bill viewing time to specific multicasts and help content providers in setting advertising rates. A valuable aspect of the system is its ability to monitor problem areas on the multicast tree. This type of management tool calls attention to specifically network routers where adjustments must be made.

Anticipating User Operating Problems

Developers should be aware that the end user is exposed to many problems when using some webcasting services that offer free access and carry advertising. Being forced to tolerate the advertising messages is only one example.

Features that generate automatic updates can slow desktop operation significantly. Users word processing, spreadsheet, or presentation software report deteriorating performance when PointCast is used.

The most common complaint is the increasing amount of hard disk space that is required. Even when a limited number of topics are selected from a service such as PointCast, the information may consume as much as 24 MB of storage. The continual refreshing of screen saver notifications also requires additional disk drive space.

How Much Push?

The question of user notification is not a trivial one. A variety of alternatives differ in their intrusiveness to the established computing routines of the users. The intrusiveness of one method against another cannot be assessed because the perception depends on the overall application. The screen saver, for example, originally popularized for push notification by pioneer PointCast Network, is considered very popular in some environments and is unwelcome in others.

Considering the targeted subscriber audiences is important: If users spend a large amount of time at their desks or actively use their PCs, the screen saver can be effective. It may, however, require excessive bandwidth if a large number of users schedule their alerts and downloads during the same time period.

When users are distracted by a screen saver or when they include extranet subscribers outside of the secure company environment, other formats of alert – E-mail messages, pager alerts, or fax delivery – may be more practical because they require less bandwidth to be effective. However, these alternatives are suitable only for short, telegraphic-style messages. Audio and video clips used to capture users' attention are not practical.

Using headlines in a title bar or ticker tape minimizes desktop screen space and is less intrusive and less distracting. A pop-up window asking if the user wants to receive new content is another alternative and can be eliminated quickly with the click of a mouse.

The least intrusive notification method is the polite agent notification software by BackWeb; it performs the alert function in the background when other tasks are being executed on the desktop.

Selecting Notification and Delivery Features

In planning a webcasting operation, selecting the users' form of notification and the method of delivering the selected content is also necessary. Some push tools provide notification and delivery through direct hyperlinks contained in the notification message. By contrast, some webcasting tools provide only notification of a change. The user must see the alert and pull the item to view the information. Webcasting products that provide notification include Communicator, Community, and Digital Bindery.

A large number of push tools deliver only specified information without prior user notification. These tools include Affinicast, AfterDark Online, Flash Site, Gigex, InfoWizard, IntelliServ, Mercury Mail, Messenger, My Way, Net Attache Pro, and Netriever.

A large percentage of push tools provide notification and delivery options in the same package. Products in this category include Castanet, DataChannel, Driveway, Farcast, Groupmaster, HeadLiner, Highlights, INCISA, Intellicraft, Intercast, Intra Express, I-Server, Netcaster, NewCast, News Edge, and One-to-One.

Effective Web Site Development

Webcasting alerts only the clients and subscribers to changes or new items on Web sites; the objective is to entice users to visit these sites often. As a result, these Web sites must be not only well-designed, but easily accessed and navigable.

For ease of access, Web sites are reachable with standard browsers – Netscape Navigator, Microsoft IE, and browsers embedded within AOL services. The general rule is to make certain that any Web site targeted by hyperlinks is reachable via widely used versions of Web browsers. Some sites may be written in JavaScript, for example, which is the latest technology for Web site developers, but many browsers are not able to read it because not all browsers are Java enabled.

The objective is to avoid lengthy download times. Many users simply refuse to wait, and the push channel directing them to such Web sites thus becomes a wasted effort.

Web sites including extensive multimedia content should be paired with text-only versions for users who do not want to wait for graphics and animation to download. This situation can be alleviated by providing background downloading of Web pages.

Web sites design should also regard user response time. If the site does not have sufficient capacity to allow users to log on rapidly and the ability to accommodate the large number of users who may be trying to connect simultaneously, the users will be locked out. A quality Web site must continuously monitor the response it receives and add server capacity when required.

A Web site should also be easy to navigate – particularly one that consists of many Web pages. Such a site can be improved considerably with the inclusion of a site-specific search engine that quickly locates information by topic, data, or other criteria.

The architecture of a Web site should always allow quick movement between pages. A Web site map or table of contents should be readily available on every Web page to further facilitate navigation.

Selecting Authoring and Development Tools

Three generations of Web authoring tools are available: HTML tag editors, what you see is what you get (WYSIWYG) page editors, and Web site construction tools. Most are suitable for implementing push technologies that have initiated a new group of specific products, such as Web page and site construction capabilities. With time, however, the existing and popular Web authoring tools may include additional features suitable for push implementation.

HTML tag editors are the oldest generation of Web authoring tools and are primarily designed for Web page development. The ultimate appearance of Web pages designed with these tools is not necessarily what is displayed during the editing process, however.

The second generation of Web authoring tools followed quickly using WYSIWYG editors. With these tools, HTML tags can be hidden, allowing developers to concentrate on Web page layout rather than HTML tagging. More importantly, the output of those tools is representative of how the Web pages appear in popular browsers.

The latest generation of Web authoring tools focuses on construction of complete Web sites rather than individual Web pages. These tools (see Table 9.3) are required for developing intranet Web sites, although their sophistication may be overwhelming to nontechnical users. These tools also include a whole range of utilities, templates, development task management, and hyperlink checking, and they are clearly most suitable for additional facilities to handle push technology Web channel creation and operation. They do, however, require additional training and special skills to operate efficiently.

Table 9.3 Summary of Web Authoring and Development Tools

Tool Category	Description
Tag Editors	♦ First generation of tools ♦ Provide Web page editing at the HTML level ♦ Require thorough knowledge of HTML ♦ Final output uncertain
WYSIWYG Editors	♦ Authoring tools of second generation ♦ HTML tags hidden or hideable ♦ Web pages represent what is viewed in the browsers
High-end Editors	♦ Focus on Web site development ♦ Include utilities for checking hyperlinks, templates, and Web management programs ♦ Required for Web site development
Push Development	♦ New set of specialized tools ♦ Platforms, servers, browsers, and development editors designed for push technology features

The Web authoring development tools are sufficient for development of Web pages and Web sites. The high-end products feature rich facilities and are mandatory for building and maintaining attention-getting commercial Web sites. Within an intranet, only a few designated developers may require the most sophisticated tools. Most end users can be supported by more basic products, which are available free of charge or at costs ranging from $29 to $149 per system, depending on their features.

Developing Web sites and channels for webcasting requires a new set of development tools and involves more complex issues than the simple design of Web pages or Web sites. As multicasting becomes a more common method of providing information, tools optimized for multicasting also become more important. Developers must select Web authoring tools based on the applications planned for their networking environments.

Evaluating Push Technologies

At least 30 companies offer a range of push technology products. A selection of push services, servers, transports, tools, platforms, and browsers enabled to operate in push environments are now available. Although some products overlap several categories, most adequately perform a set of specific functions, but must be evaluated individually.

With the exception of Microsoft and Netscape, and their respective push-enabled Active Desktop and Netcaster product lines, most vendors are small, relatively unknown, startup ventures. As a result, limited information is available to differentiate one from another. Most are also held privately, which indicates a lack of available information about their performance, profitability, and long-term stability in the marketplace. Therefore, determining which ventures are financed by well-established, venture capital investment banking firms is wise.

Selecting the Necessary Skills

Companies developing webcasting and push technology services must also develop the skills necessary to design and maintain these systems. Two groups of skills are required for operating the technology and creating and manipulating content materials: marketing and editorial. The skills to develop the Web channels involve the collection and editing of the material. The content of a channel must also be updated at regular intervals or maintained as an expanding archive.

Many push systems and tools no longer require extensive technical knowledge of the hardware or software. In fact, some tools require only familiarity with the associated wizard to create daily updates to their push delivered hotlists. Conversely, other push tools require high levels of specialized training – particularly when multimedia content is used.

The Cost of Webcasting

Because most push client software is distributed free of charge, the assumption that webcasting is free is prevalent. Nothing could be further from the truth. Setting up Web channels and enabling clients for high-end BackWeb application services managing several hundred users can cost more than $50,000. This cost may escalate even further as more channels, subscribers, and multicasting capabilities are introduced.

The best strategy when allocating finances for such an undertaking is to visit several push technology vendors' Web sites and download their demonstrations and client software. Because push tools and their pricing differ widely from one product to another, they are very difficult to compare by any other method. Table 9.4 summarizes the various charges of representative major vendors of these products. These prices were effective during the fourth quarter of 1997 and are only representative of the variety of costs that may exist when push technology is introduced.

Table 9.4 Pricing Policies of Push Vendors

Push Product	Pricing Policy Description
Active Desktop Channels	♦ Most push features are available free in Microsoft IE 4.0
BackWeb	♦ Basic monthly channel license of $10,500 for 25,000 InfoPacks ♦ 200,000 additional InfoPacks cost $1,250 per month
Castanet	♦ Push transmitters cost $1,000 up to $25,000 for unlimited use ♦ Bongo authoring tool costs $495 ♦ Client is free
Downtown	♦ $10,000 for Web server push add-on software ♦ $1 per year per subscriber
HeadLiner	♦ Tools for developing and customizing clients cost $3,995.95 for fewer than 10,000 users ♦ Messaging costs start at $995
Communicator	♦ $995 for fewer than 500 subscribers ♦ $5,000 for more than 500 subscribers ♦ Dynamic publishing plug-in costs $25,000
Netcaster	♦ Castanet channels require transmitters at cost ♦ HTML Mail and LiveSite clients are free
NETdelivery	♦ Channel providers pay between $.01 and $.05 per delivery ♦ Rate cards control transaction sharing and branded client advertising
PointCast	♦ Connector channels are free ♦ Premium provider prices set on case-by-case basis
WebCast	♦ $195 Personal version includes advertising ♦ $995 Professional version without advertising ♦ $10,000 Commercial version creates custom advertising and reports for Webcaster

Push: An Advertiser's Nightmare

The implication of push technology is that whether any information pushed is considered timely or useful is the user's choice. As a result, push services must provide much better content than other information delivery methods because the service is easily deactivated and ignored. Although push provides a company with direct and in-depth contact with its subscribers, an additional effort is required to capture and hold their attention.

Any attempt to use push technology for competitive promotion and sales of company products and services requires top quality Web channel content. Material that may be sufficient to implement groupware communications within an enterprise intranet may not create sufficient attention and revenue streams with outside clients.

Advertisers considering push technology for promoting products and services must remember that they are competing with other companies. They may offer similar products and services using the same push technology, making the ultimate test the quality of customized presentations.

Advertisers who are not prepared to make an appropriate effort and investment to meet this marketing challenge are well advised not to become involved in push for marketing objectives.

Digital TV

Companies considering push as a way to promote their products and services must also consider the developments in digital TV (DTV) broadcasting. The U.S. Federal Communications Commission (FCC) has approved DTV broadcasting for major networks. The affiliates of the top four networks in the top 10 markets that account for 30% of all TVs owned in the United States are expected to begin DTV broadcasting by May 1999. By the end of that year, more than 50% of U.S. households are expected to use such broadcasts.

Most broadcasters initially plan to offer high-definition TV (HDTV), but will also experiment with digital data services for reception by DTV-compatible PCs. As a result, significant activity on the part of PC manufacturers is underway to sell network TV station operators on virtues of interactive data broadcasting and associated push technologies.

These trends are leading to the development of new PC products (for example, PC Theaters and Broadcast PCs) when targeted at consumer households. These products are being designed to exploit all digital channels available, including cable, various digital subscriber line (DSL) alternatives, satellite, terrestrial broadcasts, and the Internet.

Microsoft, which is developing the Broadcast PC, promotes a Windows-based system using TCP/IP because it will allow for interactivity with synchronized HTML page and video transmissions.

Monitoring Digital Broadcasting Services

Any organization wanting to use webcasting as a marketing vehicle must consider the rapid pace of DTV development before making major investments in webcasting infrastructures of their own. The most critical aspect of these new markets is the access to sectors of the population with digital, interactive, and multimedia transmissions of broadcast TV quality. This market will define a whole new calculus of online marketing and advertising and may render individual attempts to set up local competitive systems cost prohibitive by comparison.

Considering these recent and future developments, designing intranet-based Web sites and channels on servers designated for enterprise push applications to enhance company communications is logical. This will provide experience in push technology implementation without extensive investments until nationwide services offering DTV marketing are available.

Specialized, digital, interactive broadcasting channels providing complete services to advertisers will prove to be more cost effective in the long term than attempts at developing specialized systems. Complete services will offer immediate national and global distribution via all digital networks and will use the most current equipment to remain competitive.

This type of service is also preferable to company marketers and advertisers because they are accustomed to contracting radio and TV networks. This arrangement allows them to concentrate on designing the most effective content rather than focusing on overall distribution and demographics.

In addition, third-party services will have precise user psychographics to develop their services, relieving company executives from developing their own statistical programs and databases.

The RealNetwork service, introduced in August 1997, allows users to support live or on-demand video broadcasts over the Internet and can handle up to 50,000 simultaneous streams, enabling content suppliers to reach audiences that may be too small for analog cable or satellite TV. With DTV, this type of service will be able to reach large audiences easily. Already, RealNetwork services can be used for broadcasting infomercials.

UUCast Service, which supports audio and video broadcasting, can distribute up to 250,000 simultaneous streams to customers of an ISP or online service. Another multicasting service on the Internet is offered by Digex Communications, which is available on a per-event basis to business users and content providers. Clearly it represents another source for DTV.

The @Home Network, WebTV, and the NetChannel are even closer to DTV than Web-based digital channel services.

@Home selected Progressive Networks for providing audio and video streaming software because it relies on multicasting protocols that convert unicast streams into multicast broadcast.

WebTV has developed a technology that circumvents bandwidth limitations to deliver high-quality, high-speed Web images and video. It is based on a microchip that combines the capabilities of a TV tuner, cable modem, and high-speed PC modem into a single, low-cost unit. Microsoft acquired the venture in late 1997.

NetChannel is a TV-Internet service competing with the WebTV Network. It offers personalized Web content over TV from sources such as Internet Shopping Network and Intuit Quicken Financial Network enhanced for TV.

Evaluating Digital Broadcasting Alternatives

Now available are tools and services that use existing broadcasting infrastructures for delivering digital information, regardless of its sources. Monitoring these developments is important because they offer cost-effective alternatives for distributing digital content.

Multimedia Datacasting is offered by The WavePhore Channel through wired or wireless means, including FM Radio, broadcasts, satellite, microwave, and cable. This approach provides an end-to-end solution for distributing and receiving digital data.

TV broadcasters can add digital data to their existing broadcast systems to deliver news, newspapers, magazines, games, software, training, and advertising to anyone able to receive their signals. WavePhore system (*http://www.wavephore.com/*) claims to be the most powerful one-to-many digital data distribution system. It is designed to provide content providers and TV broadcasters additional revenue stream opportunities by reaching households and businesses that already receive conventional TV signals.

The Multimedia Datacasting system offered by WavePhore uses in-band and vertical blanking interval technologies for transmitting at a speed of up to 500 Kbps when the two are combined. All that is needed is WaveCeiver software installed on standard PC platforms. Figure 9.2 illustrates the Multimedia Datacasting concept as offered by WavePhore.

Figure 9.2 The Multimedia Datacasting Concept of WavePhore

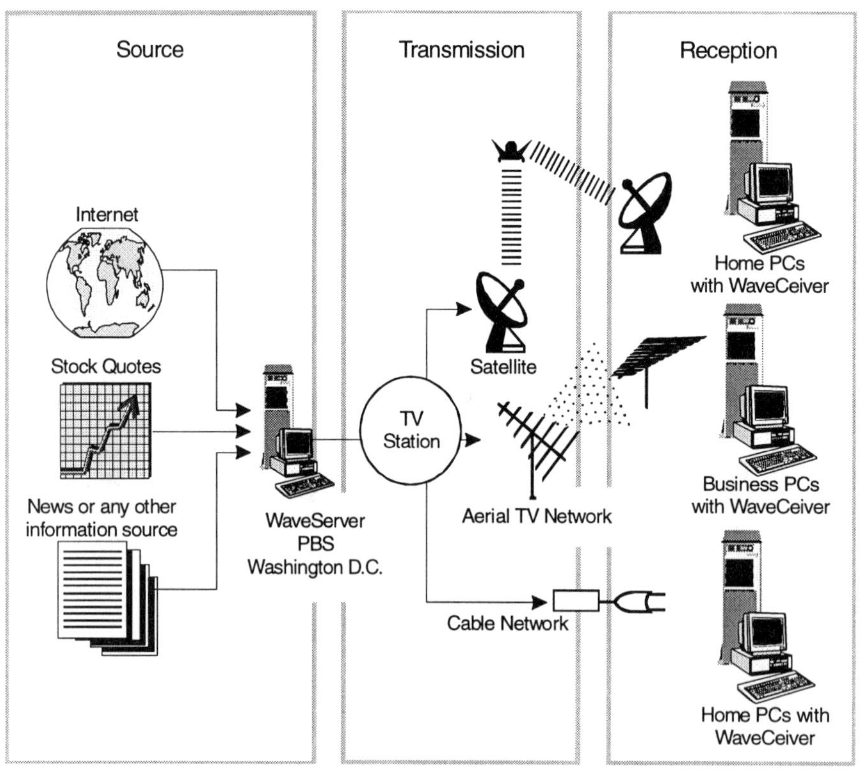

End-user Orientation

Potential users and subscribers to push services should be forewarned about the disadvantages and resource demands on their systems. This is a function of webcasting developers who are responsible for providing user platforms that can efficiently receive webcasting or push service.

Even with intranets where push technologies are controlled, users must be educated about the consequences of using push technologies. Distributing software electronically is a case in point because it has the potential of creating a bandwidth shortage in a network.

Immature Push Industry Instability

The push industry is very young, and emerging ventures and products are often untested for the long term. Most should be viewed as beta solutions that are being introduced by early adopters to enhance their intranet or Internet operations.

The instability in the industry is underscored by the rapid pace of product development and the need to finance development and testing of new releases in a competitive market. Some new ventures do not succeed alone, regardless of the products they produce. Lanacom, the vendor of HeadLiner push technology, has been acquired by BackWeb technologies after a very brief existence as an independent firm. Intermind, which developed the Communicator push technology, reduced its staff to a skeleton crew after Microsoft and Netscape introduced browser-based push products that use similar technology. Intermind believes it will receive a patent for its technology and will then move to license the use of that technology. If large companies engage in legal action as a result, however, the company may not survive.

Consequently, webcasters seeking to develop their own channels and provide that kind of service should select products from vendors who will be in the market for a few more years and whose products will have service support and updating in the future.

Maintain Awareness of Future Developments

While evaluating existing Internet connectivity is of great importance when implementing marketing Web channels, watching potential future developments is also necessary.

Cable TV Internet access with high-speed links is only one alternative being tested. Services that use wireless technology to link the user to the Web – of particular importance to mobile audiences – are also under development. Unfortunately, ISPs are not assured of a definitive future.

Another utility service also reaches virtually every household and office in the world: the local electric power service. In fact, it is beginning to pose a threat to existing Internet access providers.

In October 1997, engineers at United Technologies, Plc. and Northern Telecom Ltd. proved that transforming existing power lines around the world into major backbones and local delivery links on the information superhighway is commercially viable. The concept has already been tested in the United Kingdom and power line telephony is seen as a viable alternative to existing telecom networks.

A commercially viable utilities phone system requires that the power utility register 40% or more of its household customers and offices in a community – a difficult, competitive task, considering the telephone companies' success. Webcasting promoters must be aware of the promise of such technological developments, however.

International Webcasting Association

The mission of the International Webcasting Association (IWA) is to promote the effective and efficient delivery of interactive multimedia content over the Internet and other digital networks. It exists as a membership organization to provide services to individuals, companies, and other organizations using the technologies, services, and content of this industry. IWA committees focus on technology, broadcasting, advertising, content, legal policy, and educational issues of webcasting and are a solid starting point when developing a webcasting organization.

Individual members and companies include AT&T Solutions, Apple Computers, Arlen Communications, AudioNet, Broadcast.net, Canadian

Association of Broadcasters, CBS Radio, Channel Africa, DigiMedia/MIMS Switzerland, Freedom Forum, Intervov Communications, ITU-Geneva, National Association of Broadcasters, NetRadio.net, Paxon Communications, Sakai Interactive, SYPHA-Great Britain, UCLA EXT, and Xing Technologies. For more information, contact *http://www.webcasters.org/*.

Conclusion

The objective of webcasting is to draw user attention to content that will generate revenue for Web channel promoters – a difficult task that demands strategic planning. Creating a professional organization to implement it and maintain it regularly may also be required.

Initial tasks are to evaluate the webcasting objectives and select specific push facilities. This type of analysis can be accomplished only by pairing webcasting objectives with existing networking infrastructures. Bandwidth capabilities, multimedia content requirements, non-Internet LANs, and the potential for specific push communities all affect push technology selection and implementation.

In addition to selecting an appropriate push development tool or service, operators must consider end-user issues – intrusiveness of the notification and delivery modes and the availability of necessary skills to implement and maintain a competitive program.

Webcasting and push technology are only now emerging. They are immature and unstable; small vendors and providers are offering untested products and inadequate financing. How much of an impact alternative DTV and wireless services may have on push and webcasting remains unclear. Regarding this uncertainty, webcasting promoters should consider all conceivable aspects of this new technology before making a mission-critical commitment.

Chapter 10

Webcasting and Push Browser Capabilities

Intrinsic push tools and features in the latest Web browsers obviate the need to install and support a separate webcasting solution in an enterprise. These webcasting browser tools allow users to easily configure built-in push tools to receive Web-based news and information.

With these tools, webcasters can leverage Web capabilities, including Active X, JavaScript, and dynamic HTML, to create sophisticated, interactive applications and services, which are then pushed to user desktops. The most recent versions of IE and Communicator are examples of such webcasting-enabled browsers.

Built-in browser push capabilities are basic in their function, however, and more comprehensive push tools should be introduced when advanced applications are considered.

Netscape Communications

Netcaster is the built-in push technology available in the Communicator 4.0 browser for Windows 95 and NT. It is the first push client software based on open Internet standards, including HTML, Java, and JavaScript. Virtually any Web site can become a channel for direct delivery to the desktop.

Netcaster can be launched from any browser component and provides relatively easy and intuitive access to all push functions in a single graphical interface. As such, analysts consider it to be more user-friendly than the fragmented push interface offered by the competing IE 4.0 browser from Microsoft.

Netcaster users can subscribe to dynamic real-time channels, access channels, and Web sites offline, and create a Webtop channel anchored to a desktop. These capabilities allow constant monitoring of information flows, regardless of actual applications.

Netcaster offers Premier Channels, additional Marquee Channels accessible through Channel Finder and hundreds of other Netcaster-enabled channels. In addition, three types of channels are offered: Netcaster-specific channels, regular Web pages, and Marimba Castanet applications. Users can specify how often information is pushed to the desktop, the amount of data, and the number of levels.

Netcaster uses a basic Web crawl, but does not have notification capabilities and cannot be configured to screen content automatically. Using JavaScript 1.2, Web developers define Netcaster channels that control content, format, and updating for the client.

The Netcaster desktop is the Webtop and any page configuration is achieved by a Web crawl and specifyied display formats. The Webtop is designed to provide a functional push alternative to the Windows desktop. Channel Wizard is a development tool that quickly produces JavaScript for defining a channel. Developers simply cut and paste them on Web pages to place Add Channel buttons. Webtop Genie is a similar development tool for creating customized Webtops. Both are free to content and application developers.

Netcaster is fully customizable and can be managed centrally using Mission Control. Netcaster is also used by other push tools for developing solutions for managing user and channel profiles or content aggregation systems. For more information, contact *http://www.netscape.com/*.

Microsoft

Webcasting is the basic information feature of IE 4.0 and provides a way to subscribe to Premium Channel providers, who deliver content to the desktop in the background; download frequencies and volume can be customized. It is now available for Windows 95 and NT platforms; Windows 3.1, NT 3.51, and Mac versions will follow. However, users must know how to manipulate IE 4.0 browser menus and fill out dialog boxes to subscribe to specific Web resources.

The IE 4.0 push architecture consists of several levels. The lowest level, which is transparent to users, provides basic Web crawl capabilities, including notification, notification via E-mail, content screening, user scheduling, offline browsing, a unified cache, and a means to specify download levels. Other features are part of the browser used and change constantly. As a result, these levels are best explored using the *http://www.microsoft.com/ie* Web site.

Depending on a schedule specified by the user, the Web crawler uses standard HTTP query to determine changes in Web pages. It also notifies the user of site changes and downloads updated information according to level depth and screening parameters specified.

IE 4.0 also provides a number of push enhancements, including desktop integration, channel definition, administrative controls, built-in channel finder, and a Castanet Tuner. These enhancements require Active Desktop and CDF capabilities and allow Web channel developers to control the timing of updates and provide a channel map to the user. An API that facilitates multicast transmission of push channels is also available. More information can be obtained at *http://www.microsoft.com/ie/*.

Table 10.1 outlines browser-based information delivery technologies.

Table 10.1 Summary of Browser-based Delivery Technologies

Tool	Vendor	Basic Characteristics
Netcaster	Netscape Communications Corp.	♦ Communicator 4.0 browser-based; handles virtually any Web site as a channel ♦ Webtop channel on desktop ♦ Supports Marimba Castanet and Channel Wizard development tools
Webcasting	Microsoft Corporation	♦ IE 4.0 browser-based ♦ Multilevel architecture with notifications and schedule features ♦ Channel definition format (CDF) ♦ Numerous enhancements in development

Comprehensive Webcasting Tools

A number of recently introduced push products are tools from independent vendors. Because these vendors are not associated with any specific browser, these tools are usually more comprehensive than the push tools available within browsers. Most are developed for organizations to increase worker interaction productivity.

However, most ventures offering these tools are very small and relatively new, often with little or no understanding of the market for such products. In many cases, they are driven by the technology and exploring other capabilities of the Internet model rather than trying to meet a specific company need. Other ventures offer push services that focus on content channels and their agglomeration using some of those tools; yet others have developed proprietary services and processes.

Several dedicated push servers and multicasting tools are available (see Table 10.2). Those interested in evaluating these products should access the vendor Web site to obtain current details of the products and their performance. Many vendors offer free software demonstrations.

Table 10.2 Representative Webcasting Tools

Webcasting Products	Vendor	Basic Characteristics
Affinity Interaction Manager (AIM)	Affinicast, Inc. http://www.affinity.com/	♦ Application server for managing user profiles, cataloging media assets, and matching users in realtime with desired content ♦ Annual fees are $10,000 to $30,000
BackWeb	BackWeb Technologies http://www.backweb.com/	♦ Powerful push broadcasting system with a high degree of customization ♦ Open system supports various business models and provides extensive content management and controls ♦ Minimum $10,000 server cost
Castanet	Marimba, Inc. http://www.marimba.com/	♦ Java applet viewer system ♦ Targets software distribution in businesses ♦ Tools for implementing and maintaining interactive applications and services works with different platforms and devices ♦ Basic Transmitter $995, extensions $5,000
DataChannel	DataChannel http://www.datachannel.com/	♦ A Webcasting management system for allocating Web channels, news feeds, PC applications, and legacy systems
HeadLiner	Lanacom http://www.lanacom.com/ (acquired by BackWeb Technologies in mid-1997)	♦ Scans news-oriented Web sites and delivers headlines linked to stories ♦ Operates as a user agent for customizing source selection and delivery times
INCISA	Wayfarer http://www.wayfarer.com/	♦ Designed for use in sales, marketing, and company communications ♦ Excludes advertising or disruptive content and delivers headlines linked to stories ♦ Extensive customization of channels and delivery with polling and surveying capabilities ♦ $5,000 per 100 seats
IntraExpress	Diffusion http://www.diffusion.com/	♦ Designed for distributing information from company sources to business partners and customers ♦ Complements existing browser, messaging, and groupware technologies

Webcasting Products	Vendor	Basic Characteristics
Intercast	Intel Corporation http://www.intel.com/	♦ Transport technology for digital data associated with TV signals ♦ Allows transmission of Web pages with TV broadcasts
IntelliServ	Cognisoft, Inc. http://www.cognisoft.com/	♦ Server-based intranet application for acquiring and distributing information to users according to their preferences ♦ Identifies and monitors company sources and provides administrative tools
MindShare	My Way Online, Inc. http://www.myway.com/	♦ Server product for operating branded online networks and push services ♦ Delivers digital content and notifies clients, eliminating distracting material

Affinicast

Affinicast Interaction Manager (AIM) software allows an organization to add a complete profiling and personalization solution to its Web infrastructure. Using models based on psychology and personal communications, AIM claims to outperform standard demographics by 400% in predicting user preferences. The methodology supports profile creation through a variety of measurement techniques, including psychographics, questionnaires, customized registration information, and clickstream log files.

Affinicast tailors its delivery to individual clients' customers and relationship objectives. The system typically integrates Affinicast psychographics with existing customer data to create an effective profile. AIM is an application server that manages user profiles, catalogs media assets, and matches users with media assets through personalized real-time Web pages. Written in Java, AIM works with existing Web infrastructures and can run on any major OS. For more information, visit *http://www.affinicast.com/*. Figure 10.1 illustrates AIM implementation concept.

Figure 10.1 AIM Implementation Concept

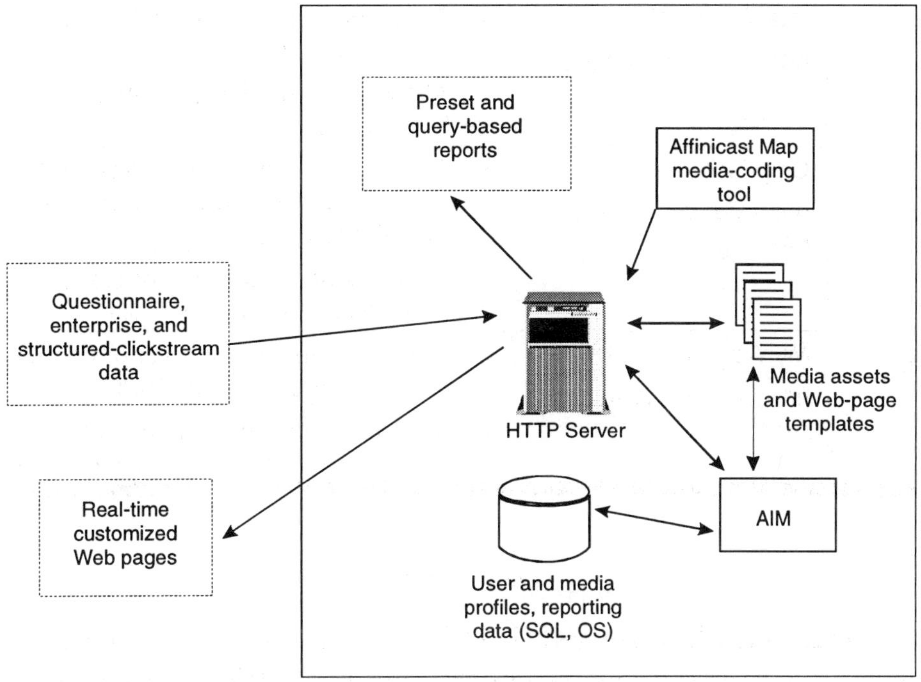

AIM is a set of models that can be licensed at an annual fee ranging from $10,000 to $30,000, depending on the application and use level. It is also available on a service basis for audience analysis or for serving personalized media.

BackWeb Technologies

BackWeb (*http://www.backweb.com/*) is a powerful broadcasting system with a great degree of customization and flexibility on both the server and client side. BackWeb consists of servers and clients that can be customized. The server product allows individual content providers to operate and administer their own channels.

BackWeb is an open system that supports advertising, direct marketing, and subscription business models. It is a robust and flexible solution with a server cost starting at $10,500 for minimum traffic and subscriber volume.

The server can be managed with a special BackWeb Console client, which monitors and controls server operations consisting of a database of InfoPaks. InfoPaks are files broadcast from channels as content to clients. The actual content of InfoPaks can include standard graphic, sound, and multimedia files, Java applets, HTML files, or binary files for software distribution.

BackWeb provides content management and control features, including customization. Channel developers can also define content delivery.

BackWeb also provides scheduling capabilities, content versioning, and mechanisms to control how long InfoPaks remain on client systems and when updates are made. Sources of information can also be defined to determine content generation for scheduled broadcast to clients. Tracking and reporting capabilities integrated into the BackWeb server provide detailed statistics on channel activity and end-user interactions.

BackWeb Polite Agent is a free client tool that allows users to specify channel names or browse and register for channels in a directory. Several methods are available for modifying users of channel updates. Users can also specify the limit of space on disk consumed by a channel.

In July 1997, BackWeb Technologies acquired Lanacom, the creator of the HeadLiner product line being incorporated into a single product. This acquisition introduces information relevance features for managing information from the Internet and company data systems.

Cognisoft, Inc.

Cognisoft, Inc. offers IntelliServ, a server-based intranet application for acquiring and distributing information to users. The system integrates, monitors, and tags information from internal and external data sources and coordinates delivery, which is selected by the user.

IntelliServ identifies, categorizes, and continuously monitors company sources, which may include file servers, Web severs, open database connectivity (ODBC) databases, Lotus Notes, and Microsoft Exchange. It also provides access to a network of broadcast sources maintained by Cognisoft partners, which provide additional information that can be monitored and integrated with internal company content.

IntelliServ includes administrative tools for adding and deleting data sources, synchronizing user directory, and implementing security.

Administrators can optimize the configuration of IntelliServ to maximize its value to the enterprise. More details on IntelliServ can be found at *http://www.cognisoft.com/*. Figure 10.2 shows the potential of IntelliServ implementation in an enterprise.

Figure 10.2 IntelliServ Implementation Example

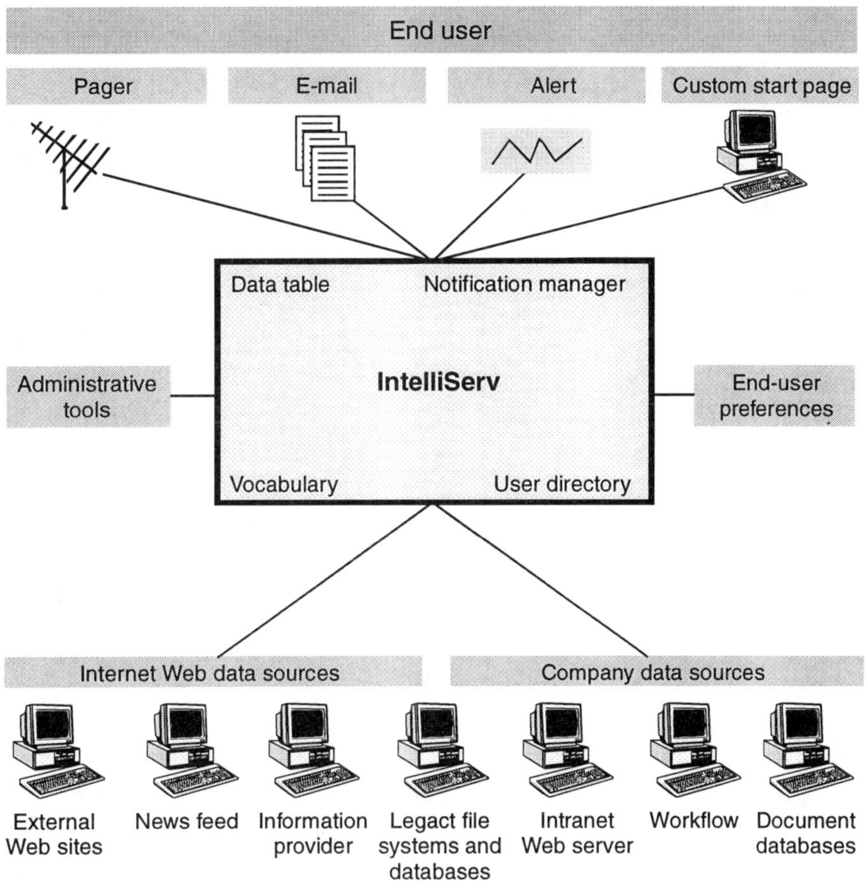

DataChannel

DataChannel offers company webcast management solutions that allow administrators to manage Web channels, news feeds, PC applications, and company legacy databases.

This tool set is available as a customizable desktop and provides a way for the end user to build departmental or personal channels to receive critical, real-time, company information. Visit *http://www.datachannel.com/* for further details.

Diffusion

Founded in 1995, Diffusion developed IntraExpress server product designed to distribute business information from any sources located within the enterprise. This system targets company workgroups and distribution partners and customers using their preferred communications channels.

IntraExpress is designed to complement and leverage existing browser, messaging, and groupware technologies as a single information delivery server. Content developers retain full control of distribution channels.

IntraExpress is effective for companies with multiple products or for which information is the primary product. It is an extranet information delivery solution targeting Fortune 1,000 sales and marketing organizations that need to distribute information to audiences inside and outside the corporation. More information about Diffusion can be found at *http://www.diffusion.com/*.

Intercast

Intel developed this transport standard for digital data associated with TV signals. Intercast technology is a series of protocols and formats that allow transmitting Web pages with a TV broadcast and qualifies as a form of webcasting. Such webcasts are received using PCs equipped with a special tuner.

Users can receive or interact with content created around existing TV programming. Intercast depends on TV producers' integrating Web-formatted content into their programs. The back channel is used as the link to Web sites that are mentioned in TV broadcasts and initially transmitted with the TV signal for desktop storage. In short, users can interact with Web channels that are announced on TV screens, providing additional data on running TV programs.

Intercast technology links the Internet and TV on a PC, targeting primarily the consumer market. Intercast was launched originally in the United States in 1996 and was introduced in Korea in the second quarter of 1997. In both cases, these are National TV Standards Committee (NTSC) standard transmissions, but PAL standards – TV standards in Europe and Asia – will be supported by this technology also.

With Intercast technology, the user controls the interactive experience. It takes advantage of digital power of the PC to converge Internet and TV using existing communications infrastructures including TV antennas, cable, or C-band satellite systems. The PC hard disk can store hundreds or thousands of broadcast Web pages and present them to the user on demand. High-resolution graphics of a PC are also superior to conventional TV displays.

Most existing Pentium PCs can be upgraded to this function level with add-in boards. PCs with built-in Intercast technology offering cost-effective video delivery and display are also available. Required hardware platforms include 100-MHz Pentium processors, peripheral component interconnect (PCI) bus system, 16 MB RAM, a very fast graphics adapter, Soundblaster audio, an 800-MB hard drive, and an 18.8-Kbps modem. Point to *http://www.connectedpc.com/* for additional information.

Lanacom

Lanacom offers HeadLiner products, which are pure push technology but compete successfully with other push products. HeadLiner scans news-oriented Web sites for new information and delivers only the headlines, which are the links to full stories. This stage is free of advertising, and content providers do not need a push server to broadcast information. More details can be found at *http://www.lanacom.com/*. HeadLiner use is illustrated in Figure 10.3.

Figure 10.3 HeadLiner Use in Enterprise Applications

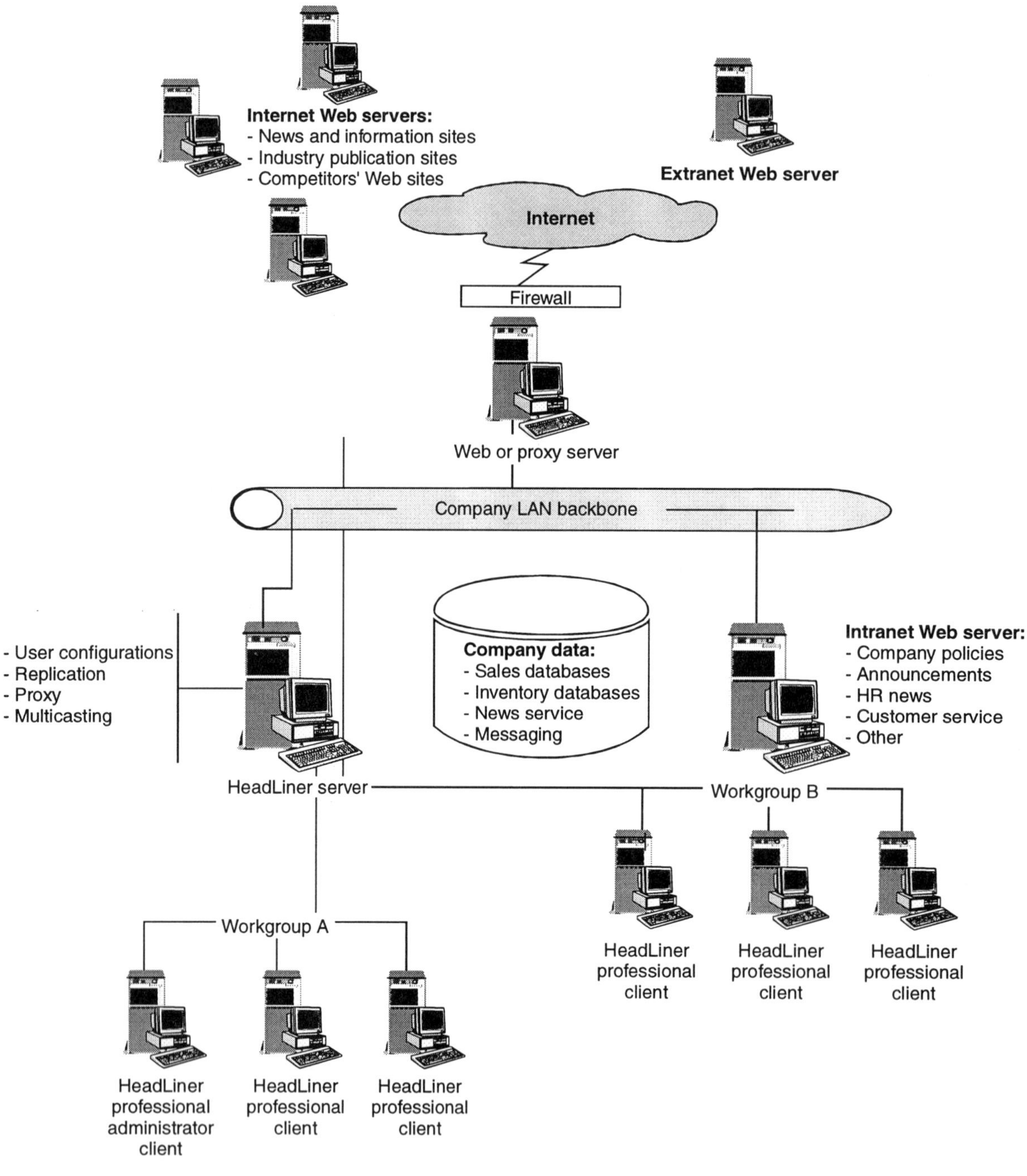

HeadLiner client operates as an agent of the user and delivers updated headlines only when new information is posted at Web sites scanned by Lanacom. HeadLiner also has the ability to display new information from specified Internet news groups in the ticker window. In addition to standard push features, HeadLiner also provides a scrolling display of story headlines and a screen saver option.

The product provides an easy-to-use management system that allows administrators to select what their users will access from more than 700 sources.

Marimba, Inc.

Castanet offered by Marimba is among the most hyped push technologies largely because of significant initial funding from the Java Fund. Castanet is a Java applet viewer concept that allows users to select from a wide variety of content channels. Each channel can offer its own content and updating schedule.

The Castanet model is particularly suitable for software distribution – a valuable business application. It is a platform of tools for implementing and maintaining interactive applications and services, including full-featured productivity programs, sophisticated internal business applications, and rich multimedia experiences. Castanet is designed to work across different platforms and varied devices, including PDAs, cellular phones, pagers, printers, and NCs.

Castanet distributes and maintains applications and services within an organization's intranet or across the Internet. It guarantees that subscribers automatically have the most updated tools and information.

Castanet tools include a channel, a transmitter, and a tuner. The transmitter is the Castanet server, which manages the distribution and maintenance of Castanet channels. The tuner is the Castanet client that monitors, receives, and manages channels by end users. Castanet elements and their relationship are illustrated in Figure 10.4, and further information can be found at *http://www.marimba.com/*.

Figure 10.4 Marimba's Castanet Elements

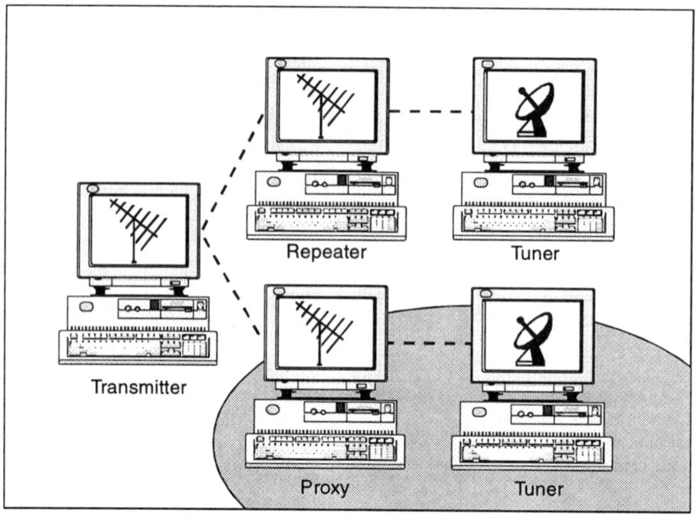

Castanet channels are applications or information distributed by Transmitters, and they support Java applications, applets, and HTML. Additional types are supported through the Castanet Update Now extension of the Transmitter. It allows delivery and updating of programs written in C, C++, and Visual Basic over intranets and the Internet. Channel creators update channels only on the transmitter and those changes are distributed to subscribers automatically. Plug-ins on a subscriber-by-subscriber basis can personalize channels.

A core Transmitter can support up to five channels and can be supplemented by transmitter extensions. A back channel transmitter extension captures subscriber feedback, which may include user preferences and most popular channel features. Castanet transmitters can be scaled to accommodate millions of subscribers through the use of numerous Castanet Repeaters. Marimba's special reconciliation of code tranmitted to clients is a unique advantage. The company awaits approval for this process.

The Castanet Transmitter is available for Windows NT, Windows 95, and Solaris 2.5 environments. They require 16 MB of memory and a minimum 10 MB of hard disk with additional storage for channel content. The Castanet Tuner is available free for the same platforms and the Mac OS and also requires 16 MB of memory and 10 MB of disk space. A Castanet proxy, which reduces the burden of firewall computers, is also available for these platforms. The Castanet

Tuner is bundled by Netscape in its Communicator browser, making Marimba one of the primary push product vendors.

Marimba sells the transmitter software and licenses Castanet technology for company use on a royalty basis. The basic server price is only $995, but the Update Now extension and the associated Guardian security features cost $5,000.

Castanet is still considered the most effective push technology to support Java applications. Unfortunately, only 15% of browser users in mid-1997 were estimated to have used Java. As a result, Marimba has difficulties convincing enterprises that its product presents an immediate value. As a reflection of these difficulties, Marimba introduced the extensions for handling non-Java programs.

My Way Online, Inc.

My Way Online, Inc. offers the MindShare server product, which allows organizations to operate branded online networks. It delivers digital content to audiences with a specifically branded push service.

The vendor defines the product as a virtual courier service that can deliver any digital content, including text, images, audio, video, animation, or executable software. Branding can apply to notification messages, dashboards, customization wizards, channel guides, tickers, and screen savers.

Content providers give precise shipping instructions to the Dispatcher of the MindShare system, which functions as a hub, aggregating and filtering content packages and notifying clients. When a branded online network expands, additional Dispatchers and Replicators are added to maintain operating efficiency.

The MindShare client, known as Courier, receives notifications, retrieves the information on its own initiative, and notifies the user of a delivery. Courier can distinguish between information priorities and eliminate distracting and other than company content. Deliveries are always performed in the background; large files are sent in parts and assembled automatically to minimize bandwidth congestion. The MindShare concept is illustrated in Figure 10.5.

Figure 10.5 The MindShare Concept

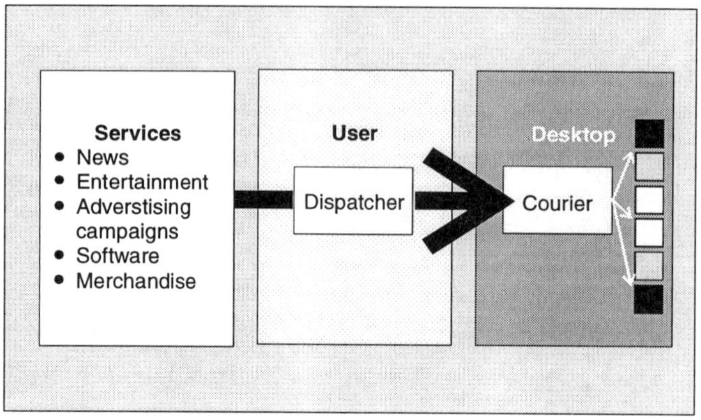

Users select notification methods and can customize their choice of channels and information packages. In addition, MindShare tracks online use and provides automatic feedback to the Dispatcher. More information is available at *http://www.myway.com/*.

Wayfarer

INCISA is Wayfarer's push technology and is designed for use by business managers or marketing, sales, communications, and human resource departments. INCISA pushes information in realtime and allows the companies to manage, filter, and deliver relevant information to user desktops. Sources of information can include legacy databases, other company data systems, and public information sources. INCISA also saves bandwidth by initially sending only a headline, which typically averages only 350 bytes.

INCISA is a turnkey solution specifically designed for company markets. Unlike many webcasting products, it contains no advertising. All information can be customized, and intranet data from company sources are provided through INCISA DataBridge. INCISA WebWatch delivers immediate alerts to users about changes and updates. INCISA HeadLinks provides headlines with links to full information for a more productive system. Figure 10.6 illustrates the INCISA architecture.

Figure 10.6 INCISA System Architecture

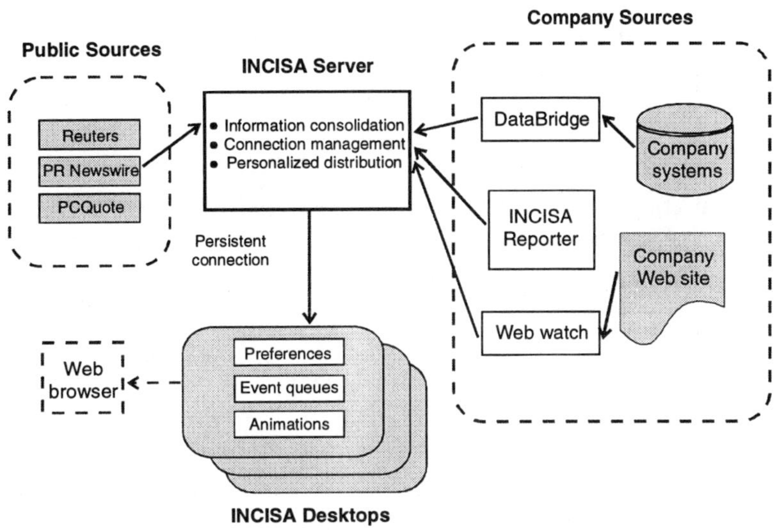

INCISA allows customization and information delivery. Its features include profiles of individuals, groups, or departments that can control what information they receive and when they receive it. It also provides a way to survey or poll employees for real-time, two-way communications.

INCISA incorporates RSA encryption and security technology, which allow businesses to authenticate company users and encrypt data messages for secure delivery of critical company data over intranets, guaranteeing the ability to push highly sensitive, confidential materials directly to specific departments, managers, and individuals.

INCISA server runs on Windows NT and Sun Solaris and supports Windows 95 and NT 3.1 clients. Prices start at $5,000 for 100 seats; discounts for higher volumes of use are available. Encryption is available for an additional fee of $10 per seat. Contact *http://www.wayfarer.com/* for further details.

Other Webcasting Tools

The need to conserve bandwidth is paramount in webcasting tools, but is only the most obvious and visible problem being solved. Caching techniques have been introduced to reduce bandwidth shortages, but they also create other management concerns.

For example, the need for mechanisms that guarantee integrity and synchronization of content when information is distributed among several servers is increasing. Another concern is the amount of disk space required for caching downloaded information. Some push tools offer default amounts of disk space, but customizable tools will be needed for the long term.

Tools to determine the length of time that cached information should be stored and the configuration of access rights for users are necessary. Some vendors are working to include those features in their tools.

Conclusion

Webcasting and push technology tools are increasing rapidly. They are, however, often offered by new ventures that have only been in business for a short time and are more focused on technology than business needs of company information systems. These products are in early development stages and do not meet all the requirements of an interactive enterprise.

The most logical solution is to assess the need for push technology and design a program of testing and selecting various push technologies. It is quite probable that no single approach will provide all the webcasting solutions desired. It will be some time before leading vendors will have push technology tools that provide all possible solutions. Which new ventures have the staying power to provide a reliable product line? The answer remains undetermined.

Chapter 11

Webcasting and Push Services

Introduced in 1996, PointCast is generally considered the first push technology service. In fact, several services have provided similar products for some time. These providers are primarily specialized financial services developed for financial organizations and operated on private networks.

These and the latest webcasting services target the end user, providing an opportunity to push only specified information. In professional push services, the approach eliminates advertising, although fees are associated with their use. In the case of consumer-targeted push services, users access them free of charge, although prime information sources are accessible only to paid subscribers.

Growth of Third-party Webcasting Services

By mid-1997, an estimated 500,000 commercial sites were available on the Web. In addition, virtually every Fortune 1,000 company used an intranet. With regard to these developments, staying abreast of all these dynamic and often valuable information resources has become nearly impossible. Webcasting services offer many solutions to this particular aspect of information overload.

Such services interactively manage, organize, and deliver global information. Some develop their own technology software, while others use existing tools. Most operate as the aggregators of Web channels and sites, making arrangements with third-party publishers and merchants to facilitate information selection and Web channels. They accomplish this goal by offering specialized interfaces to deliver the information users need when they need it, without their involvement. Downloads take place in the background, and users are notified about the information arrival.

A number of characteristics differentiate those services, including services with advertising and those that require monthly or usage fees. Another category includes information services that specialize in specific communities of interest (music or sports, for example) and are targeted primarily at consumers. In many cases, webcasting services offer a combination of operating modes for business and consumer markets.

Differences in the control a user has over the available channels have also been identified. Some webcasting services offer a specified number of free channels but require subscriptions or special fees to access Premium channels. This business model was pioneered by the original online services – AOL, CompuServe, and Prodigy – before these services provided Internet activity.

The various services differ greatly (see Table 11.1). Some allow users to select channels that are grouped in specific service categories, such as financial or news. Other webcasting services provide agents that are capable of searching for information based on keywords and phrases rather than only the headlines in a channel. The more sophisticated the service, the more expensive it is and the larger the storage requirements for the downloaded content.

Table 11.1 Representative Webcasting and Push Services

Vendor	Service	Basic Characteristics
AirMedia, Inc. http://www.airmedia.com/	News Catcher	♦ Wireless system distributes information from leading news feeds and financial sources, but requires special hardware
Amulet http://www.amulet.com/	InfoWizard	♦ Automated research service using agents to acquire content specified by users from technology and newswire sources
AudioNet http://www.audionet.com/	AudioNet	♦ Live broadcasts from 175 radio and TV stations and events to viewers and listeners worldwide
Berkeley Systems http://www.afterdark.com/	AfterDark Online	♦ Automatic news delivery with channel customization based on user preferences and updating frequency

Vendor	Service	Basic Characteristics
		settings
BroadVision http://www.broadvision.com/	One-to-One	♦ Offers branded intelligent marketing services to consumers ♦ Personalized information enhanced by human editors
Caravelle http://www.caravelle.com/	TRANSCEIVE	♦ Monitors Web-based content from all intranet or Internet sources ♦ Notifies specific audiences through means of their choices
Desktop Data, Inc. http://www.desktopdata.com/	NewsEDGE	♦ Provides customized, real-time news and information to workers via company LANs and WANs ♦ Filtered according to interest profiles
Desktop News http://www.desktopnews.com/	Desktop News	♦ Provides more than 150 specific channels in major subject categories, allowing users to define specific interest areas
DoubleClick, Inc. http://www.doubleclick.net/	DoubleClick Network	♦ Internet Advertising Network provides targeted, measurable advertising in several defined categories
Empirical Media http://www.wisewire.com/	WiseWire	♦ Uses collaborative, neural net filtering to determine user interest and deliver the most relevant content ♦ Investigates push technology for delivery
Farcast http://www.farcast.com/	Farcast	♦ Customized search and retrieval service from news sources and company directories for a monthly fee
inCommon http://www.incommon.com/	Downtown	♦ Open framework for publishing on the Web ♦ Providing leading Web news and research channels
Individual, Inc. http://www.individual.com/	First!	♦ Personalized news service using fax, E-mail, groupware, intranets, and the Internet for delivery from more than 700 sources worldwide
InfoBeat http://www.infobeat.com/	InfoBeat	♦ Delivers current news on selected topics at specified times to existing E-mail addresses ♦ Uses major news feeds and wire services
Intermind http://www.intermind.co	Communicator	♦ Subscribers can select from more than 200 channels and Web site publishers

Vendor	Service	Basic Characteristics
m/		♦ Covers news, merchants, and events
NETdelivery http://www.netdelivery.com/	NETdelivery	♦ Offers community marketing concept for automated presentation delivery for enhancing relationships between suppliers and clients
News-Alert http://www.newsalert.com/	Clip Alert	♦ Provides customized information for managing stock portfolios
Open Sesame http://www.opensesame.com/	Open Sesame	♦ Specialized entertainment service updating users on new music and events
PointCast, Inc. http://www.pointcast.com/	PointCast Network	♦ The original push technology service ♦ Supported by advertising, offering major news feeds and financial sources
Tibco Software http://www.tibco.com/	TIBnet	♦ Claims to have invented the first generation of push technology offering multicasting of content over LANs and WANs
WavePhore http://www.wavephore.net/	WaveTop	♦ Uses vertical blanking interval in TV to transmit content at a high speed to users with appropriate devices and software

Intelligent Search Engines

Some webcasting services resemble intelligent search engines, which depend on feedback from users to enhance search productivity. In fact, all webcasting services must use some form of search engines and search agents to deliver information to clients. As a result, the two forms of Web searching and data selection are converging: intelligent search engine ventures are expanding into webcasting services, and webcasting services are constantly looking for the most efficient and intelligent search agents and engines to present a competitive offering.

Users should evaluate intelligent search engines before making a final decision about a webcasting service. Some push services seem to offer productivity enhancement by downloading information in the background. However, an efficient and intelligent metasearch engine that controls several search engines and eliminates advertising may prove to be as efficient and even more up do date if properly used. In addition, this approach does not consume large amounts of bandwidth – one of the major problems with unrestricted push technology.

AirMedia, Inc.

AirMedia, Inc. offers its AirMedia Live News Catcher, which receives information from a wireless receiver and can operate without an Internet connection.

The primary information sources of this service include Business Wire, CNN, Knight-Ridder, Newsbytes, PR Newswire, and Reuters news feeds, sports scores, lottery information, weather, entertainment, and lifestyle reports. Financial and stock information is also available and can be linked directly to any online trading accounts of the users. Personal Portfolio software allows monitoring of stocks and mutual funds and links to Quote.com for additional information.

News Catcher requires hardware that costs $149 and includes an annual subscription to the basic plan. The company's Premiere Plan extends this service to financial information, stock quotes twice every hour, and up-to-the-minute sports scores and weather forecasts.

AirMedia also links to E-mail accounts for an additional $9.95 per month. The service delivers E-mail as long as the user is within reach of its wireless network, which uses PageNet for transmitting news to the PC. AirMedia software requires 20 MB to 33 MB of disk space for all animation, graphics, and sound capabilities. More information can be found at *http://www.air media.com/*.

Amulet

Amulet offers InfoWizard, an Internet-based, automated research service that uses agents to acquire data and information. Channels include CMP Media, Computer Review, CorpTech, Comtex, Faulkner Information Services, Information Access, International Computer Programs, Information Sources (Softbase), Lycos, Newsbytes, PR Newswire, and Reuters. Users pay only when they order and download specific reports. Prices range from $5 to $25 for a single report, and further details can be obtained at *http://www.amulet.com/*.

AudioNet

AudioNet was the first company to take advantage of audio and video streaming technologies and has become a leading Internet broadcasting service. The service delivers broadcasts live and on demand to viewers and listeners all over the world.

AudioNet information includes live broadcasts from more than 175 radio and TV stations, play-by-play university and professional sporting events, live music concerts and club performances, on-demand music from 1,600 CDs, live and on-demand shows and webcasts, and company and special events broadcasting.

In addition, AudioNet produces many large-scale events, including the Super Bowl, National Hockey League (NHL) Stanley Cup Finals, and basketball tournaments. It made history by attracting more than 500,000 listeners worldwide to its coverage of Super Bowl XXXI, making it the largest Web audience.

Broadcasting on AudioNet provides the ability to reach listeners far beyond the range of local radio and TV stations. It also provides access to certain office buildings and other sites where broadcast signals are not normally received.

AudioNet offers intranet and Internet broadcasting services to businesses and all types of organizations. It adequately accommodates live broadcasts of special events, shareholder meetings, conference calls, speeches, press conferences, product introductions, conventions, trade shows, political debates, and award ceremonies. For further information about AudioNet's capabilities, visit *http://www.audionet.com/*.

Berkeley Systems

Berkeley Systems offers AfterDark Online, an automatic news delivery service that broadcasts content directly to the desktop as a screen saver. The user can select source channels and customize each channel. Users can also determine the frequency of updates, which can be automatic or scheduled. Any Web browser or Internet access through an ISP with 14.4-Kbps or 28.8-Kbps modem is sufficient to use the service.

AfterDark Online delivers national and international news, business news, financial news, technology news, weather, and sports. It also tracks stock quotes and sports scores, which are displayed as ticker tapes scrolling across the bottom of the screen saver. The screen saver is available free of charge from the vendor site.

AfterDark Online sources include DBC Financial News, E! Online, *Sports Illustrated* Online, *USA Today*, *Wall Street Journal* Interactive, and ZD Net. Contact *http://www.afterdark.com/* for more details.

BroadVision

The One-to-One service is the first application system for dynamic, personalized Web marketing and selling. The objective of this service is to transform static electronic brochure sites on the Web into interactive One-to-One marketing communities. It runs on Sun SPARC 1000 platforms.

BroadVision communities include NetRadio Network, VirginNet Ltd., Channel 4000 Internet community information service, and the ANGLE personal information service.

ANGLE is a free information-retrieval service designed to demonstrate the One-to-One intelligent marketing technology. It combines One-to-One technology and selections from a staff of more than 20 editors nationwide to provide a personalized, Web-based information service. Users select information styles, choose graphics for customizing the site, and select an editor or personality to suggest sites based on their interests.

BroadVision intends to generate revenues through advertising and co-branding with Web publishers. ANGLE allows advertisers to target their messages to individuals, but does not compare them to users and depends on rule-based filtering, which reduces the transmission of irrelevant information by filtering out many items collected by search engines. Additional information on BroadVision can be found at *http://www.broadvision.com/*.

Caravelle

This Canadian venture offers WATCHER line of products for services designed to guard company network investments. It continuously monitors devices and applications, identifying weaknesses, and immediately notifies the system administration about failures.

The latest feature of the WATCHER service explores groupware tools for Caravelle customers. InfoWATCHER monitors Web sites for new and updated information and automatically publishes it. This task is completed in intranet or proxy servers, and users are advised by E-mail, pager, or screen tools.

The TRANSCEIVE product line monitors Web-based content from any Internet or intranet source. The system notifies targeted audiences when defined types of changes are detected. For more information, visit *http://www.caravelle.com/*.

Desktop Data, Inc.

Desktop Data, Inc. is an independent provider of customized, real-time news and information services for workers linked to LANs and WANs. Its NewsEDGE service delivers more than 650 news and information sources in realtime. The news is automatically filtered based on interest profiles and is targeted at company executives, salespeople, marketers, attorneys, accountants, consultants, bankers, and financial professionals. Users can personalize their requests.

NewsEDGE claims to be the most widely installed enterprise solution for intranet-based broadcasting, serving more than 140,000 professionals in over 388 organizations. Its content is acquired from news and information originating from more than 120 leading publishers and over 650 authoritative news sources.

Because the service supports a wide range of computing platforms, companies can establish centralized information broadcasting and response services with its internal channel capabilities. Figure 11.1 illustrates Desktop Data services.

Figure 11.1 Desktop Data Service Overview

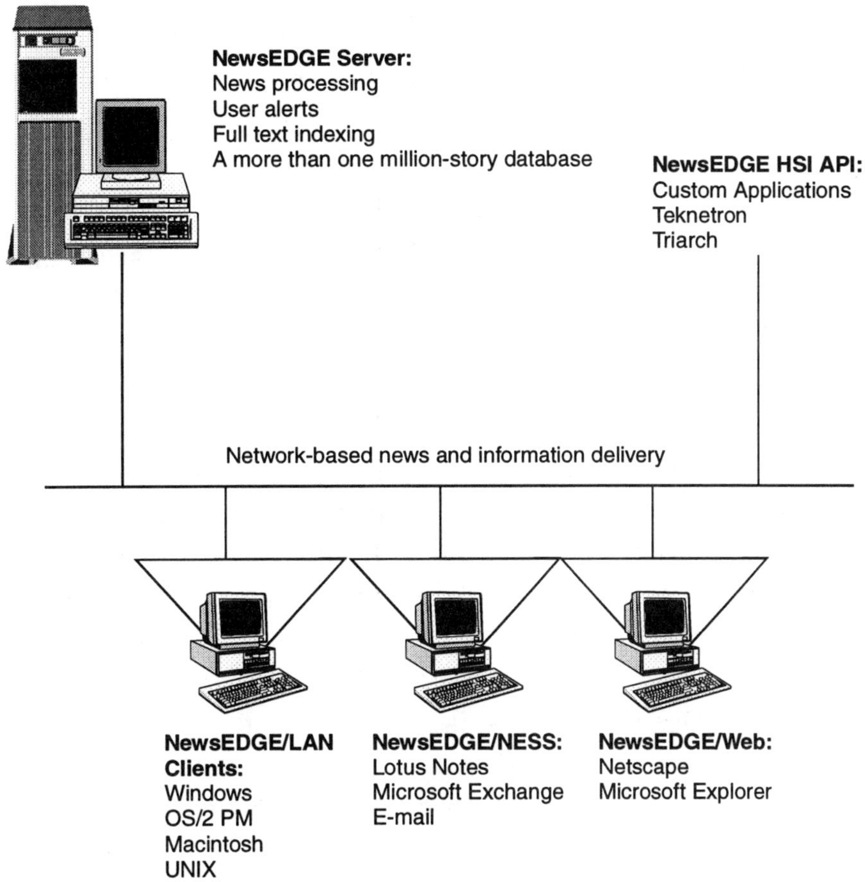

Since September 1996, Desktop Data has provided NewsEDGE/WEB, the NewsEDGE product line for seamlessly integrating real-time news into intranets. The line is being adopted as a standard platform in commercial enterprises because it supports Web server software, requires minimum bandwidth, and can be scaled to support more than 2,000 users per server. It operates inside firewalls on company LANs and WANs.

Desktop Data also leverages Lotus Notes, Microsoft Exchange, and E-mail information for distribution and delivery. NewsEDGE can deliver to end-user platforms including Windows, Windows 95, Windows NT, OS/2, Mac, and UNIX. It is also integrated for investment customers with specialized services such as TFinancial, Comstock, Reuters, Teknetron, and Triarch. Contact *http://www.desktopdata.com/* for more information.

Desktop News

Desktop News is a simple, free push technology solution for customized content delivery. It delivers a customized news feed directly to a desktop in compact headline ticker format. Users define their areas of interest and the service employs its sophisticated News Agent software to seek and deliver custom content continually.

The Desktop News open publishing model accommodates an unlimited number of subscribers and publisher content channels. Ticker headlines are expanded into full multimedia content coming directly from the source Web site.

Desktop News requires Windows 3.11, Windows 95, NT 3.5, or 4.0 versions and interacts with Navigator 3.0 and IE 3.0 browsers. It requires less than 4 MB of storage space for client software and content updates. According to the company, the service offers more efficient resource management than other push technology models.

Current content of Desktop News is indexed and accessible under major subject categories, including business, technology, finance, education, entertainment, health, science, and U.S. and world politics. They represent more than 150 specific channels of sites that include sources such as *Business Week*, C|Net, CNN, *Forbes*, Fox/Business, MSNBC, *PC Week*, *Money*, the History Channel, and Insurance News. Additional categories in development include arts, fashion, food and beverages, hobbies, media, real estate, religion, and travel. For more information, visit *http://www.desktopnews.com/*.

The DoubleClick Network

The DoubleClick Network is the first Internet advertising network to provide targeted, measurable Internet advertising. It consists of seven categories of interest defined as affinity groups. To help advertisers target their Internet promotions, the service provides a single contract, invoice, standard advertising banner, and comprehensive daily campaign reporting.

The DoubleClick Network sites include Premium, Business and Finance, Technology, Directories and Search Engines, Sports, Travel and Leisure, Entertainment, News, and Information and Culture. This service acts as a single source for reaching diversified audiences from more than 60 Web sites. Contact *http://www.doubleclick.net/* for additional information.

Empirical Media

Empirical Media offers the WiseWire search technology, which applies collaborative neural net filtering to determine user interests and deliver relevant Web information. It is based on NewsWeeder technology developed at Carnegie Mellon University using artificial intelligence and collaborative filtering. WiseWire is an adaptive search system that learns how a user rates information as it is displayed. Every time a user interacts with the service, the personal profile is further defined to improve the quality of subsequent deliveries.

WiseWire examines the ratings of the other users and develops interest patterns determining relationships between people and content. Profiles used to filter content are also used to deliver targeted advertising.

The service filters content from a wide variety of proprietary and public sources, including Web pages, newswire articles, news and entertainment, premium content, Usenet news groups, WiseWorld chat rooms, mailing lists, and other Internet sources.

In mid-1997, WiseWire had not incorporated a notification feature. However, the company is investigating ways of providing push technology services through Netcaster or CDFs. Contact *http://www.wisewire.com/* for updated information.

Farcast

Farcast targets information overload by providing a customized search and retrieval for a monthly fee of $9.95. Users decide what to look for and receive unlimited access to news, stock quotes, weather, sports, and other data. Sources include the Associated Press, United Press International, the New York Stock Exchange, NASDAQ, and company directories. No advertising is involved in this service, and it is accessible through individual E-mail. For more information, contact *http://www.farcast.com/*.

inCommon

inCommon's Downtown is an open framework designed to publish information on the Internet. It includes automatic content delivery and information customization. Downtown uses leading Web content publishers, including the Auto Channel, Billboard, CBS Sportsline, CBS UTTM, News.com, DBC, Envirolink, The Gate, *The L.A. Times*, Motley Fool, Movie Link, *The New York Times*, *PC World* Online, Research, TechWeb, and *USA Today*.

Downtown is a comprehensive push service that delivers information from sites designated by the user. The service searches designated channels for new content, automatically downloads it, and notifies the user when it is available. Visit *http://www.incommon.com/* for additional information. Figure 11.2 illustrates Downtown channel selector screen.

Figure 11.2 Downtown Channel Selector Screen

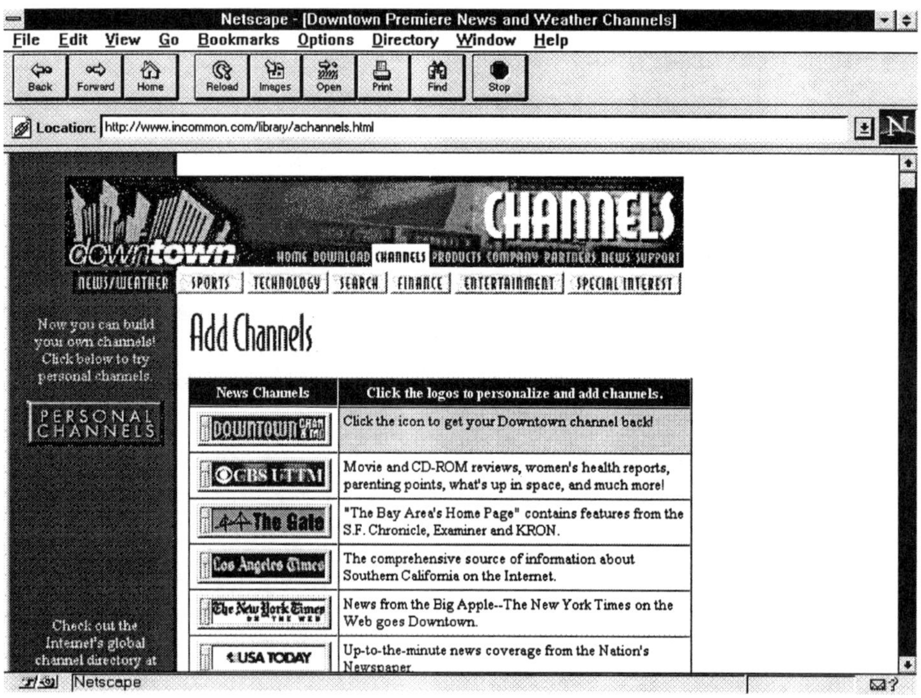

The Personal Channels feature of the service allows users to create their own channels for virtually any site on the Web. These channels include scrolling headlines, new content alerts, navigational summaries, rapid Web access, off-line browsing, and persistent presence on the desktop. Personal Channels can also be used to control information flow on intranets and the Internet.

Individual, Inc.

In operation since 1989, Individual, Inc. (*http://www.individual.com/*) provides personalized information services, which were originally pushed to subscribers using fax machines. The services now provide several variants, including First! Intranet, First! for Notes, First! Alert, and First! for Fax or E-mail. Users can select information delivery in a variety of forms. No advertising is involved, and subscribers pay a monthly fee for each service. Additional fees are charged for materials over the monthly limit.

Individual uses SMART agent software to select daily the most relevant news for each customer from more than 700 sources, including worldwide network of newswires, newspapers, and magazines scanning more than 20,000 stories every day. The First! service claims to achieve an 80% to 90% relevance level for customer profiles – about twice the level achieved by traditional search methods.

Individual also offers a special search service called CompanyLink, which provides access to company databases such as Hoover's Online publicly traded companies and CorpTech Database of technology companies.

InfoBeat

Originally started as Mercury Mail in 1995, InfoBeat delivers news. The user can customize the information by selecting specific categories. For further information about InfoBeat, visit *http://www.infobeat.com/*. The home page of InfoBeat is illustrated in Figure 11.3.

Figure 11.3 InfoBeat Home Page

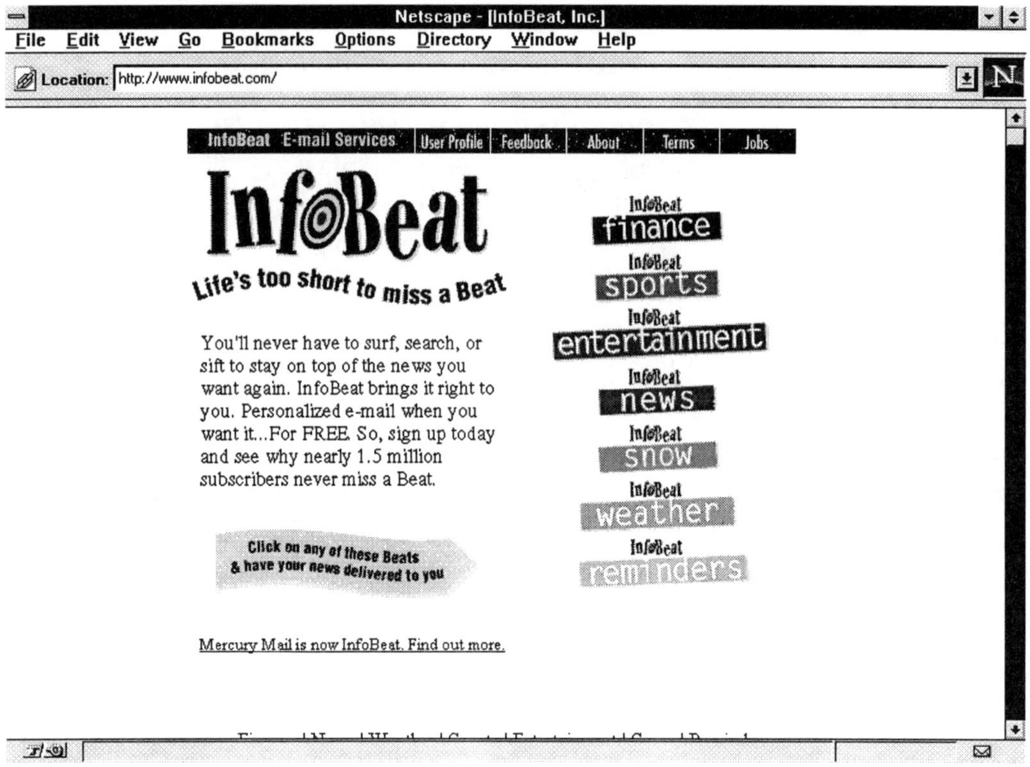

Although an advanced filtering system is used to sort and personalize information, this selectivity remains at the source and headline levels. Human editorial intervention ensures that subscribers receive personalized information that accurately reflects their needs and overcome the limitations of automated filtering.

InfoBeat service is free of charge to users because revenues are generated from service sponsors and advertising. Highly personalized advertisements are embedded in E-mail messages delivered directly to subscribers. InfoBeat's custom E-mail messaging handles more than one million messages daily and is expanding to process one million messages per hour.

Intermind

In October 1996, Intermind released its first push technology product: Communicator. It is a Web publishing, subscribing, and feedback system in which content providers pay licensing fees according to the number of visitors to their site. The service provides all levels of operations; content providers do not need their own Web sites to use with this service.

Users can select and subscribe to information and automatically receive notification of any updates on their desktop browsers. Subscribers can select from more than 200 participating channels and Web site publishers can use the system to push new content to distribute information.

Content provider channels include Times Mirror Magazines including *GOLF*online, *Sporting News*, SkiNet, Transworld SNOWboarding, *Field and Stream*, *Yachting*Net, PopSci.com, and even special channels (the Ryder Cup and Tournament, for example). Other channels include CBSNews Up to the Minute, PBS Online, HotWired, RealAudio Timecast, Virtual Vineyards, Micro Tempus, The Republican National Committee, Spiegel, Jupiter Communications, The Sierra Club, Visio, Discovery Channel Online, Web Review, DealerNet, and Cybergolf.

Some of the channels created by Intermind have a short life, sufficient only to cover the duration and commentary of specific events. This capability demonstrates the uniqueness of Intermind technology, which is flexible enough to allow for such levels of granularity.

The Communicator Personal Edition is free to users and allows subscriptions to specific channels. In addition to updates from Times Mirror sites, users can choose from 200 channels. Contact *http://www.intermind.com/* for further information.

News-Alert

News-Alert allows subscribers to receive Clip Alerts for managing personal stock portfolios. Users enter stock symbols or company names to add to their online portfolios. Once a stock portfolio is created, subscribers can set up Personal Topic searches to collect related headlines. Once Personal Topics is set up, they can use the Clip Alert option to alert them.

Netscape 3.0+ or Internet Explorer (IE) 3.0+ mail programs are required for this notification process. Additional information is available at *http://www.newsalert.com/*.

NETdelivery

NETdelivery from Netcast Communications automates the delivery and presentation of information. In an attempt to position itself as a leading electronic delivery service, the company offers applications that help create, sustain, and enhance one-to-one relationships between suppliers and clients.

NETdelivery is developing an easy-to-use delivery service that links communities with common interests to providers of relevant content, merchandise, or services. The communities of interest formed by the service include providers, company partners, community partners, and subscribers. According to the company, NETdelivery is pioneering this community marketing concept. The first community is called CyberSeniors and is comprised of Internet users who benefit from 50+ years of insight, knowledge, and wisdom. Other communities of interest are developing also.

NETdelivery services are available free of charge. The service does not depend on a specific browser, E-mail, or OS; it processes interactive multimedia content, eliminates unwanted content, and provides useful demographics to content and merchandise suppliers. Visit *http://www.netdelivery.com/* for further details.

Open Sesame

Open Sesame *(http://www.opensesame.com/)*, also from Netcast Communications, is a specialized entertainment service that informs users about new books, CDs, upcoming concerts and events, soon-to-be-released movies, and upcoming TV programs. The service responds to a personal interest profile provided by the user and to the record of interactions at the Web site. The system is designed to learn about the preferences of the user as time progresses. It uses proprietary learning agent technology to determine the optimum delivery content. This process involves both user clustering and collaborative filtering techniques to determine the most effective combination for a particular profile. Profiles are updated daily, which makes this service more timely than some comparable services. Open Sesame acquires information from established sources, including Atlantic Records, Borders, Sony, and MovieFone.

While Open Sesame currently delivers its results through a standard Web browser or E-mail package, it is also developing push technology clients for its services. Future coverage is also intended to expand to include health, travel, and personalized business information.

PointCast

PointCast is the original push technology service and offers news and information delivered to the desktop in form of screen savers and a channel guide. PointCast Network (PCN) launched its service in February 1996 and captured a significant lead in the push service marketplace – estimated at more than one million active users.

PointCast service revenues result from advertising and subscriptions sold to premium content providers, including Business Wire, Accuweather, Reuters New Media, CNN, PR Newswire, Standard & Poor's Comstock, Time Warner's Pathfinder, *The Boston Globe*, *The L.A. Times*, *The New York Times*, *Chicago Tribune*, Newsbytes News, Quote.com, and EDGAR Online.

The PCN service initially created significant bandwidth shortages and networking bottlenecks, and overloaded individual storage capacities. To relieve this problem, PointCast introduced the I-Server, which is company installed and operated and includes Windows-based management tools. The I-Server locally caches PCN content and relieves the bandwidth congestion when it is accessed directly by many users simultaneously. I-Server also provides log file tools and reporting systems and allows simultaneous presentation of data to many users.

The I-Server also provides content customization in the form of a company channel. Only one such channel can be set up, although it may contain numerous subject groupings. Basic HTML tools are used to create articles, and graphic logos can be included. Other forms of multimedia content, such as Shockwave, are not possible. After installation, users must be redirected to receive their feeds through the I-Server.

The PointCast environment is considered limiting because of the availability of only a single channel, which provides little flexibility for organizations with varied content disciplines. In addition, controlling access to public channels that may distract users from focusing on work-related information streams is also impossible. In short, PointCast is now being seen as more of a consumer push technology, despite its initial launch in the business environment.

To compete effectively PointCast is developing its PCN to provide more customization to the company client. This effort is reflected in the PCN 2.0

version of the service, which is an update of the I-Server product line. Although PointCast is a leading push technology service, it is also becoming a provider of tools to manage the selection and reception of its channels. As a result, it is becoming a more acceptable operation, although the main issue of advertising and distracting content in its services remains.

PCN 2.0 allows network managers to schedule updating, caching, and filtering of PointCast content and is designed to reduce the intensity of traffic downloads on company networks. New features include PointCast Company Broadcast Manager, which sends internal updates; PointCast Administrator, which allows configuration of clients and sets the filters; and PointCast Caching Manager, which enables distributed RAM caching among several intranet servers.

The company also provides some tools, including PointCast Studio for content development and client advertising screening. PointCast Connections enables any Web site to become a channel broadcasting its content through the PCN. Figure 11.4 illustrates the PointCast home page.

Figure 11.4 The PointCast Home Page

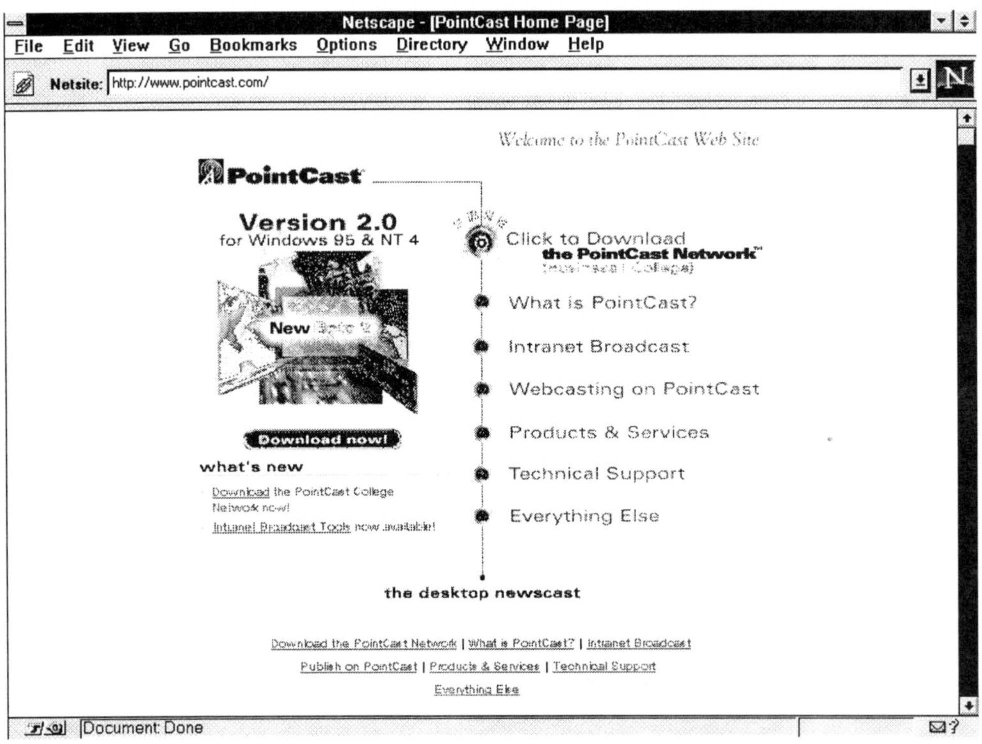

Tibco Software

This company was founded in 1985 and claims to have invented the first generation of push technology long before PointCast or Marimba. In contrast to other push services, Tibco offers multicasting, which allows a server to send a packet of information only once, even if it is broadcast to thousands of users.

Tibco (*http://www.tibco.com/*) is an example of the publish and subscribe approach to push technology. This method allows users to publish data to a list of people who have requested it and can be delivered to computers operating on a variety of platforms (see Figure 11.5).

Figure 11.5 Illustration of TIBnet

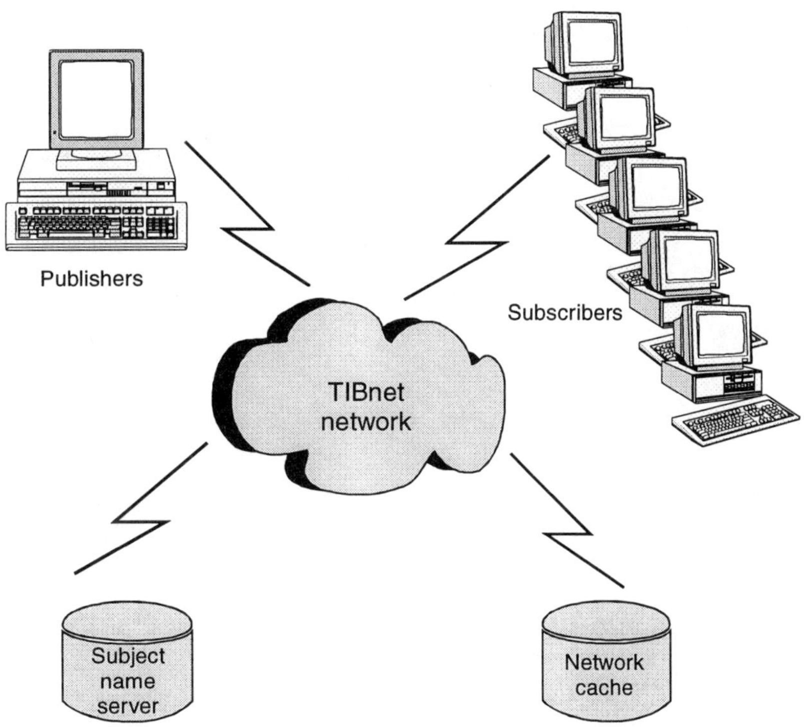

Source: Tibco, Inc.

Tibco operates as an independent division of Reuters Holdings, Plc., which is among the largest news and information companies in the world. Tibco is a leading supplier of digital trading systems to financial firms and developed and patented the publish and subscriber push technology variant.

In December 1996, Tibco announced TIBnet for implementing content-based, event-driven networks over LANs and WANs. Adding content-based information to intranets and Internet communications, users can receive instant updates to critical data as it changes without asking for it. Tibco provides online stock quote delivery through Yahoo!.

WavePhore

WavePhore (*http://www.wavetop.net/*) was originally founded in 1990 to use proprietary coder/decoder (codec) technology for point-to-multipoint distribution of data over broadcast channels. Currently, WavePhore Networks division provides business-to-business broadcast data delivery; its Newscast divisions delivers real-time business news to 52,000 business users. WavePhore distributes digital data and information over the Public Broadcasting System (PBS) and its network of more than 250 member TV stations that reach 99% TV households in the United States.

WavePhore Consumer Group is a combined effort of WavePhore technology departments and WebTop Home PC Broadcast Network is supported by major channels and advertisers. Initial Internet content providers include PBS Online, CBS SportsLine, Quote.com, and The Weather Channel. The overall network intends to offer approximately 20 channels, with two or three providers on each.

WaveTop uses the vertical blanking interval (VBI) in TV signals to transmit content at high bandwidth speeds. The system provides speeds of up to 150 Kbps and uses 10-VBI lines. WavePhore in-band data broadcasting is another technology; it inserts data into an active portion of the analog video signal with speeds up to 384 Kbps. The system can accommodate both transmission concepts simultaneously with speeds of more than 500 Kbps.

As such, this system differs from Intercast, which combines TV and Internet content on the PC. The goal is to offer a service for Internet content providers who want to reach PC users who already have TV tuners on their platforms. WaveTop also intends to target small office/home office (SOHO) markets in the future.

Conclusion

Webcasting services gained the attention of the press and Internet users in 1996 when PointCast launched its screen saver and became successful literally overnight.

Since then, a large number of software ventures have introduced similar push technology services. Heavy bandwidth and desktop storage requirements were the major disadvantages of early push technology services. Later, competitors introduced improved services with lower requirements for these resources.

Initial push technology services were primarily targeted at consumers and offer free client software and heavy advertising and entertainment content as a result. This abundance of superfluous material, in effect, became an important issue within enterprises whose workers have access to those services because the distraction lowered interaction productivity.

Nevertheless, webcasting is a valuable technology being introduced in intranets and Internet transactions. The continued demand for these services led to the rapid emergence of new push technology software designed specifically for business implementation. These services eliminate advertising and distracting content and provide alternative client notification schemes, webcasting management, and user demographics and reporting systems.

The webcasting service and push technology industries are in an emerging state, although several well-established push technology services have served the company networks environment for some years. These services are now developing Internet-based variants of their offerings. As a result of established databases and revenues, those services have the business experience and resources to provide effective products in those markets.

Some of the new push technology ventures are introducing valuable features and financed by leading venture capital funds. Whether they have the staying power for the long term, however, remains to be seen. Several webcasting services discontinued operations after a relatively short time. As a result, companies contemplating the use of outside webcasting services should thoroughly evaluate the products and staying power of the ventures it considers.

Chapter 12

Webcasting and Push Case Studies

While webcasting applications vary widely depending on the company and the industry in which they operate, most are designed to enhance company sales and marketing processes. Distributing new product and services information to employees, business partners, and customers appears to be the most common use of push technology.

A summary of some typical webcasting implementations are presented in the Table 12.1. Details about each of the push technology applications have been identified following the table.

Table 12.1 Early Adopters of Push Technology

Company	Push Technology and Applications
ABN-AMRO	*NewsEDGE and Tibco* • Financial trading support system
AT&T Wireless Services	*Communicator* • Technical data distribution selectively to developers about new products and updates
Barnes & Noble	*Firefly* • Creation of communities of like-minded readers for pushing book recommendations

Company	Push Technology and Applications
Bechtel	*Tibco* • Updating engineering and project management documentation for integration of all work projects
Ben & Jerry's	*INCISA* • Distributes news feeds, stock quotes, and inventory updates to employees and business partners
Bloomberg	*NewsEDGE* • Special service to Open Bloomberg customers for personalization of information needs
Capital Market Risk Advisors	*Farcast* • Distribution of personalized news and information to designated E-mail addresses for mobile consultants
Chicago Board of Trade	*INCISA* • Distribution of memos and commodity prices to 4,000 members of the organization
Compaq Computer	*PointCast Network* • Special Compaq Channel created to broadcast information, news, and software updates to Compaq users
Conference Plus	*INCISA* • Scheduling and managing customer conference calls for minimizing wait times
Dell Online	*IE 4.0 Browser* • Branded push channels in new desktops for broadcasting software updates and marketing materials
Dow Jones Interactive	• Operates three online services • Company is considering introduction of push technology
Ernst & Young	*IntelliServ* • Developing push technologies for internal communications with 75,000 workers worldwide
Ford Motor	*FOCALpt* • Special webcasting service designed to serve 15,000 Ford dealers worldwide to support sales and services
Fruit of the Loom	*PointCast I-Server* • Distributes latest inventory information and enables distributors to place individual orders
Heineken	*BackWeb* • Use of push technology to inform subscribers of upcoming regional events

Company	Push Technology and Applications
IBM	*TRANSCEIVE* • Use of push technology for marketing intelligence and monitoring competitive product Web sites
IntelliHealth	*PointCast* • First Internet broadcast service for the healthcare industry targeted at healthcare professionals
KPMG	*NewsEDGE/Web* • Business news and information for 5,000 intranet users in the United Kingdom
Lufthansa	*BackWeb* • Introduces push technology for airline customer service information about tickets and flight schedules
Merrill Lynch	*NewsEDGE* • Incorporates push technology for real-time news and information to 25,000 TGA terminal users worldwide
NationsBank	*INCISA* • Special NationsCast channel for internal communications of customized content to employees

ABN-AMRO Bank NV

ABN-AMRO Bank NV is a global financial institution with 60,000 employees. To compete more effectively, ABN-AMRO is implementing push technology from Desktop Data that integrates the NewsEDGE service with the TIBCO market sheets that provide details of stock performance or company data. This approach allows the bank's traders to access authoritative information directly from their online trading environments. The solution is available to a variety of user platforms, including Windows 95, Lotus Notes/Domino, and the company intranet.

Although this is a major investment for ABN-AMRO, it is considered a key element for ensuring efficient information flows across the enterprise. NewsEDGE is the critical service to provide traders, financial consultants, and relationship managers with personalized news alerts and filtering capability. This is expected to increase user productivity by providing each with only the most relevant information.

AT&T Wireless Services

This service company is an early adopter of push technology as a means of sending members of the AT&T Developer Program the latest technical data, sample codes, and other operational information. AT&T Wireless Services uses the Communicator push technology from Intermind. The publisher-subscriber webcasting model is run on a notebook PC, updating technical and product information that is then posted on an intranet Web site.

AT&T developers can download the subscriber software from the Web site and specify which information they want to receive. Whenever AT&T Wireless Services has products or news updates that are relevant to those specifications, the Communicator publisher sends it to the developer's desktop.

Using push technology AT&T solves one facet of the information overload problem. Before the introduction of the Communicator technical bulletins were distributed through E-mail, CD-ROMs, and other conventional distribution methods. Consequently, all the developers received all the information generated whether it was required or not. Push technology gives AT&T developers more control over the amount of information received and gives them a chance to eliminate irrelevant content.

Barnes & Noble

This major bookstore chain – selling $2.5 billion in books annually – recently created a Web site that is developing specialized reader communities. It uses the Firefly tool kit to set up an icon on its home pages for consumers to register for a Firefly Passport. Users provide some personal data about themselves, receive a password, and are assigned a virtual intelligent agent. Whenever each consumer visits Barnes & Noble Online and enters his password, the agent starts assisting in selecting books and topics.

The Firefly Passport concept of Barnes & Noble is based on the idea of creating subcommunities of like-minded customers. Over time, the intelligent agent learns customers' preferences and makes book recommendations based on past purchases. The recommendations are pushed to the user screen when the Barnes & Noble Web site is entered and the Firefly Passport password is recognized.

This is an interactive push technology implementation in E-commerce. The agent asks the user to rate books in inventory that fit within a category in which the consumer demonstrated an interest. By creating common interest communities, consumers interested in a certain subject receive the benefit of collective recommendations of other consumers with the same interest without having to search for them.

For more information, visit *http://www.barnesandnoble.com/*.

Bechtel

This global construction company introduced webcasting to keep its engineering and project management documents updated. They selected the publish and subscribe model for communicating updates through an intranet. This capability was originally for new projects, but it is beginning to link with company suppliers through extranets. The objective is to tightly integrate all work processes. Bechtel considers push technology implementation a strategic necessity.

The implementation is based on TIBCO middleware, and the intranet model proved ideal because the company uses a variety of computer platforms in many remote locations. It is built on a Microsoft Windows NT service linked with an Oracle database. Bechtel discovered that this was a complex project and it required significant research about how people use information. The company sees this as larger issue than evaluating products, technical analysis, and data flows.

Ben & Jerry's

Since 1978, this ice cream company has become one of the most well known in the United States. It now employs thousands of workers nationwide and supplies to numerous supermarkets. Because of a constant problem of competition, the company needs to educate its employees continuously about competitive and market issues with an efficient communications method.

Previous use of E-mail did not prove efficient enough. Ben & Jerry managers need a system that ensures the right information is delivered to the right people in a timely and efficient manner and that it will not be ignored. The company considered PointCast, which was unexpectedly unwieldy when distributing the technology to a large numbers of clients. It was also expensive.

The primary objective of the company's use of push technology is to ensure that key company messages, including human resource policies, internal news, and new product information, are delivered immediately to the employees.

Ben & Jerry's introduced INCISA push technology for distributing news feeds, stock quotes, and inventory updates directly to employees and business partners' desktops. It is able to distribute specific information at specified times to specified recipients who need to know. Because employees are known not to read all the conventional memos received by them, the company uses the INCISA feature for displaying messages across the computer screen to gain user attention.

Another important criterion for push technology selection was the ability of INCISA to work within the context of Web browsers on PCs, Macs, and other terminal equipment so that additional client integration effort could be avoided.

The company also uses push technology in its human resources department to send messages about healthcare, new policies, forms required by employees, and similar information. It is also developing a worldwide system that will link its suppliers and retailers with the inventory database using INCISA DataBridge feature. The company will use it to publish daily ice cream sales data, product trends, and a Top 10 favorite flavors list. The push technology will also extend to sales, marketing, and other departments of the company.

Bloomberg

Bloomberg is a global, multimedia based distributor of information services that combines news, data, and analysis for businesses and financial markets. The service provides real-time pricing, historical pricing, indicative data, analysis tools, and electronic communications through more than 76,000 Bloomberg systems used by approximately 250,000 financial professionals in 100 countries.

In mid-1997, Bloomberg announced that its Bloomberg News service will use NewsEDGE push technology from Desktop Data for real-time news applications. It is being made available to Open Bloomberg customers exclusively and gives them an opportunity to customize their specific information needs to better serve their clients.

This personalization includes the ability to search agents using specific words and phrases, ticker symbols, company names, and specific information sources. Bloomberg selected NewsEDGE for its push technology service because the system reads the stories, proactively tracks information uniquely important to each user, and creates appropriate alerts.

Bloomberg believes that the combination of its Open Bloomberg system and NewsEDGE gives its business customers a superior real-time news solution and a competitive advantage in making business decisions.

Capital Market Risk Advisors

Capital Market Risk Advisors (CMRA) is a financial risk management advisory firm in New York City that monitors fast-breaking news. The group is an industry-watcher operation, keeping abreast of the financial markets. Like most advisory and trading firms of this ilk, CMRA uses both Bloomberg and Dow Jones services that provide the required depth of information and financial trading tools.

Because advisory firms spend a large amount of time traveling, they are also frequently away from the terminals. Although Bloomberg and Dow Jones are now also offering associated push technology within their services, they are not mobile as yet.

CMRA conceived a push technology solution to alleviate this problem by using the Farcast webcasting service, which delivers personalized news and information to a designated user E-mail address. The firm pays a monthly fee of $9.95 and can instruct up to 15 agents to perform autonomous searches on specific subjects and deliver the results at particular times of day to E-mail accounts. Farcast service does not offer the depth of Bloomberg or Dow Jones services, but it is sufficiently comprehensive for use by highly mobile financial consultants. It also has the advantage of portability.

CMRA uses Hewlett-Packard (HP) palmtop and a Megahertz modem card to access the Web and transmit the information to E-mail locations. This activity can be performed readily wherever access to a telephone is available, most commonly at airports and hotels. In the absence of an effective, portable Web browser Farcast is considered a useful alternative.

Chicago Board of Trade

The Chicago Board of Trade (CBOT) continually distributes memos and commodity price information to its 4,000 members. It has created a Web site for public distribution of commodity prices, but the memos flooding the members are not organized. Therefore, members must scroll through each message in search of which is appropriate for them and which is inefficient and wastes valuable trading time.

As a result, CBOT is implementing a push technology based on the INCISA tool from Wayfarer Communications. The objective is to have an alert icon, perhaps a pop up headline, appear on the user screen whenever a new memo of significance to a particular member is generated.

Compaq Computer

Compaq uses the PointCast services to deliver information directly to end users on a regular basis. For this purpose, the company created a Compaq Channel on the PointCast Network, which distributes news broadcasts to North American commercial desktop customers. Compaq, however, has an equity investment in PointCast venture.

Compaq continually broadcasts information directly to its customers and end users. The company has a branded version of PointCast Network software that is shipped with most configurations on the Compaq Desktop 2000 and Deskpro 4000 PCs.

The dedicated Compaq Channel distributes articles, news or software updates, and other information of importance to Compaq users. The push service also offers news, company, weather, and lifestyle channels. The PointCast software is available for downloading from Compaq Web site (*http://www.compaq.com/us/pcn/*).

The Compaq Channel notifies users about driver updates, product enhancements, new product announcements, and special information designed to enhance Compaq ownership experience.

Conference Plus, Inc.

Conference Plus, Inc. (CPI) provides reservations for teleconferencing services for retail and wholesale businesses. Considering its primary customers, it must schedule and manage customer conference calls globally. Because CPI's clients are busy executives meeting tight deadlines and cannot afford to waste time during the conference call reservation process, the company has reduced the waiting time to no more than 15 seconds for its customers.

CPI introduced push technology to distribute real-time customer service statistics to managers. This information is obtained from its Fujitsu 9600 ACD switch, which provides it through a DataBridge feature to an INCISA service from Wayfarer Communications. The INCISA system pushes the new statistics to the managers and interested groups that are in the best position to act on this information.

The customized system displays the number of customers waiting in the telephone queue – the longest time customers are on hold – and CPI managers can take immediate corrective action when the wait queues become backlogged. The purpose of the push technology application is to resolve backlogs and problems before callers experience unacceptable hold times, which is critical for retaining existing customers and attracting new ones.

Dell Online

Dell Computer is a leading manufacturer of PCs and servers and a pioneer of selling those products over the Web. It is now developing a continuous personal link with the buyers using push technology because consumers can indicate what level of information they will accept on an as-needed or as-required basis.

The company is loading branded push channels into its new desktop systems; the channels will broadcast navigational tools, software updates, and marketing materials to customers. The goal is to exploit the latest push clients being incorporated in IE 4.0 browsers, which are shipped with every Windows systems.

Dell is using the Web no longer as a revenue generating storefront, but as an interactive relationship building medium. The company now already knows its customers and push technology will provide the least expensive communications vehicle. Dell push channels will focus primarily on customer service and support.

The push component on Dell's Web site automatically records customer data the first time it is used. Afterward, it delivers tailored content to the customer. It becomes a powerful marketing platform that other companies are expected to match. Dell's push approach follows its strategic business plan and is an excellent example of how Web technologies can be used to develop emerging markets.

Dell considers push to be a means to deliver help desk materials from its 35,000-page database. It also uses the push technology as a vehicle for distribution of software patches and customized marketing messages. The objective is to approach a level of service and support for consumers that until recently was only possible with individual customers.

Dow Jones Interactive

Dow Jones Interactive Publishing, a division of Dow Jones, has three online products: *The Wall Street Journal* Interactive Edition, Dow Jones News/Retrieval, and Dow Vision. All the services use a pull form of delivery, but the company is investigating push delivery alternatives.

In the case of Dow Jones, customer's system uptime and fast access are critical to business decisions. The company sources can deliver information to the Internet through a 25-Mbps backbone, but it is concerned about what happens when the information arrives at the service providers, which are outside of Dow Jones control; Dow has not implemented leading edge technology, preferring to wait until push technology is stable and reliable. Nevertheless, few doubt that push technology is suitable for this type of service.

Ernst & Young

This professional services firm, one of the Big 6 accounting organizations, is developing push technologies for internal communications with its 75,000 desktop workers worldwide. It is based on IntelliServ information filtering technology from Cognisoft, which is being designed for company knowledge managers.

Ford Motor

This auto maker developed FOCALpt, a special service provided by Ford and participating Ford dealers. It is a leading webcasting application that is used in a company environment. FOCALpt pushes critical company information to dealerships quickly and reliably over the Internet. FOCALpt enables dealerships to provide customers with personalized service and more informed sales and service interaction. The FOCALpt system is designed to serve 15,000 dealers worldwide for supporting, selling, and servicing automobiles.

When a presentation is made to a customer, information is being updated in the background also; therefore, the salesperson does not need to ask and search for the specific information. The goal is to improve customer retention by providing support for the lifetime of a Ford automobile.

The system also offers promotional, inventory, and financing information to help close a sale or agreement. While communicating with the customer, the system can locate the make, model, and configuration of choice anywhere in the region.

Ford bases its FOCALpt system on QuickServer from Wayfarer Communications, developer of the INCISA turnkey webcasting solution for business applications. Andersen Consulting assists Ford by providing strategic, technical, and system integration expertise in the development of company push technology applications.

Fruit of the Loom

This apparel manufacturer is among the early adopters of push technology to deliver production reports, inventory analysis, and other company data to its employees using an intranet. The company has selected PointCast service as a basis for its applications.

Prior to introducing webcasting, Fruit of the Loom generated paper reports based on inventory information resident on an IBM AS/400 intranet Web server – a task that became increasingly difficult.

Fruit of the Loom installed the PointCast I-Server, and network administration now enters the data into HTML templates, indicating where and how often to acquire information from company sources. The I-Server software resides on a Compaq P-100 Deskpro running Windows NT and automatically downloads the latest inventory from the AS/400 system every hour. Simultaneously, it notifies all managers when updated information is available.

Fruit of the Loom is expanding its I-Server usage to distributors over the company extranet as part of its overall program to streamline inventory management and product ordering. The company provides its PCs to distributors loaded with a proprietary software that allows them to dial in to the Fruit of the Loom database for checking inventory and placing orders. This part of the process does not yet incorporate push technology, but the company considers it a powerful marketing tool for the future. Webcasting would alert distributors to new products, inventory changes, and other company news as soon as these take place.

Heineken

Heineken, an international beer brewer in Amsterdam, sponsors sports and music events in many of the 170 countries in which its beer is distributed. It uses BackWeb push technology to deliver updates of Heineken events and provides subscribers a means to receive other popular features from its Web site.

The company uses its Web channel to inform subscribers of upcoming regional events, primarily a promotional and marketing use of push technology. The company also pushes its popular screen savers, which are downloaded in the background, at the beginning of each season. The channels are also used to notify subscribers of last-minute, live events.

IBM AS/400 Division

IBM, located in Rochester, New York, evaluated several push technologies for its own internal use. The division selected TRANSCEIVE from Caravelle, Inc., because it offered the features of interest to that organization specifically.

IBM uses push technology to monitor changes to Web content on specific sites of competing corporations. As soon as competitors' hardware and software updates or new products are announced on their Web sites, TRANSCEIVE system identifies those changes and notifies the appropriate IBM employees. This is an example of push technology as a business intelligence tool.

IntelliHealth

IntelliHealth is a joint venture between Aetna U.S. Healthcare and John Hopkins University and Health Systems. It was established in 1996 to create the first Internet broadcast service targeting the healthcare industry. The service creates a single user-friendly news and information service for healthcare professionals.

The resulting PointCast Network Health Care Insider is an array of channels that focus on the needs, concerns, and interests of the entire health industry. Perot Systems is the prime systems integrator of the service, working with clients to implement the technology for operating Health Care Insider and enterprisewide intranets for critical applications and data mining.

Perot Systems recently announced the Healthcare Solutions Model, a scalable, Web-based solution that includes Health Care Insider. The model is designed to give healthcare organizations the ability to access company news, eligibility records, referral information, clinical records, educational and training programs, scheduling tools, and other functions.

The Health Care Insider will offer several specialized channels, including news of associations and medical journals; topical channels about allergies, cancer, and medical products; and channels about health-related professions, including pharmacy, nursing, and transactions.

The Healthcare Solutions Model is designed to provide dynamic E-commerce capabilities within the integrated healthcare networks enterprise. Physicians will also be able to communicate and settle claims with payers in the network.

KPMG

KPMG is one of the world's largest professional services firms, with more than 1,000 offices in 829 cities of 145 countries. Its staff includes more than 74,000 partners and associated employees.

In early 1997, KPMG installed NewsEDGE/WEB push technology from desktop Data for more than 5,000 users of its intranet for news and information in the United Kingdom. The sources include *Financial Times*, Reuters RBA, and Dow Jones, and company content.

KPMG initially introduced push technology with a pilot project making NewsEDGE/WEB available to three independent teams within the company. The system provides users with news about clients, competitors, markets, industries, and individuals in response to individual demand and interest profile and alerts. The objective of this system is to provide all KPMG users with real-time news and information that is relevant to each individual, workgroup, or department on an unlimited license basis.

Lufthansa

Lufthansa, based in Frankfurt, Germany, is the first in the industry to employ push technology for customer service. The airline delivers updates on ticket pricing, flight schedules, and new programs and services using its own BackWeb channel. Personalized content about special offers is delivered directly to its customers, who can make reservations through hyperlinks.

Lufthansa's primary objective of the push initiative is to provide personalized information desired by customers and prospects all over the world. The airline provides localized content in the international markets where it operates.

MagicMaker

MagicMaker is a small, multimedia production company located in Palo Alto, California. It is one of the first to implement push technology for creating interactive online entertainment.

The company periodically broadcasts episodes of *The Marexx*, a Web-based multiplayer title, via ATM networks. This production is based on science fiction writings of Alan Dean Foster and include 2-D and 3-D animation, in addition to audio and video content. A chat service is also associated with the production, and all of the features are pushed to users desktops.

Merrill Lynch

This leading financial services and management organization created a state-of-the-art technology platform known as Trusted Global Advisor (TGA). It includes NewsEDGE push technology from Desktop Data, which delivers real-time news and information to 25,000 TGA users worldwide.

The TGA platform is a major investment of Merrill Lynch that supports its policy of providing sophisticated tools and assists in implementing its performance-based strategies. It is designed to substantially increase the efficiency and effectiveness of financial consultants to assist them in better servicing the needs of their clients.

The NewsEDGE push technology is seen as an important component of the TGA platform, which is an integrated tool. It provides Merrill Lynch financial consultants with a personalized news alert system and the ability to perform searches of the universe of financial markets news and the massive research generated daily within Merrill Lynch.

NationsBank

This major national banking organization employs 80,000 people and requires an efficient means of communications using secure internal systems. At the time of upgrading its communications the bank used eight incompatible E-mail systems and an obsolete company information database.

NationsBank implemented push technology for its internal communications needs for customizing messages, managing content, and direct delivery to employee desktops. The company also insisted on integrating their logo and brand name on the system, known as NationsCast. Availability of RSA encryption for securing financial information transactions was a major factor in this decision.

The bank evaluated several push technologies and rejected PointCast I-server solution specifically because it offered no discretion over the content pushed to the employees; it also included cumbersome advertising and distracting materials in the form of sports, weather, and horoscopes. As an alternative, NationsBank selected INCISA from Wayfarer. The company uses its HeadLinks feature to provide headlines of information and links that connect employees to sources of information that they specify. In addition, the company provides links to relevant news feeds, stock quotes, and updates from its Lotus Notes and Oracle Databases that can be accessed through INCISA DataBridge and delivered automatically to employees.

NationsBank uses push technology to send targeted messages about new banking products, departmental projects, and critical company information to employees selected by groups, departments, or individuals.

TCI, Ingenius

TCI, Ingenius is a subsidiary of TCI, which has delivered news and information to public and private schools for more than a decade. It continues to search for better and more efficient methods for broadcasting information to customers. A major system requirement is to enable principals and teachers to customize and administer the information to students and to deliver it on typically small bandwidth networks that are predominant in school districts. Another requirement is to eliminate advertising and distracting content from the process at all times.

An important consideration is the ability to brand specific school districts with their own channel names. Ingenius evaluated several push technologies for this purpose and selected INCISA from Wayfarer as the system most suitable to meet all the requirements of that particular environment.

The superintendent, the principal, and the teacher can use the system to select specific information sources for narrowcasting the messages to those that are most appropriate for their district, school, or even an individual classroom. This approach is efficient also because customized feeds deliver only information of specific interest to teachers and classrooms, avoiding flooding them with information that is irrelevant.

The Ingenius service also allows school administrations to selectively broadcast administrative messages to specific schools and districts when required. In other cases it provides outside content from news services throughout the world to support specific programs such as social studies. In addition, school administrations can communicate directly with parents who are equipped with home desktops and can inform them precisely about their children's progress.

Conclusion

Push technology is first and foremost understood and implemented by the large, multinational corporations that must distribute information continuously.

Webcasting, in any form, offers these companies the unique opportunity to reduce costs of distribution because push technology, properly implemented, reduces bandwidth and time spent by employees searching for relevant data.

Nevertheless, push technology is in its infancy. This is also reflected by the continuous evaluations of the early adopters of webcasting tools and services. They continue to search for the product or service that will provide productivity enhancements at a reasonable cost. Conversely, these products vary in what they can offer in specific company environments and must be evaluated and compared before final decisions are made.

Chapter 13

Conclusions

E-commerce is the dream within which webcasting can become a profitable reality. At the end of 1997, 60 million people were estimated to be connected through the Internet into a seamless digital network. By the end of year 2001, this number is expected to increase to 175 million.

According to the latest projections from IDC, the amount of commerce on the Web will skyrocket from $2.6 billion in 1996 to an estimated $220 billion during 2001. This growth is expected to result from more than 300 million devices that will be used to access the Web by that time.

The advantage of Web commerce is that it does not matter where the users live or in what time zone they conduct business. A Web channel can reach people at any time. Initial market studies suggest that up to 73% of Internet users had used the Web for purchases.

Web marketing and enterprise communications are entering the next generation of operations. New webcasting and push technology business models represent another attempt to justify E-commerce on the Web after the passive information and search engine Web site models failed to generate major revenue.

If You Build It, They May Not Bother to Come...

Although primary research suggests that 50% of E-commerce transactions are being completed via the Web rather than fax or telephone, it does not necessarily follow that a Web presence generates buyers. By 2001, IDC estimates that almost 80% of all E-commerce will be performed on the Web, making it a very competitive marketing environment.

Those who will not be able to push their products and services effectively will most likely become ineffective. Interest in webcasting and associated push technologies as a means to provide some advantages on the Web is mounting.

The Virtual Mall Lessons

While the mass consumer cyberspace markets are constantly in the news, Web publishers are aware that selling via the Internet does not resemble traditional selling methods. Most have learned by observing the failures of virtual malls and interactive TV pilots during the last three years.

Clearly, online marketing requires consumer communities with shared interests, user interaction, and competition within such electronic environments. In addition, goods that cannot be touched and tested are not ideal online products. Complex services – finance, travel, insurance, real estate, for example – and high-price items, including automobiles, boats, and airplanes, are more appropriate for those markets.

Information about user experiences with products is emerging as a more powerful endorsement than discounted prices. Webcasting and push technologies are effective mechanisms for maintaining user interests.

Business-to-Business Success

While consumer spending through the Web is gaining attention from the media and appears to show impressive growth, it pales in comparison with business-to-business activity, which will account for a growing percentage of Web commerce. In summary, intranets and extranets are where E-commerce will be conducted.

Intranets and extranets reflect the real world where business transactions have been performed remotely by fax, phone, EDI, and postal services for years. The Web is a more convenient, easier, faster, and less expensive vehicle.

As a result, intranets and extranets are being targeted by savvy webcasting tools and service suppliers as their most promising market. The consumer market is also expected to embrace this technology, but the most lucrative opportunities for the immediate future are in the business arena.

Controlling employee use of intranets and having the capability to prepare reports about network use for management is necessary. Conserving network bandwidth and eliminating distracting advertising and other nonbusiness content from webcasting services must also be addressed.

These problems require a new set of solutions: webcasting or push technology products and services that are now available. The push alternative is considered the next Web-based business model.

Streaming Multimedia Will Make It Happen

Whether in networking environments or via the Internet, capturing user attention and explaining the benefits of products and services is difficult without video presentations. Many companies now support their sales, marketing, training, and customer services with VCR or CD-ROM video presentations. Unfortunately, this approach is not as efficient as it seems because these products are often out of date when they reach their destinations.

Within the last year or so, Microsoft, Motorola, Oracle, Silicon Graphics, and Tektronix have announced streaming video products. These products enable Web publishers and producers to distribute video presentations directly to users with Web browsers. As a result, the time between production of the video and its delivery to end users can be reduced significantly.

Streaming multimedia is an important development, as are real-time videoconferencing and collaborative computing products. Fewer users are willing to download software before viewing it and may be concerned about disk space availability. Streaming video eliminates those issues and also enhances the webcasting market.

However, streaming video remains dependent on available bandwidth. In intranets where Ethernet connections are 10 Mbps to 100 Mbps, bandwidth availability is no longer a major problem. In the consumer markets, the latest development in digital TV and cable modem access to the Web may remove those obstacles to acceptable streaming video on the Web.

The Importance of Multicasting

Multicasting communications consists of a broadcasting Web server site targeting multiple client sites as recipients. This form of webcasting involves one site that is actively sending out messages or instructions while all others passively receive. The message, however, is sent only once and continues to be relayed to all recipients through routers and switches, saving a considerable amount of network bandwidth.

For establishing a reliable multicasting service, all clients must have a means of learning when a multicast will take place. They must also be able to indicate their wish to receive it, and the network must be able to route multicast data to them efficiently. Multicasting requires implementing multicast-enabled routers and specialized protocols. Router manufacturers are now adding multicasting capabilities to their products; older routers can be upgraded with additional software and memory.

The Internet, which constitutes an enormous networking environment, will be the last to acquire full multicasting capabilities, although telecom equipment vendors are creating reliable multicasting services for public access and use.

Web Content Provides the Real Challenges

Webcasting offers solutions to Web merchants and publishers facing rapidly growing cyberspace sources and numbers of users. They face many challenges that must be resolved:

1) Attract the user's attention to the Web site

2) Entice users to stay long enough to absorb the content

3) Encourage users to return repeatedly

Push delivery schemes are expected to manage information retrieval and filtering for the user and should make particular Web channels easier to use and create a stronger user link. Merchants that webcast directly also establish their brand images and control revenue streams.

Webcasting is expected to simplify locating a Web site by pushing it to users. Push delivery is the process, but the content is broadcast to users in form of channels comparable to those of conventional TV, the familiar business model that is expected to work in cyberspace also.

Creating Web Channels Is Not a Trivial Task

The Internet as a webcasting delivery channel with real-time, multimedia content is possible technically. The questions are whether it is needed in many instances and whether it can be created cost effectively. Each application must be evaluated considering new developments in digital TV and alternative Internet broadcasting solutions.

The driving force for implementing webcasting originates with Web publishers and Internet merchants striving to increase revenue garnered from Web sites, search engines, and online advertising. The webcasting concept is seen as a more dynamic business model for the future and has the familiarity of conventional broadcasting.

To use webcasting for advantage, companies must transform Web sites and rapidly increasing Web pages to be more defined, organized Web channels that target specific markets. Web channels, around which special Web communities of interest can be constructed, are considered the most effective solution to the information overload taking place.

Web channels also offer a better basis for user psychographics and are expected to lead to superior E-commerce results. They require a full interactive multimedia webcasting environment, which is possible within intranets based on LANs with adequate bandwidth capacities. Creating Web channels is not a trivial task, and companies must be committed to the effort before undertaking it.

Webcasting Money-making Potential

Push technology products and services are appearing in business and consumer market environments, and many are free to the users. They attract users by offering customized delivery and features within Web channels. Who can make money on the Web and how is it done? That question remains unanswered.

Most webcasting services are hoping to license push technologies to content publishers or marketing organizations. Others are trying to generate revenues through interactive targeted advertising, subscription fees to specialized communities of interest, or combinations of these techniques. In fact, little evidence that any of those solutions is guaranteed to make money exists, but Web content publishers and merchants cannot ignore this marketing approach in a very competitive cyberspace environment.

The Risk of Webcasting

Whether a company can benefit from implementing webcasting is not easily decided. The potential revenues are generally unknown and difficult to estimate.

Nevertheless, the potential for revenue reduction in traditional marketing channels of the business must also be considered. If the potential for new revenues on the Web is greater than potential loss of business elsewhere, webcasting is clearly worth implementing.

Unstable and Emerging New Industry

Webcasting services represent an emerging industry, although some examples of well-established push technology services that existed in the professional financial services arena for years have been identified. These services are now developing Internet variants of their offerings and offer the business experience and resources for the most effective combination of webcasting products and services.

Some push technology ventures are financed by leading venture capital funds. Whether they have the stamina to stay in such a fiercely competitive market is unknown, however. Several webcasting services discontinued operations after a relatively short time, while others were quick to merge with competitors to stay in business. Outside webcasting services should be evaluated with great care before a commitment is made.

Watch the Early Adopters

Push technology is implemented first by the large, multinational corporations that must continuously distribute information to remain competitive. Webcasting offers them the opportunity to reduce distribution costs. It reduces the bandwidth and the time spent searching for relevant data and collaborating with distant colleagues.

The Webcasting Idea Is Widespread

The rapid growth of the Internet, Web sites, and their users is a tantalizing incentive to marketers. The failures of previous approaches to E-commerce gives new impetus to webcasting and push technology, making it one of the key ideas of the day.

Radio and TV broadcasting are proven, effective business models. Now, cable TV and digital TV concepts are bringing the Web to the masses through their existing TV sets. This development cannot be ignored; it keeps the push technologists working overtime to develop effective tools to promote customized products and services.

Microsoft invested $1 billion in Comcast, a cable TV operator, and is in discussion about investing another $1 billion in Tele-Communications Inc., one of the largest cable TV organizations in North America and the world. Those services are already on their way to providing high-speed Internet access to cable TV customers through digital set top devices.

The effort to bring the Internet into the living rooms of most households is approaching success. As a result, webcasting becomes a strategic concept that most organizations marketing consumer goods and services will eventually be required to implement. Using cable and TV sets for connectivity with the Web is expected to accelerate consumer use of the Internet for commerce and entertainment. Any company that wants to stay in business tomorrow must ensure that it has the means to compete in that future environment today.

Glossary

address – Indicates unique location of a particular system on the Internet. See also IP address.

agent – A program designed to act on behalf of a user with specific search objectives. Agents are used to collect information for users in a webcasting network.

alert – A method of informing a client of a push service or Web channel that new information is available.

algorithm – A sequence of processing steps that performs a particular operation, such as compressing a digital image.

applet – A program that runs within a Web browser. These are often written in the Java programming language.

artificial intelligence – Reproduction of methods or results of human reasoning and brain activity using symbolic manipulation in computers.

auto retrieval – A search procedure whereby the search engine performs searches in the background and notifies users when results are available.

backbone – A high-speed segment of a network linking lower speed subnetworks.

bandwidth – The range of frequencies that a given system is able to reproduce. The communications capacity of a transmission line or a specific path through a network measured in bits per second (bps). In a LAN, bandwidth is analogous to throughput.

BLOB – *Binary Large Object* – Very large data files consisting of many megabytes of data.

Boolean operator – A symbol for logical rather than arithmetic operation that is used to define or limit information sought in queries. Examples are AND, OR, and NOT.

browser – A Web client that includes a routine to create a view of data in a database without ability to make additions or changes. It allows hypertext to be read.

case-based reasoning (CBR) – Reasoning based on analogy and previous experience within a domain; used as a problem-solving method; important in pattern recognition, learning, and predictions.

channel definition format (CDF) – Specification designed to allow third-party push products to interoperate and certified by the World Wide Web Consortium (WWWC) as an official Internet standard. It defines how and when information will be automatically delivered to desktops.

click rate – The number of advertisement clicks as a percentage of advertisement views in Web browsing.

click-through – The rate at which users click on Web advertisements that take users to the advertisers' Web sites.

client/server – An architecture that distributes computing responsibility between a front-end and a back-end program. With two or more machines, client/servers can dramatically reduce network traffic and increase performance.

clusters – A method of presenting search results where similar type of hits are grouped and headlined together.

compression – The translation of video, audio or digital data singly or in combination to a more compact form for storage and transmission. Computer algorithms and other techniques are used to accomplish this compression process. (See JPEG, MPEG also.)

concept search – Program that automatically amplifies a query with related words to focus on relevant sites.

concurrence – Simultaneous transmission or occurrence of two or more events or activities within the same time period.

cookies – Information about users stored on their hard disk that indicate their Web browsing patterns.

company IQ – Collective organizational effectiveness resulting from information distribution.

CPM – *Cost Per Thousand* – A measure of the number of exposures of an advertising banner of graphic to a user.

crawler – See robot.

crawling depth – The level of penetration to which a search engine is instructed to reach when collecting data.

dial-up connection – A temporary connection between two computers established over the telephone line.

directory – A search engine that consists of a list of major topic categories within which subtopics facilitate searching.

DNS – *Domain Name System* – An Internet application that translates verbal Internet addresses into numeric addresses for data routing.

domain – Portions of verbal Internet address separated by dots. Basic domains include .com, .edu, .net, .mil, .gov, .org and national domains such as .au, .uk, and .us.

E-commerce – Online activity involving orders and payments for goods or services.

encryption – A mathematical routine that transforms original text into unintelligible cyphertext.

exclusion term – Search operator that designates words that must be specifically excluded from documents. Usually the minus sign (-).

expert system – Problem-solving application based on knowledge of a task and rules for using it to reach a solution.

extranet – A secure network using TCP/IP to link intranets with outside business partners' intranets.

FAQ – *Frequently Asked Questions* – Used in USENET groups recommended before asking questions on the Internet for newcomers.

filtering technique – A procedure to eliminate Web sites that are spamming or word stuffing.

filters – Software agents to select requested information or withhold undesirable content from company users in a webcasting system.

firewall – A hardware and software system that protects an internal network or intranet from inside or outside unauthorized access.

forum – Any discussion group accessible through dial-in bulletin board, mailing list or news group.

fps – frames per second. See frame rate also.

FTP – *File Transfer Protocol* – An Internet tool for sending and retrieving files on networked computers.

full-text search – Search engines that search full text of Web pages.

fuzzy logic – System of logic for quantifying possibilities often used in neural networks.

fuzzy search – A search based on imprecise query terms.

GIF – *Graphics Interchange Format* – Developed by CompuServe, this format is the most common graphics file format used on the Web. All graphical browsers support embedded .GIF files known as inline images.

Gopher – Popular tool from the early 1990s for searching a variety of text-based data on the Internet before advent of the Web.

home page – The first screen of a Web site which provides links to other pages.

HTML – *Hypertext Markup Language* – Allows users to specify the appearance and formatting of a document, including special tags for input, tables, and indexing.

HTTP – *Hypertext Transport Protocol* – The language of Web servers used by browsers to request documents or post information to the server.

hyperlink – A link between Web resources often underlined or displayed in different color on a Web page. When a hyperlink is selected, the Web browser retrieves the page to which the links points.

hypermedia – Defines hypertext, which contains a large percentage of multimedia content such as graphics, images, audio, and video.

hypertext – Pieces of text joined in non-sequential manner that are accessible by navigation through a series of menus.

IETF – *Internet Engineering Task Force* – Subgroup of the Internet Society responsible for developing Internet standards.

indexing – Keeping track of files in an organized table.

inferencing engine – A logical program within an expert system that makes artificial intelligence decisions.

infoclutter – Information overload.

information overload – A flood of data and information.

inline interstitial – An advertisement displayed during downloading of immersive environments such as Java or Shockwave.

intelligent search engine – A search engine with artificial intelligence elements that makes some decisions in rating the results of a search.

interactivity levels –Interactive design features available with hardware configurations.

Internet – An international network using TCP/IP.

intranet – An in-house network of networks based on TCP/IP; makes seamless linking with the Internet possible.

intermercial – See interstitial.

interstitial – An advertisement that loads in the narrow space between a Web page requested and the page being loaded.

IP – *Internet Protocol* – The network layer protocol that sends and receives packets of data on the Internet and other TCP/IP-based networks.

IP Address – Physical address of an Internet system expressed in the form of xxxx.xxxx.xxxx.xxxx. Domain names are verbal translations of IP addresses and are easier to remember. Each system has a unique IP address.

Java – A computer language that allows users to add animation, moving text, and interactive games to Web sites. Developers can create applications that can be embedded on Web pages and users with Java-enabled browsers can run them as applets.

keyword – A word that is entered as a query term in a search engine to match with identical words in documents being searched.

latency – Present, but not visible or active; applies to a power or quality that has not yet come into sight or action; used to describe the delay in network transmissions of data.

lossy – A compression technique in which a displayed, decompressed image does not contain all the original digitized data.

lossless – Any compression scheme that allows full recovery of original data packet.

mailing lists – Online dissuasion groups whose interactions are distributed to subscribers through E-mail.

metasearch engine – A Web site or program that simultaneously submits a query to several search engines.

middleware – An application server software that serves as an intermediary between Web servers and legacy databases.

MIME – *Multimedia Internet Mail Extensions* – Additions to Internet E-mail standard that allow multimedia objects to be encapsulated as text; provides reliable delivery.

multicasting – Transmission of content to a selected group of subscribers only once and forwarded by routers and switches, saving bandwidth.

narrowcasting – Customized or personalized broadcasting to a group of individuals or clients.

natural language – Structured spoken, written, or signaled communication between people consisting of vocabulary alphabet or symbolic representation.

natural language processing – Use of computers and artificial intelligence to analyze natural language meaning and structure.

netiquette – The conventions of politeness recognized on the Internet .

neural networks – Networks of nodes and weighed links used for pattern matching, classification, and other non-numeric problems.

newbie – An Internet newcomer.

news group – A collection of online discussion groups or forums.

parallel processing – Simultaneous performance of different sequences of instructions or operations on different sets of data through multiple processors.

parsing – Analysis of structures and decomposition into constituent parts especially applied to linguistic elements such as statements or phrases.

pattern recognition – The use of knowledge of previous patterns to solve new problems. Associated with neural networks.

phrase searching – Searching according to strings of words next to each other rather than single keywords.

posting – Broadcast rather than point-to-point E-mail message.

proximity – A search feature that locates documents with keywords appearing within a specified number of words from each other in a document.

proxy server – A dedicated server for Internet client software and managing Internet connections to produce additional security.

psychographics – User profiles indicating preferences and patterns of Web browsing and basic demographics.

push publishing – Print media terminology for webcasting or narrowcasting.

push technology – Technology that enables users to select their own content from an array of information sources, including news, weather, sports, and stock quotes. Content of this type contains extensive advertising.

query – The keyword or phrase that is used by search engines to locate matches in text.

real-time – The transfer of data that returns results so rapidly that the process appears as instantaneous to the user.

relevance – A rating of results according to statistical frequency relative to keyword in query.

resolution – A measure of image quality of a display. It refers to the number of pixels available on the display and controls the level of detail that can be presented.

robot – Also known as spider, worm, crawler. A program that explores the Web automatically, retrieving documents.

robot exclusion protocol – A program that excludes robots from access to a particular Web site.

screen saver – A program or utility that prevents the cathode ray tuby (CRT) from being etched by an unchanging image.

search – Examination of text or data to discover items that meet specific criteria.

search assistant – Programs that augment, enhance, and help track searches.

search consolidator – See metasearch engine.

search engine – Software program designed to search files and databases that reside on network servers.

search-in-context – Search results that include related topics.

semantic network – A method for simulating associative memory used to represent data, analytical, and logical structures.

SGML – *Standardized General Markup Language* – Defines text for formatting and hypertexting.

site search engine – Software for searching documents and files resident and indexed at a particular Web site.

SNMP – *Simple Network Management Protocol* – Provides specifications and formats for collecting network management data as an alternative to CMIP.

spamdexing – Manipulating a Web page to obtain the greatest possible recognition by search engines.

spamming – News groups flooded with irrelevant or inappropriate messages or crashing a program by overrunning a fixed-size buffer with excessive large input data.

spider – See robot.

spoofing – Sending E-mail that appears as if someone else sent it.

spider blocker – A program that denies access to a Web site and makes including an index impossible.

SQL – *Structured Query Language* – A non-procedural computer language used for accessing relational databases.

stop words -- Short and common usage words that are ignored by certain search engines.

streaming – Continuous rather than bursty transmission of data traffic; particularly important in delivery of time sensitive multimedia audio and video.

switching – Transfer of data via addressed packets or blocks of information. This differs from circuit switching because the network interprets some data and determines the routing during the transfer of a packet.

syntax – A grammatical structure of phrases, sentences, and clauses including relationships among words whose structure is revealed by parsing.

TCP/IP – *Transmission Control Protocol/Internet Protocol* – A protocol developed by the U.S. Department of Defense (DOD) to connect dissimilar systems on a network commonly used in UNIX networks and as the basis of the Internet.

Telnet – A protocol that offers access to an array of databases, including library catalogs on the network.

thread – Abbreviation of topic thread, a continuous chain of postings on a single topic in a news group.

turnkey solution – A complete system delivered to the user in a ready-to-run condition.

unicasting – Transmission of content separately from one Web site to each user.

URL – *Universal Resource Locator* – The specific location of a Web resource and the appropriate network protocol.

USEnet – A distributed bulletin board system supported by UNIX computers; considered the largest decentralized information utility in the world.

virtual – Existing or resulting in an effect although without factual basis. A virtual device may exist in a computer memory only representing a hardware peripheral.

virtual reality – Also known as artificial reality, cyberspace, and telepresence. The use of computers to simulate actual environments in which a user can interact.

visit – A request made by one user at one Web site.

VPN – *Virtual Private Network* – Use of encryption on an Internet connection to provide a secure channel between systems as a less expensive alternative to leased lines.

wanderer – See robot.

webcasting – A method to harness an intranet to deliver relevant internal and external business information to employee desktops without employees actually requesting it. The push technology works in the background mode.

weblicator – A free client application that allows users to copy Web pages. It is similar to PointCast in allowing the sharing of content cached to a server.

webmaster – Person in charge of maintaining the content found on a Web site or of keeping it updated and operating.

Web site – A collection of Web pages consisting of a home page and other linked pages. May contain more than one Web home pages.

World Wide Web – A system for accessing Internet files using hypertext allowing users to navigate the Internet by following links from documents on one computer to documents on others.

World Wide Web Consortium (WWWC or W3C) – A working group responsible for setting Web standards .

WYSIWYG – *What You See Is What You Get* – A user interface of many authoring systems where the author sees the screens as he develops them exactly the way they will appear to the user.

XML – *Extensible Markup Language* – A lightweight language for structuring and describing data for content or applications; developed by the W3C.

Computer Technology Research Corp.

6 North Atlantic Wharf, Charleston, South Carolina 29401 U.S.A. • Tel: 803/853-6460; Fax: 803/853-7210

REPORT EVALUATION

Dear Valued Customer:

It is our continued desire and top priority to provide you with the most current and accurate computer technology information in our reports. Please assist us by taking a few minutes to answer the enclosed questionnaire. Your participation will help us to continue to provide professional service and quality reports to you. Please return the completed questionnaire by fax or mail. Feel free to attach additional sheets if you would like to add more comments. Your time and input are greatly appreciated.

Sincerely,

Edward R. Wagner

Edward R. Wagner
President

Report Title: ____________________

Customer Name: ____________________

Address/Phone: ____________________

____

Rating System: **1**=poor, **2**=fair, **3**=good, **4**=above average, **5**=outstanding.	1	2	3	4	5
1. How would you rate your overall satisfaction with this report?	☐	☐	☐	☐	☐
2. How would you rate the informational content?	☐	☐	☐	☐	☐
3. How would you rate the technical content?	☐	☐	☐	☐	☐
4. Overall, how up-to-date is the report?	☐	☐	☐	☐	☐
How would you rate the quality of data provided regarding: a) product releases?	☐	☐	☐	☐	☐
b) price/performance data?	☐	☐	☐	☐	☐
c) product evaluations?	☐	☐	☐	☐	☐
d) management issues?	☐	☐	☐	☐	☐
5. How would you rate the quantity of illustrations?	☐	☐	☐	☐	☐
6. How would you rate the quality of illustrations?	☐	☐	☐	☐	☐
7. To what degree did this report provide the information which you were desiring to obtain on the subject matter?	☐	☐	☐	☐	☐

Continued on next page

Rating System: **1**=poor, **2**=fair, **3**=good, **4**=above average, **5**=outstanding.	**1**	**2**	**3**	**4**	**5**
8. How would you rate the readability of the report in terms of general appearance (type style, layout, etc.)?	☐	☐	☐	☐	☐
9. How would you rate the report's international coverage?	☐	☐	☐	☐	☐
10. To what extent will the material in this report figure into your decision-making?	☐	☐	☐	☐	☐
11. To what extent did you save time or money by reading this report? (Please explain briefly if possible)	☐	☐	☐	☐	☐

12. Is this the first CTR report you have purchased?	Yes ☐	No ☐
13. Would you purchase other CTR reports?	Yes ☐	No ☐
14. Would you recommend that other information technology professionals purchase this report?	Yes ☐	No ☐
15. Do you believe the information provided warrants the report's cost?	Yes ☐	No ☐
16. Were you satisfied with the service you received from our staff in fulfillment of your order?	Yes ☐	No ☐
17. Did your shipment arrive in good condition?	Yes ☐	No ☐
18. Were you satisfied with the delivery time of your shipment?	Yes ☐	No ☐

19. What additional information or topics would you have desired to see in this report that were not adequately covered?

20. What topics would you like to see us cover in future reports?

21. If you know of another individual whom you believe would be interested in receiving information concerning our report series, please list his/her full mailing address below:

Fax your completed questionnaire to: **(803) 853-7210**
or mail your completed questionnaire to: **Computer Technology Research Corp.**
6 North Atlantic Wharf
Charleston, SC 29401-2115 U.S.A.

Thank you for your time and input!